Issues in the Social Sciences: 10

Series Editor: *Katherine Harrison*

Edges of Identity:
The Production of Neoliberal
Subjectivities

Issues in the Social Sciences

Titles in the Issues in the Social Sciences series are published periodically. The peer-reviewed series presents current academic research into contemporary social issues in an accessible and engaging style that is designed to immerse researchers and students alike in active debates in the Social Sciences.

Editorial Advisory Board

Eric Allison, *The Guardian*, UK
Lisa Blackman, Goldsmiths, University of London, UK
Stephen Edgell, University of Salford, UK
Rosalind Gill, City University London, UK
Graeme Gilloch, Lancaster University, UK
Dan Goodley, University of Sheffield, UK
Jane Kilby, University of Salford, UK
Clement Macintyre, University of Adelaide, Australia
Ross McGarry, University of Liverpool, UK
Catherine McGlynn, University of Huddersfield, UK
Caroline Miles, University of Manchester, UK
Andrew Mycock, University of Huddersfield, UK
Jayne Raisborough, Leeds Beckett University, UK
Stuart Shields, University of Manchester, UK
Jonathan Tonge, University of Liverpool, UK
Imogen Tyler, Lancaster University, UK

Edges of Identity:
The Production of Neoliberal Subjectivities

Edited by

**Jonathon Louth
and Martin Potter**

University of Chester Press

First published 2017
by University of Chester Press
University of Chester
Parkgate Road
Chester CH1 4BJ

Printed and bound in the UK by the
LIS Print Unit
University of Chester
Cover designed by the
LIS Graphics Team
University of Chester

Editorial material
© University of Chester, 2017
Foreword, introduction and individual chapters
© the respective authors, 2017
Cover images © Khvay Samnang, 2011–2012

All Rights Reserved
No part of this publication may be reproduced, stored in a retrieval system or transmitted in any form or by any means without the prior permission of the copyright owner, other than as permitted by current UK copyright legislation or under the terms and conditions of a recognised copyright licensing scheme

A catalogue record for this book is available
from the British Library

ISBN 978-1-908258-24-3

CONTENTS

Preface — viii

Acknowledgements — x

Contributors — xii

Introduction — 1
The Production of Neoliberal Subjectivities:
Constellations of Domination and Resistance
Jonathon Louth and Martin Potter

Chapter One — 25
Consuming Environmental Citizenship, or
the Production of Neoliberal Green Citizens
Benito Cao

Chapter Two — 52
'Empowered Girls' in Neoliberal Times:
Malala as the *Effect* of Heterogeneous Discourses
Shenila Khoja-Moolji

Chapter Three — 84
Our Borders: Neoliberalism, Identity and
Asylum Seeker Policy in Australia, 2001–2013
Ben Revi

Chapter Four — 106
"The Way You Make Me Feel": Shame and the
Neoliberal Governance of Disability Welfare
Subjectivities in Australia and the UK
Karen Soldatic and Hannah Morgan

Chapter Five 134
Subjects or Subjected? The Puzzle of Identity
in Neoliberal Times
Tom Brock and Mark Carrigan

Chapter Six 161
Ejaculatory Timing and Masculine Identities:
The Politics of Ab/normalising Sexual Performance
Hannah Frith

Chapter Seven 181
Neoliberal Ideology and Shifting 'Salarymen Identity'
Under Corporate Restructuring in Japan
Nana Okura Gagné

Chapter Eight 207
Urban Transformations, Work and the Idea of Social
Solitude Among Two Generations of Men in Surabaya,
East Java
Matteo Carlo Alcano

Chapter Nine 230
Neoliberalising Mostar: Governmentality,
Ethno-National Division and Everyday Forms
of Resistance
Giulia Carabelli and Rowan Lubbock

Chapter Ten 254
Urban Transformations in Phnom Penh:
Creative Collectives, the White Building and the
Production of Space
Jonathon Louth and Martin Potter

Contents

Chapter Eleven 285
Exploring the Formation and Reproduction of
Neoliberal Subjectivities: A Socio-Cognitive
Approach
Rodolfo Leyva

Index 313

PREFACE

It is a real pleasure and a privilege to introduce the tenth volume in the Issues in the Social Sciences (ISS) series: *Edges of Identity: The Production of Neoliberal Subjectivities*. This is an exciting, peer-reviewed edited collection that gathers together the voices of academic researchers working in and across Europe, Asia, Australia and North America. As such, it is a landmark in the series' development and represents what I hope to be the shape of things to come. When the first volume of ISS was published in 2003, the modest intention of the then-series editor, Anne Boran, was to create an opportunity for colleagues working in the Social Sciences at the University of Chester to publish research in a format that was useful, accessible and affordable for our own undergraduate students. Since then, the series' horizons have widened and while it maintains its original mission to present cutting-edge research to scholars working at all levels, the books now welcome the contributions of researchers from across the UK and worldwide. Correspondingly, the series' readership has expanded internationally, meaning that its capacity to share ideas with Social Sciences students across the world has increased far beyond original expectations. It is therefore both appropriate and gratifying that this tenth instalment in the ISS series takes a truly global perspective and draws on theoretical analyses and fieldwork conducted in countries including the UK, Bosnia and Herzegovina, Pakistan, Cambodia, Japan and Australia.

The publication of the tenth ISS book also presents a timely – if not overdue – opportunity to thank and congratulate everyone who has been integral to the series' development since its inception. All of the individual authors and editors who have generously contributed their research over the last 14 years in order to produce such a fascinating range of volumes deserve recognition and gratitude. Particular thanks are due to

Preface

the editors of the current volume, Jonathon Louth and Martin Potter, for ensuring the international scope of *Edges of Identity*, which necessitated working closely with authors across four continents while they themselves were often operating across two – no mean editorial feat. Likewise, the anonymous peer reviewers, who have provided insightful feedback on each manuscript since the series' re-launch in 2013, have been crucial to maintaining high academic standards. Members of the Editorial Advisory Board have acted as perceptive sounding boards for new ideas and directions in the series and I thank them for their continued support. Acknowledgement is also due to Alessandro Pratesi, who organised the conference from which the idea for the current volume originated in 2013, as well as several earlier conferences that inspired other books in the series. Finally, it is essential to recognise the long-standing support of the University of Chester Press and to express appreciation for the hard work and expertise of the managing editor, Sarah Griffiths, without whose tenacity the series would never have achieved such longevity or success. I hope that readers will enjoy the present volume and look forward to the next 10 books in the ISS series as eagerly as I do.

Katherine Harrison
Series editor
Chester, United Kingdom, 21 June 2017

ACKNOWLEDGEMENTS

This book has been a long time in the making. This initial idea was borne from a student-led conference held at the University of Chester in 2014 where I was working as a senior lecturer of international politics. From the subsequent call for chapters the beginnings of a distinctive and unique volume emerged. However, following a sudden change of personal circumstances, the project was shelved for a period of time. I would like to thank each and every contributor for their patience and commitment to this book. Without their understanding it would not have been possible to revive this excellent volume. My thanks are also extended to series editor Katherine Harrison for her patience, faith and assistance; likewise, Sarah Griffiths from the University of Chester Press has supported the production of this volume despite numerous hurdles. Adding to this, Evan Smith's proof editing skills proved invaluable. Yet, it is to Martin Potter, who came on board as a co-editor very late in the piece that much of my thanks are reserved. Without his involvement, dedication and enthusiasm to bring this book back to life, it is unlikely to have ever made it to press. Finally, I would extend my heartfelt thanks and appreciation to Mary and Eli for their support and for always being there.

Jonathon Louth
Phnom Penh, Cambodia, 25 April 2017

Acknowledgements

In mid-2016 Jonathon approached me to come on as co-editor of this volume. It has been a joy to be a part of reviving this volume and I'd like to echo Jon's thanks to all the contributors for their patience. Their enthusiasm and responsiveness when I contacted them for revisions after a long hiatus was an enormous relief, to say the least. Thank you again for your understanding, and for the quality of your work. I'd also like to thank Katherine, Sarah and Evan. Thank you Jonathon for inviting me on another beautiful journey. And thanks to the myriad other humans who show similar patience and understanding towards me in my everyday life.

Martin Potter
Phnom Penh, Cambodia, 25 April 2017

CONTRIBUTORS

Matteo Carlo Alcano is a postdoctoral fellow in anthropology at the University of Milano – Bicocca (Italy). Since 2008 he has been conducting ethnographic research in South Bali and East Java (Indonesia) where he has studied gender, mobility and work. Between 2013 and 2016 he was funded by SEATIDE (Southeast Asia: Trajectories of Inclusion, Dynamics of Exclusion) a 7th Framework Programme of the European Commission. His most recent publication is *Masculine Identities and Male Sex Work between East Java and Bali: An Ethnography of Youth, Bodies and Violence*, published by Palgrave Macmillan in 2015.

Tom Brock is a lecturer in the Department of Sociology at Manchester Metropolitan University. He holds a doctorate in sociology from the University of Durham and his research interests include social theory, digital culture and political protest. He has authored publications on critical pedagogy, student movements and populism and is the co-author of the book *Structure, Culture and Agency: Selected Papers of Margaret Archer* (Routledge, 2016). Tom currently co-convenes the BSA Realism and Social Research Group and steers the BSA Theory Study Group. He is also an associate at the Centre for Social Ontology at the University of Warwick.

Benito Cao is lecturer in politics at the University of Adelaide. He has received several teaching awards and has published articles in the fields of cultural studies, identity politics, critical thinking, environmental politics and citizenship studies. He is the author of *Environment and Citizenship* (Routledge, 2015), and is currently working on a book entitled *Mediating Environmental Citizenship*.

Contributors

Mark Carrigan is a digital sociologist and social media consultant. He is a research fellow in the Centre for Social Ontology at the University of Warwick and digital fellow at *The Sociological Review*. He convenes the Independent Social Research Foundation's Digital Social Science Forum and co-convenes the Accelerated Academy with Filip Vostal. He is an assistant editor of *Big Data & Society*, associate social media editor of the *International Journal of Social Research Methodology* and a founding member of the editorial boards of *Discover Society* and the *Journal of Applied Social Theory*. His research interests include asexuality studies, digital universities, digital social science, digital capitalism and subjectivity. He is a regular blogger and podcaster.

Giulia Carabelli is a research fellow at the Max Planck Institute for the Study of Ethnic and Religious Diversity and a member of the 'Empires of Memory' research group. Her PhD thesis (Queen's University Belfast) developed as part of the 'Conflict in Cities and the Contested State' project and it examined the process of reconstructing Mostar in Bosnia Herzegovina. Giulia's research interest is located at the intersection of urban sociology, cultural studies and political theory; her work has so far explored the roles and potential of grassroots movements and civil society actors in the making of urban spaces, especially in contested and politically fragile environments such as Bosnia Herzegovina.

Hannah Frith is a critical social psychologist and feminist researcher based at the University of Brighton, UK. Her research examines the interrelationships between identity, embodiment and sexuality. Her *Orgasmic Bodies: The Orgasm in Contemporary Western Culture* (Palgrave, 2015) examines the socially constructed meanings which orgasm has for men and women in neoliberal contexts which demand that individuals work on and improve their sexual selves. She has previously published work looking at the mediation of dying, makeover television, clothing and identity, sexual refusals and adolescent sexuality. She has co-edited *Critical Bodies: Representations, Identities and Practices and Weight and Body Management* (Palgrave, 2009).

Nana Okura Gagné is a cultural anthropologist who received her PhD from Yale University. She is an assistant professor in the Department of Japanese Studies at the Chinese University of Hong Kong. Her research interests include gender and sexuality, exchange and consumption, and globalisation and neoliberalism in Japan and the United States. Her work has been published in *Asian Anthropology, American Ethnologist, Ethnography,* and the *Journal of Language and Communication.*

Shenila Khoja-Moolji is a postdoctoral scholar with the Program on Democracy, Citizenship, and Constitutionalism and the Department of Gender, Sexuality and Women's Studies at the University of Pennsylvania. She draws on transnational feminist and postcolonial theories to write about the intersections of gender and education in the global south and immigrant diasporas. Her work has appeared in *Signs: Journal of Women in Culture and Society*; *Comparative Studies of South Asia, Africa and the Middle East*; *Compare*; *Discourse*; *Feminist Teacher*; *Girlhood Studies*; and *Gender and Education,* as well as in the form of several book chapters.

Rodolfo Leyva is a political sociologist-psychologist and lecturer of criminology and sociology at Middlesex University, and holds a PhD from King's College London. His research synthesises quantitative, experimental and qualitative methods and leading paradigms from political-economy, sociology, media studies and the cognitive sciences to explore the socio-cognitive and structural reproduction of neoliberal societies and political socialisation.

Contributors

Jonathon Louth is a research fellow at the Australian Centre for Community Services Research at Flinders University. Previously he was a senior lecturer in international politics at the University of Chester in the United Kingdom. His research focusses on intersections between international political economy and the philosophy and history of (social) science. This informs his research on Southeast Asia and the politics of wider economic integration (with an emphasis on Cambodia), which has generated work on gender, everyday lives, neoliberal governance, financialisation, constructions of order and the impact of economic thought upon social structures.

Rowan Lubbock is a PhD student at Birkbeck College, University of London. His doctoral thesis focusses on the struggle for food sovereignty within the Latin American regional organisation of the Bolivarian Alliance for the Peoples of Our America (ALBA). Through 12 months of fieldwork in Venezuela, the research examines the relationship between agrarian social movements and the state in the process of transforming the agricultural base of Venezuela through the specific institutional structure of the ALBA space. His research interests include International Relations Theory, historical sociology, Marxism and the geopolitics of Latin America.

Hannah Morgan is senior lecturer in disability studies in the Department of Sociology and Director of the Centre for Disability Research (CeDR) at Lancaster University. She is the lead organiser of the biennial international disability studies conference held at Lancaster since 2003. Hannah is a member of the Executive Editorial Board of *Disability & Society* and the Editorial Board of *Disability Studies Quarterly*. Hannah's research explores how social policy, and particularly professional practice, affects the lives of disabled people.

Martin Potter is lecturer in creative arts and media at James Cook University and creative director of documentary production company Big Stories Co. He has an extensive publication record as a media producer with 20 hours of commissioned broadcast television. He is also a director and producer of transmedia and media for development projects including *Big Stories, Small Towns* (Winner Community Champion, SXSW Interactive 2012), *Stereopublic: Crowdsourcing the Quiet* (TED City 2.0 prize, 2012), *Island Connect* (US-AID and ChildFund Sri Lanka), *Youth Today* (UNICEF, Cambodia) and the acclaimed *White Building* participatory media and arts programme in Phnom Penh (whitebuilding.org). His research and media making explores relational and participatory cultural practices.

Ben Revi is a visiting research fellow at the University of Adelaide. His research involves questions of identity in social policy, the relationship between technocracy and political debate and citizenship theory.

Karen Soldatic is a senior research fellow at the Institute of Culture and Society, Western Sydney University. Karen is currently undertaking a three-year Australian Research Council DECRA Fellowship to examine the impact of the interstice of global economic restructuring and national welfare reform on the lives of Indigenous Australians with a disability living in rural and remote areas. Karen is on the Advisory Board for the Critical Disability Studies Network of the Centre of Human Rights Education, Curtin University, Australia and an Affiliated Professorial Fellow with the Centre for Disability Research, University of Colombo, Sri Lanka. Her research in the area of disability and global economic restructuring has been published widely.

INTRODUCTION

THE PRODUCTION OF NEOLIBERAL SUBJECTIVITIES: CONSTELLATIONS OF DOMINATION AND RESISTANCE

Jonathon Louth and Martin Potter

The last 50 years have been marked by many remarkable events, historic shifts and technological breakthroughs that have challenged societies and driven change. Over the course of this period a revolution – sometimes quiet, other times violent and vicious – has also taken place. The rich ecology of our economic, political and social systems has become imbricated and enmeshed by a particular outlook; an outlook that has reshaped behaviours and expectations across scales – from the global to the most intimate of spaces. Neoliberalism, whether rolled out through the establishment of institutions to further the project, or rolled back via de-regulatory measures (Peck, 2010), has penetrated the worlds in which we live. There is the roll call of familiar names: economists, beginning with Friedrich von Hayek and Milton Friedman through to leaders who uncompromisingly pushed the ideas, making them 'fit' with reality: Augusto Pinochet, Margaret Thatcher and Ronald Reagan. Yet, it is not the macro-level policies and change that this volume is concerned with. It is the absorption of neoliberal thought and the co-constituting processes that have contributed to a common-sense acceptance of neoliberal policies, not just through the subsequent actions of elite interests, but through the interiorisation of neoliberalism into our very beings. Thus, the development, production and reproduction of neoliberal subjectivity is a key point of interest herein. And intertwined with this subjectivity, at the edges of hegemonic processes, lie grey areas of domination and resistance. These constellations allow the exploration of identity in the face of this expansionary neoliberal project. And it is here, at the edges of identity of neoliberal subjectivity, that we situate our study.

Locating neoliberalism

The rich liberal tradition acts as a convenient touchstone for the neoliberal project: the production of the good society through the actions of self-interested individuals is a common claim. However, the push to an extreme form of methodological individualism (see Ferguson & Mansbach, 2004) ignores how neoliberalism shapes and influences structures and the world within which people reside. Individuals are extracted from traditions, cultural contexts and their sense of place. Instead, individuals are seen as 'utility maximisers' that are autonomous, self-regarding and self-actualised decision makers. A core belief is the removal of constraints: that we, as individuals, should be free to act as we choose; with the state seen as the structure that most severely impedes our freedom. In place of society and the state is an appeal to a universal market; with the consequence of its reification being the absorption of the multiple, differentiated and often localised markets that predate the expansionary pressures of neoliberalism. Of course, all of this is predicated – whether liberal or neoliberal – upon an idea of constant growth. Reagan, paraphrasing John F. Kennedy, claimed that a rising tide lifts all boats; a catch cry for those who have argued for the further rollout of the project, including by mainstream parties on the left (Sperling, 2007), but with little consideration for rising inequality. What is not recognised is that the fictional construction of the individual in a world of perfect functioning markets has to, at some point, give way to the "spiraling social and environmental problems of contemporary capitalism" (Harvey, 2010, p. 114).

The charge of 'neoliberalism' is often levied as a term of derision and its usage has been dominated by those who wish to critique an ideological perspective – one which has come to define the last 50 years of capitalist expansion. Yet it was a label first applied by the Mont Pelerin Society, the elite liberal society founded by Hayek to push back against a perceived ascendancy of socialist ideas (Mirowski, 2013; Peck, 2010). Thatcher, who emerged as one of the most prominent flag bearers of neoliberalism, repeatedly echoed this fear and laid bare the ideological contest at play, declaring socialism to be economically inefficient and morally corrupt (Berlinski, 2011). The absorption of neoliberal thought by political elites in the United Kingdom became startlingly evident when Cabinet Minister under Tony Blair, Peter Mandelson, claimed that "We are all Thatcherites now" (Tempest, 2002). This claim was followed by revelations that Thatcher, when asked what was her greatest achievement, allegedly quipped "Tony Blair and New Labour" (Burns, 2008). This aphorism can be seen as part of a wider trend of absorption and the production of a view of neoliberalism as common sense. Indeed, with the use of the term becoming decidedly more commonplace in mainstream media, by politicians and even by the International Monetary Fund (IMF), a full circle has almost been reached (Peck, 2010; Rowden, 2016).

However, how might we define, historicise and understand neoliberalism as an overall project? A recent eyebrow-raising article in an IMF in-house journal, which asks if neoliberalism has been oversold, articulates in the opening paragraph the broad economic aims of the project with brevity:

> The neoliberal agenda—a label used more by critics than by architects of the policies—rests on two main planks. The first is increased competition—achieved through deregulation and the opening up of domestic markets, including financial markets, to foreign competition. The second is a smaller role for the state, achieved through privatization and limits on the ability of governments to run fiscal deficits and accumulate debt. (Ostry, Loungani, & Furceri, 2016, p. 38)

It is a neat and concise explanation, but what it does not reveal is that neoliberalism is a historical project. While there will always be some contention as to a starting point, the establishment of the Bretton Woods institutions in 1944 was an act that represented the confident reaffirming of a liberal internationalist order. It represented the establishment of the American-led rules of the game with the idea being to create favourable trade conditions for capitalist states in the post-war era. The 1973 overthrow of the democratically elected Salvador Allende by Augusto Pinochet in Chile has become, by detractors at least, the marker for the commencement of the neoliberal period. From the 1970s onwards, it is a period that has been epitomised by the rolling out of privatisation programmes coupled with the deregulation of national economies. Moreover, it was a process that was exported 'under the rules of the game' – most notably under the Washington consensus of the late 1980s: a set of fiscal guidelines often attached to financial assistance for (primarily) developing states via Bretton Woods institutions, most notably the World Bank and the IMF (Beeson, 2007). Importantly, this historical evolution is not simply driven by coercion, as was the case in Chile, but through the production of a common-sense view that, to quote Thatcher, 'there is no alternative' (see Berlinski, 2011). This was, and continues to be, an integral part of this project: developing authenticity and a view that neoliberalism represents an economic orthodoxy.

However, what is often lost is that neoliberalism is first and foremost a political ideology. As an ideology it adheres to a convenient mix of convictions, which incorporates a shared belief – but not necessarily practice – of the fundamentals of neoclassical economics (see Brenner & Theodore, 2002). What neoliberalism takes from economic neoclassicism is not 'accuracy', but the (selective) reassurances of a scientific paradigm that parades as certainty (Hay, 2004). As part of this quest for authenticity the

Introduction

influential Chicago School[1] – especially through the work of Friedman – played a decisive role in the development of neoliberalism by linking it with neoclassical economics, on the one hand, and by celebrating neoclassical economics as a "core scientific theory", on the other (Van Horn & Mirowski, 2009, p. 139).[2] Through these selective reassurances of 'science', neoliberalism gains the impression of authenticity. It is this authoritative ideological framework that has underpinned the deep marketisation of state and society on a global scale (Carroll, 2012b). The advance of neoliberalism since the 1970s has sought to depoliticise and entrench a view of the market as ahistorical and universal (Tickell & Peck, 2003). In many respects the project has been successful – even as it is blended and integrated in different forms (see Peck & Tickell, 2007). Yet the 2008 financial crisis has placed the political and corporate class under scrutiny with questions around inequality, viability and sustainability.

The 2008 financial crisis and the ongoing Euro crisis – particularly in relation to the treatment of Greece by the Troika[3] – have been cited as a 'Berlin Wall' moment for neoliberalism (Peck, 2010; Rowden, 2016). As mentioned above, an article in the IMF's own journal, *Finance & Development*, asked if neoliberalism had, in fact, been oversold. Was it conceivable that the wholesale deregulation and privatisation of economies might be a feedback-driven cause of many of the problems being experienced by national economies around the world (Ostry et al., 2016)? Of course, the writers quickly concluded that balance was the answer and the IMF leadership quickly responded to interest in the article to assert that the views expressed were not reflective of broader IMF positions (Rowden, 2016). Neoliberalism, as a form of capitalist expansion is resilient and while 'schisms' exist between the conceptualisation of a universal totality and the very real material issues experienced by people every day, they are often ignored or simply papered over by elites (Louth, 2012; Louth, 2015). Key to this is consent. This can be expressed in Gramscian terms within which civil society is central to the "production of hegemony" (Jessop & Sum, 2006, p. 161). Put simply, middle-class consent was central to the acceptance of Thatcherism in the United Kingdom (Harvey, 2005). Similarly, the global expansion of neoliberalism has required the consent and involvement of indigenous – and often emerging – middle classes (Cox, 1981). The neoliberal idea was sold spectacularly well to a self-interested, individualistic middle class who absorbed the idea as an economic inevitability.

So where does the self-interested, utility maximising individual fit into all this? While neoliberal 'freedoms' have been rolled out, the position of elites has only become more entrenched. As this 50-year experiment has been rolled out (or rolled back, as the case might be) global inequality has only been exacerbated (Harvey, 2005). Could it be that the aspirational freedom-loving consumer is a product of this neoliberal experiment?

The production of neoliberal subjectivities

How, then, do we understand our own 'subjectivity' especially if we accept as a starting point that neoliberalism is 'everywhere' (Leitner, Peck, & Sheppard, 2007)? Where do our neighbours, our family, and our community fit with how we negotiate market-orientated societies? Ontologically, it is not difficult to place the individual – the neoliberal subject – as a product of neoliberal ideology. Society itself becomes the image of neoliberalism; in this, subjectivity becomes productive in and of itself, with social and cultural existence inextricably tied to the primacy of the market (Hardt & Negri, 1994). A number of the chapters in this volume turn to Foucault, where the universal, self-actualising individual is a liberal mirage born of the Enlightenment. For Foucault, the individual is an atomised fiction that within our reality is "fabricated by this specific technology of power that [he] called 'discipline'" (Foucault, 1977, p. 194).[4] The neoliberal subject, in this context, is coerced to conform. To resist, or to simply not fit in, is to be punished, shamed or abnormalised.

Jean-Paul Sartre expresses how the self and our subjectivity is bound by the interiorisation of our social existence. The quote, in full, from an interview when asked what constitutes subjectivity:

> You said that sociality deeply penetrates subjectivity and that an abstract subjectivity would be meaningless; that it could not exist. I am wholly of the same opinion as you. In the sense that, for me, subjectivity is interiorisation and retotalisation, that is to say, fundamentally ... you live; subjectivity is to live your own being, and to live what you are in a society – because we know no other state of man, he is precisely a social being, a social being who, at the same time, lives the whole of society from his point of view. I think that any individual, or any group, or an ensemble, is an incarnation of the total society, since they have to live where they are. Moreover, it is only because we can conceive the dialectical play of an enveloping totalisation – that is, a condensing totalisation, which I call incarnation – that each individual is, in a certain manner, the total representation of her epoch; it is only reason that we can conceive a true social dialectic. In these conditions, then, I think that this social subjectivity is the very definition of subjectivity. Subjectivity at the social level is a social subjectivity. (Sartre, 2016, pp. 99–100)

The chapters that follow take a range of insightful perspectives on how an economic outlook becomes interiorised as part of the self within the context of its constituting society. Of course, this is a non-linear affair with multiple feedback processes that drive and push the formation and reconstitution of identities, cultures and even the state itself.

How do we then deal with neoliberal rule? If we live in an era of "marketized subjectivity" (Leitner et al., 2007, p. 316) that is part of an 'enveloping totalisation', how do we recognise opportunities to resist? Foucault – with his focus on discourse, power and knowledge – represents a voice to shift our understanding of how subjugated groups can resist power. Henri Lefebvre, upon whose work two chapters draw, makes the claim that new ideas are only possible if utopias are imaginable (Lefebvre, 1976). Roberto Unger suggests the possibility of incremental change within institutions, that by building "plasticity" into institutional infrastructure enables "ongoing destruction of all privileged claims on the resources – of capital, power and expertise – with which we make and remake society" (1987, p. 8).

Through a series of investigations this volume explores a rich constellation of how competing forms of self and society are repressed or exploit niche opportunities. In each case, how agency is expressed or is repressed is the point of fascination. Space, in this sense, is multidimensional and is sustained by discursive practices. This speaks to how we understand the enormity of international relations and social structures through to the intimacy of relations in the private sphere. The normalisation and the reproduction of particular social practices are linked to the expansion and penetration of a neoliberal hegemony that rationalises, atomises and homogenises the world around us. This volume critically explores how a range of subjectivities is formed, constrained, reshaped or resisted when confronted by the expansionary logic of neoliberalism.

Outline of the book

In Chapter One, the neoliberalisation of environmental citizenship is at the heart of Benito Cao's exploration of 'green subjectivity'. Cao outlines the relation between citizenship, subjectivity, and neoliberal governmentality and how citizenship is reshaped by the expansionary logic of neoliberalism. Highlighting tactics of particular government campaigns, ecological footprint calculators and media texts, Cao finds that models of

Introduction

neoliberal consumption and production elucidate the manufacturing of 'green citizens' and define the role they perform in the governing of the environment. As an opening chapter, Cao's account grounds the volume with an appreciation of the nexus between citizenship, subjectivity and neoliberal governmentality.

Increasing preoccupation regarding human impact on the environment is redefining citizenship in ways that, Cao observes, resemble a revolution, only this time informed by environmental concerns and ecological values. In the face of this revolution governments, acutely aware of the need to address environmental concerns, are adopting the language of citizenship as they frame their response via social engineering techniques. This approach has been defined as 'environmental governmentality' (Darier, 1996) or 'environmentality' (Agrawal, 2005). The neoliberal context in which environmental concerns and renewed interest in citizenship have converged profoundly shapes our current understanding of environmental citizenship. The neoliberal turn translates into a shift towards the language of individual and corporate responsibility through self-regulation, and a shift towards economics in general and consumption in particular. Cao argues that while sustainable consumption might be compatible with notions of environmental citizenship, this requires governments to shift social values, set an example by developing green infrastructure, and force corporations to change their behaviour rather than rely on self-regulation. And although this shift may be possible, Cao highlights, through a series of examples across technology, media and pedagogy, a dominant tendency towards the opposite.

Chapter Two explores the homogenisation of identity and how this intersects with a heroic feminised neoliberal construct of the 'Other'. In the story of Malala Yousafzai, the young Pakistani girl shot by a member of the Taliban, Shenila Khoja-Moolji finds a 'floating signifier'. A constructed identity of female, muslim[5] empowerment that articulates diverse hopes and fears for a wide range of people and institutions. Khoja-Moolji asks what makes Malala so *productive*? What gives her such appeal and reach? What does Malala promise and to whom, and how does she come into being? Khoja-Moolji offers a nuanced analysis of the 'Malala effect' and concludes that representations of Malala manifested through discursive structures of neoliberal governmentality, girl power and adolescent sexuality produce and give effect to a monolithic, homogenous 'othered' vision of muslim girls. This flattening of identity brings with it a depoliticisation around issues such as education, which require political analysis and political solutions. Foucault (1978) notes that this "tactical polyvalence of discourses" (p. 100) is intended to produce specific effects and subjects, and consequently directs us to think about discourse as "practices that systematically form the objects of which they speak" (p. 49). Images of empowered girls like Malala do not exist in isolation. Khoja-Moolji explores broader political and ideological appropriations of Malala's story and the manner in which she is presented as an individualised and empowered girl; in effect, a homogenised story about muslim girls for western audiences that melds with neoliberal sensibilities.

Ben Revi's chapter, 'Our Borders', looks at recent asylum seeker policy in the context of Australia's longer history of immigration, and a broader global history of neoliberalism and identity. Revi argues policy under the Australian Labor Party (ALP) governments between 2007 and 2013, presented a 'social democratic paradox', where 'fairness' in domestic politics provokes harshness toward migration. Revi interrogates the notion of 'fair'. This is a word that in the Australian context carries great weight due to the alignment of a 'fair go' with Australian sociocultural identity. He finds that 'fair' becomes redefined in terms of 'fair' access by neoliberal citizens to markets in goods and labour. No longer is there any space for fairness towards

Introduction

asylum seekers even when they are found to be refugees. The logic of neoliberal citizenship holds every activity to be, first, an economic activity. The movement of displaced persons is seen not as an act of desperation made necessary by collective repression, but an economic choice made by individuals. Every component of an asylum seeker's journey – the cost, the route, the destination, the use of 'smugglers' – is seen as an avoidable economic choice. Such identity politics limits the capacity for the Australian government to resettle asylum seekers, who are constructed as incapable of performing as neoliberal citizens, into Australian social and economic life. Revi's chapter demonstrates the ability of neoliberalism to appropriate discourse more familiar to the social democratic tradition, such as 'fairness'. It shows the power of individualism as a discourse that converts collective welfare into individual services, and presents a zero-sum view that constructs the welfare of others as antagonistic to the welfare of the self.

In Chapter Four, Soldatic and Morgan look at lived experiences of workfare-based disability programmes in Australia and the UK. They theorise that shame is used as a form of neoliberal governance within these initiatives. Through the narratives of the disabled people in their study, they show the key role shame plays in classifying and (self) regulating the behaviour and emotions of welfare recipients. Soldatic and Morgan find, in the economic deterministic discourses of disability as unsustainable, a shift in disability from the fringes to the epicentre of economic policy across most OECD countries. Disability now features prominently in economic debates pertaining to the future 'health' of the nation. Parallel to this is a programmatic imperative towards moving people off welfare and into the world of work. As the hegemony of neoliberalism has redefined ideas of citizenship, social inclusion and social mobility, Soldatic and Morgan contend that with the trialling of new forms of neoliberal governance of disability, notably in

Australia, there is a structural collective shaming of disabled people. They argue neoliberalism actively draws upon acts of shaming to force disabled people to comply with its coercive regulating regime and to keep people 'in their place'. Shame is used to articulate the lack of a job as a private moral failure and to morally intensify social divisions. Shame, according to Soldatic and Morgan, becomes a calculated political tactic to re-imagine the disability landscape, creating new divisions to separate the deserving from the *un*deserving disabled welfare recipient.

Extending the relationship of subjectivity to culture that frames the 'floating signifier' in Chapter Two, Brock and Carrigan take up a challenge issued by Rosalind Gill. Gill (2008) points out those studying neoliberalism have a rich array of conceptual tools available for minutely dissecting cultural forms and, yet, there "is very little understanding of how culture relates to subjectivity, identity or lived embodied experiences of selfhood" (p. 433). Brock and Carrigan thus seek to address this gap and to conceptualise the production of subjectivities through a lens that brings together realist-informed biographical research and Foucault's concept of problematization, offering an insight into how individuals might affirm critical reflexivity. Using the example of the asexual community, Brock and Carrigan reflect on the state of *being* asexual and the process of *becoming* asexual, avoiding the all too common tendency to foreground one at the expense of the other. They consider the relationship that this process of coming to identify as asexual has with neoliberalism and the construction of neoliberal subjectivities.

This links with concerns raised by Frith in the following chapter in relation to the construction of sexual identity, as Brock and Carrigan consider how different eras have problematized sexuality, making it an object for thought and intervention. Trying to fit identities into a prescribed script is a process that

Introduction

can be both repressive and agentive. Brock and Carrigan unpick the interplay between the two by looking at the biographical trajectories of particular individuals over time, but in a way that recognises the ubiquity of normative power. By looking at people's biographies and the forms of communicative reasoning that they deploy when confronted with the sexual assumption, Brock and Carrigan see the often "discretionary, elaborative, and ad hoc" manner through which people come to identify as asexual (McCarthy, 1993, p. 30, cited in Barnett, Clarke, Cloke, & Malpass, 2008, pp. 648–649). Thus, subjectivity is appropriately embedded within the broader practices of self-making and personhood without any need to succumb to the 'careless nominalism of the self, characteristic of generic post-structuralism more broadly'.

Hannah Frith's chapter offers an analysis of the creation of socio-sexual (ab)norms that shape meaning-making between couples trying to make sense of their sexual interactions. Frith focusses on masculine subjects and argues that ejaculation considered 'out of time' is firmly positioned as a failure of the neoliberal masculine subject. Professional and commercial interests collude in offering mechanisms for men's rehabilitation towards the perfect intercourse performance, which permeates men's interpretation of their own embodiment and sexual subjectivity. The entry of neoliberalism into the intimate sphere has seen both a re-conceptualisation of sex, and the construction of a new sexual actor. Rather than an irrepressible force of nature, neoliberalism reframes sexuality as subject to rational management and something to be continually worked upon, improved, made efficient, invested in, and capitalised upon. This 'perfect intercourse performance' is central to hegemonic masculinity – a cultural ideal of the masculine. Within this ideal, men are depicted as being naturally driven by sex, as constantly seeking and ever ready for sex, as actively initiating and 'doing' sex to women, and as in competition with other men. 'Adequate' male sexual performance must be delivered after a deliberate period of time in order to meet the obligations and responsibilities accorded to the masculine neoliberal subject. If being 'good at' sex is a neoliberal imperative, the pursuit of an increasingly spectacular orgasmic experience – longer, more frequent and more intense – is positioned as the end product of sexual labour. 'Lasting longer' becomes a marker of neoliberal masculinity, and conversely, premature ejaculation is a failure of masculinity.

With the contrasting stories of two Japanese salarymen (Ken Fukawa and Ichiro Otsuka), Nana Gagné explores the personal impact of neoliberal reforms in Japan. While Fukawa is subject to the capricious flexibility of neoliberal restructuring, Otsuka is caught between marginalisation at work and economic woes at home. Gagné's chapter explores the increasingly precarious position of the once celebrated role of the salaryman within modern Japanese society. She observes that against the growing, global shift towards marketisation (Harvey, 2005), a hegemonic logic of neoliberalism has become a global norm. Local acceptance of this logic has been vital in what Carroll (2012a) describes as "market-deepening" (p. 3). Through the lens of the salarymen case studies held against a broader interrogation of Abenomics,[6] Gagné seeks to understand how neoliberalism has expanded in Japan, resulting in both a radical transformation of individual identity as well as corporate restructuring. Gagné asks, in the midst of this deepening, how have neoliberal reforms affected individuals and their life histories? Has neoliberal restructuring produced new kinds of subjectivities among those who are affected? What is significant is that despite the claims by neoliberal advocates that neoliberal policies might liberate individuals from feudalistic logic through the freedom of rational, economic market logic and flexibility, the actual forms of restructuring have largely resulted in freeing companies from social responsibility for their workers and in

Introduction

the increased flexibility of capital. This highlights an increasing gap between the realities of the Japanese economy on the one hand, and on the other hand the resilient expectations and aspirations of the post-war salaryman's subjectivity as the family breadwinner and as an indispensable member of the national economy.

In Chapter Eight Matteo Carlo Alcano explores shifting ideas around masculinity in the low-income neighbourhood of Kampung Malang. Echoing Ivan Illich's (1982) sublime essay *Silence is a Commons*, Alcano reflects on the impact of everyday life when streets become roads. As Illich (1982) also observes, the streets were a commons of public meetings, children playing, promenading, makeshift food stalls (warung), mobile vendors, market places and pedicab (becak). The new roads however, "were not built for people". The street itself was the result of people living there and making that space liveable, but the threshold between the intimate space of home and the common space of the street could not survive the development of a road. People are no longer tolerated on the road unless they are going to a plaza to buy or sell, or driving through – riding the progressive wave of capitalism that sweeps along this new ocean of bitumen. Alcano finds a sad irony in the idea that traffic has displaced the autonomous mobility of people. Now they can move only when they are strapped in and driven. And parallel to this, young men of this inner-city neighbourhood aspire to become 'drivers' through what the older generation describe as the *labirin* (labyrinth) of the city. What better way to integrate into a system based on traffic than by becoming the traffic itself? The city is a maze and the familiar map of the local territory has been destroyed. However, the young men attempt to embrace/resist the urban transformation and to carve their new 'niche' through making street gangs. Alcano faithfully records the conflicted inter-generational responses to the neoliberal reproduction of space, which is perhaps embodied in a son's re-telling of his father's story of training his beloved pigeons.

The Bosnian city of Mostar is the site of analysis in Giulia Carabelli and Rowan Lubbock's chapter on ethno-national divisions and everyday forms of resistance. Against the backdrop of the Balkans, Carabelli and Lubbock argue that neoliberal geopolitics also emerges in subtler and more invisible forms of geopolitical 'reconnection'. They look to Foucault's work on the subjectivity of neoliberalism in order to understand how its various contradictions are made socially comprehensible. And, like Louth and Potter in their exploration of reproduction of space in the White Building in Cambodia in the following chapter, Carabelli and Lubbock also look to Lefebvre for a critical framework. In this case, they use Lefebvre to trace the potential and limits of civil society actor strategies against nationalist division and economic exploitation in Mostar as a way of drawing out the convergent and divergent practices of neoliberalism. Lefebvre's notion of 'heterotopia' – radical spaces of subversion against prevailing power relations – informs their analysis as they explore utopian re-imaginings opening up across the Bosnian landscape that recall older ideas of Yugoslav 'community', combined with contemporary ideas of participation and non-bureaucratic popular power. From the conceptual frameworks of Foucault and Lefebvre, they dissect the sinews of power that flow between the various actors (both elite and subaltern) involved in the complex entanglements of relations within and between Bosnia Herzegovina and the European Union.

In Chapter Ten, Louth and Potter also look to Lefebvre to guide their analysis of the White Building in the heart of Phnom Penh, Cambodia. Through a detailed exploration of arts and cultural practices that have emerged in the Building post-Khmer Rouge, Louth and Potter reflect on a community of people and manifestation of their shared identity and history through their cultural work. Applying a Lefebvrian lens, Louth and Potter problematize the contested and dominated nature of the Building as a space, within which emergent forms of cultural expressions of resistance take place. Detailing a lineage of arts and cultural practices that have emerged in the Building, notably since the mid-1990s as a response to sustained pressure by external parties to evict residents, they argue that the dominant discursive acts of the more powerful can be challenged through the expression of the 'lived' and the elevation of everyday life. Furthermore, the very perception of both space and sense of place can be (re)produced through these alternative interactions. Creative programmes in the White Building play a role in transmitting an inclusive vision of a subaltern community as a form of resistance that comes from, but extends beyond the everyday. Creative resistance, however fleeting, provides an empathetic turn that offers an insight into possible emancipatory moments.

In the final chapter, Rodolfo Leyva turns attention to the collective memory and imagining of neoliberalism. Leyva asks how neoliberalism affects our political, economic and cultural common-sense understandings. He uses a unique socio-cognitive approach in an attempt to understand an apparent marginal resistance to neoliberalism, despite increased inequality. Hall (2011) claims neoliberalism is a consciously articulated political project enacting a concept of how each major component of contemporary society, including individual agents, should ideally function. If neoliberalism is as consciously articulated as Hall describes and is defined by mutually reinforcing social institutions, how has it come to pass that resistance is, as Leyva claims, 'marginal'? Why is it that we actively contribute to the manifestation of such a structurally delimiting project?

Leyva posits that answers to these questions of auto-exploitation can be found in looking at complex cognitive, affective and social processes and structures and the ways in which they enable, constrain and mediate individual thought and action. Employing a diverse range of theory and affect-based schemas Leyva argues that cognitive affective processes and structures influenced by social engagement, group dynamics and self-awareness are linked to an associative network of memory representations. These representations can be primed to have a subliminal and durable affect on attitudes. Collective memory shapes society's institutions, subjectivities and social practices. When these memories are tied together, via dominant political-economic ideologies such as neoliberalism, this creates a positive feedback loop in which the subjectivities and social practices of the people living within the formative contexts of human institutions and ideologies are shaped by the dominant ideology. People's subjectivities and social practices also have power to shape the dominant ideology and the formative contexts of the institutions and ideologies they inhabit. And so it goes on, in a sustained, self-reinforcing loop. Leyva posits that although theoretically these contexts are in constant flux and reconfiguration, a socio-cognitive approach may describe and explain the role of human institutions and human agents in the reproduction of neoliberal society.

Conclusion

The purpose of this collected volume is to allow readers to embrace a pluralistic understanding of neoliberalism. As a term, neoliberalism is all too often used to simply describe a particular economic understanding of how society should function; or, in respect to ontological assumptions derived from this dominant outlook, *does* function. This volume rejects this outlook. The impact of neoliberalism (or neoliberalisms) has a breadth that cannot be measured against a list of linear, reductive or universal consequences. Each chapter shines a light on how neoliberalism is manifested *within*, through an exploration of a diverse collection of sites, scales and spaces. While a genealogy of the broad development of the 'neoliberal project'

Introduction

is offered, its absorption as an expansionary and capitalist logic is nuanced and differentiated within each specific setting.

The following chapters illustrate the far-reaching spread of neoliberalism – across cultures and into our most personal, intimate spaces. A recurring theme within the volume is the idea that the production of neoliberal subjectivities is intrinsically tied to notions of space and place. The chapters herein explore how competing forms of self and society are repressed or exploit opportunities within the liminal space at the edges of neoliberalism. In each case, how agency is expressed or is repressed is the point of fascination. Both space and place, in this sense, are multidimensional and sustained by discursive practices. This speaks to how we might understand the enormity of international relations and social structures through to the everyday intimacy of relations in the private sphere. The normalisation and the reproduction of particular social practices are linked to the expansion and penetration of a neoliberal hegemony that rationalises, atomises and homogenises the world around us. This volume critically explores how a range of subjectivities is formed, constrained, reshaped or resisted when confronted by the expansionary logic of neoliberalism. Many critics (see Harvey, 2005) have argued that neoliberalism has failed to achieve the growth rates of the golden age of Keynesianism in the 1960s. This failure to succeed on its own merits raises serious questions about how neoliberalism has maintained legitimacy in the face of its own failed *raison d'être* – which is to ensure wealth for all through market efficiency. In light of sustained criticism of the neoliberal project it seems only reasonable to seek both tools and 'how-to' guides in order to untangle a limiting and reductive ideology from our lives and our social structures. We hope that the critical analysis and theoretical reflection embodied in this book goes some way to providing both tools and guides for readers.

Notes

1. Its full name is the Department of Economics at the University of Chicago. It is also worth noting that a group of Chilean economists, dubbed the 'Chicago Boys', who were central to Pinochet's economic reforms, were trained in this department.
2. Yet contradictions, assumptions and variation are evident in the application of neoclassical economics, which has led some to claim that: "Neoliberalism is to neoclassical economics as astrology is to astronomy. In both cases, it takes a lot of blind faith to go from one to the other" (Rodrik, 2002; Marangos, 2008, p. 238).
3. Troika in this case refers to the three key entities representing the European Union in its foreign and financial affairs made up of the International Monetary Fund, the European Commission and the European Central Bank.
4. It is interesting to note that Harvey (2016) is resistant to Foucauldian claims that locate the conditions of neoliberalism in the eighteenth century. For Harvey, neoliberalism is reflective of a distinct project undertaken by corporate capitalist elites from the 1960s onwards.
5. Khoja-Moolji makes a point of capitalising neither 'islam' nor 'muslim' "to signal that there are many different ways of being muslim and many different understandings about the religion of islam, which are betrayed by practices of capitalisation".
6. Abenomics are the economic policies of the Shinzō Abe government that have been implemented after the December 2012 election and are based on the 'three arrows' of dramatic monetary easing to increase inflation, robust fiscal stimulus and growth policies (Japan Revitalization Strategy) targeting the private sector, broader participation in the economy – particularly of women – and development of new markets.

References

Agrawal, A. (2005). *Environmentality: Technologies of government and the making of subjects*. London, United Kingdom: Duke University Press.

Barnett, C., Clarke, N., Cloke, P., & Malpass, A. (2008). The elusive subjects of neoliberalism. *Cultural Studies, 22*(5), 624–653.

Introduction

Beeson, M. (2007). The political economy of security: Geopolitics and capitalist development in the Asia-Pacific. In A. Burke & M. McDonald (Eds.), *Critical security in the Asia-Pacific* (pp. 56–71). Manchester, United Kingdom: Manchester University Press.

Berlinski, C. (2011). *There is no alternative: Why Margaret Thatcher matters*. New York, NY: Basic Books.

Brenner, N. & Theodore, N. (2002). Cities and geographies of 'actually existing neoliberalism'. *Antipode, 34*(3), 349–379.

Burns, C. (2008, 11 April). Margaret Thatcher's greatest achievement: New Labour. *Conservative Home*. Retrieved from http://conservativehome.blogs.com/centreright/2008/04/making-history.html

Carroll, T. (2012a). Neo-liberal development policy in Asia beyond the post-Washington consensus. *Journal of Contemporary Asia, 42*(3), 350–358.

Carroll, T. (2012b). Working on, through and around the state: The deep marketisation of development in the Asia-Pacific. *Journal of Contemporary Asia, 42*(3), 378–404.

Cox, R. W. (1981). Social forces, states and world orders: Beyond international relations theory. *Millennium – Journal of International Studies, 10*(2), 126–155.

Darier, E. (1996). Environmental governmentality: The case of Canada's Green Plan. *Environmental Politics, 5*(4), 585–606.

Ferguson, Y. H. & Mansbach, R. W. (2004). *Remapping global politics: History's revenge and future shock*. Cambridge, United Kingdom: Cambridge University Press.

Foucault, M. (1977). *Discipline and punish: The birth of the modern prison* (Trans. C. Raus). London, United Kingdom: Allen Lane.

Foucault, M. (1978). *The history of sexuality: Volume 1, an introduction*. New York, NY: Vintage Books.

Gill, R. (2008). Culture and subjectivity in neoliberal and postfeminist times. *Subjectivity, 25*(1), 432–445.

Gramsci, A. (1971). *Selections from the prison notebooks* (Trans. Q. Hoare & G. N. Smith). New York, NY: International Publishers.

Hall, S. (2011). The neo-liberal revolution. *Cultural Studies, 25*(6), 705–728.

Hardt, M. & Negri, A. (1994). *The labor of Dionysus: A critique of the state form*. Minneapolis, MN: University of Minnesota Press.

Harvey, D. (2005). *A brief history of neoliberalism*. Oxford, United Kingdom: Oxford University Press.
Harvey, D. (2010). *A companion to Marx's Capital*. London, United Kingdom: Verso Books.
Harvey, D. (2016, 23 July). Neoliberalism is a political project. *Jacobin Magazine*. Retrieved from https://www.jacobinmag.com/2016/07/david-harvey-neoliberalism-capitalism-labor-crisis-resistance/
Hay, C. (2004). The normalizing role of rationalist assumptions in the institutional embedding of neoliberalism. *Economy and Society*, *33*(4), 500–527.
Illich, I. (1982). *Silence is a commons*. Speech presented at Asahi Symposium Science and Man – the Computer-Managed Society, Tokyo, Japan. Retrieved from http://www.preservenet.com/theory/Illich/Silence.html
Jessop, B. & Sum, N. (2006). Towards a cultural international political economy: Poststructualism and the Italian school. In M. de Goede (Ed.), *International political economy and poststructural politics* (pp. 157–176). Basingstoke, United Kingdom; New York, NY: Palgrave Macmillan.
Lefebvre, H. (1976). Reflections on the politics of space. *Antipode*, *8*(2), 30–37.
Lefebvre, H. (1991). *The production of space* (Trans. D. Nicholson-Smith). Malden, MA: Wiley-Blackwell.
Leitner, H., Peck, J., & Sheppard, E. (2007). Squaring up neoliberalism. In H. Leitner, J. Peck, & E. Sheppard (Eds.). *Contesting neoliberalism: Urban frontiers* (pp. 311–327). New York, NY: Guilford Press.
Louth, J. (2012, 14 February). *Newtonians in a non-linear world: The perils of ignoring complex phenomena*. Paper presented at the book launch for E. Cudworth & S. C. Hobden, *Posthuman International Relations*. London, United Kingdom: University of East London.
Louth J. (2015). Neoliberalising Cambodia: The production of capacity in Southeast Asia. *Globalizations*, *12*(3), 400–419.
Marangos, J. (2008). The evolution of the anti-Washington consensus debate: from 'post-Washington consensus' to 'after the Washington consensus'. *Competition and Change*, *12*(3), 227–244.

Introduction

Mirowski, P. (2013). *Never let a serious crisis go to waste: How neoliberalism survived the financial meltdown*. London, United Kingdom; New York, NY: Verso.

Ostry J., Loungani, P., & Furceri, D. (2016). Neoliberalism: Oversold? *Finance & Development, 53*(2), 38–41.

Peck, J. (2010). *Constructions of neoliberal reason*. Oxford, United Kingdom: Oxford University Press.

Peck, J. & Tickell, A. (2007). Conceptualizing neoliberalism, thinking Thatcherism. In H. Leitner, J. Peck, & E. Sheppard (Eds.), *Contesting neoliberalism: Urban frontiers* (pp. 26–50). New York, NY: Guilford Press.

Philp, M. (1985). Michel Foucault. In Q. Skinner (Ed.), *The return of grand theory in the human sciences* (pp. 65–81). Cambridge, United Kingdom: Cambridge University Press.

Rodrik, D. (2002, 23–24 May). *After neoliberalism, what?* Paper presented at the Alternatives to Neoliberalism Conference sponsored by the New Rules for Global Finance Coalition, Washington, DC.

Rowden, R. (2016, 26 July). The IMF confronts its N-word: The International Monetary Fund admits that it's time to discard some of the old neoliberal dogmas. *Foreign Policy*. Retrieved from http://foreignpolicy.com/2016/07/06/the-imf-confronts-its-n-word-neoliberalism/

Sartre, J.-P. (2016). *What is subjectivity?* (Trans. D. Broder & T. Selous). London, United Kingdom: Verso Books.

Sperling, G. (2007, 18 September). Rising tide economics. Council on Foreign Relations. Retrieved from http://www.cfr.org/business-and-foreign-policy/rising-tide-economics/p14230

Tempest, M. (2002, 11 June). Mandelson: We are all Thatcherites now. *The Guardian*. Retrieved from http://www.theguardian.com/politics/2002/jun/10/labour.uk1

Tickell, A. & Peck, J. (2003). Making global rules: Globalization or neoliberalization? In J. Peck & H. Wai-chung Yeung, (Eds.), *Remaking the global economy* (pp. 163–181). London, United Kingdom: SAGE.

Unger, R. (1987). *Plasticity into power: Comparative-historical studies of the institutional conditions of economic and military success*. Cambridge, United Kingdom: Cambridge University Press.

Van Horn, R. & Mirowski, P. (2009). The rise of the Chicago School of Economics and the birth of neoliberalism. In P. Mirowski & D. Plehwe (Eds.), *The road from Mont Pelerin: The making of the neoliberal thought collective* (pp. 139-180). Cambridge, MA: Harvard University Press.

CHAPTER ONE

CONSUMING ENVIRONMENTAL CITIZENSHIP, OR THE PRODUCTION OF NEOLIBERAL GREEN CITIZENS

Benito Cao

The growing preoccupation with the state of the environment has overlapped with the renewed interest in citizenship since the 1990s. In the past two decades, environmental activists, governments and corporations have embraced the language of citizenship to articulate their claims, policies and positions regarding environmental issues. Conversely, environmental concerns and ecological values are inspiring new articulations of citizenship, with the potential of transforming what it means to be a citizen in the twenty-first century. However, this convergence between environment and citizenship is taking place in a historical context shaped by neoliberal forces, values and discourses that are also having a major, and arguably more significant, impact on the meaning and practice of citizenship.

This chapter explores the neoliberalisation of environmental citizenship, with a particular focus on the production of neoliberal green subjects. The chapter begins with an articulation of the relation between citizenship, subjectivity and (neoliberal) governmentality. This is followed by a brief outline of how citizenship, as a form of political subjectivity, is reshaped when confronted by the expansionary logic of neoliberalism. The chapter then examines three pedagogical instruments used to promote environmental citizenship: government campaigns, ecological footprint calculators and media texts, in particular children's animation. The analysis reveals that, in the present context, these instruments consume the concept of environmental citizenship, that is, they subject the concept to an economic rationality that reduces environmental citizenship to the act of sustainable consumption. In addition, the analysis reveals that these pedagogical instruments enable the governing of the environment through citizens (as consumers), thus making neoliberal green citizens both subjects and agents of neoliberal environmentality.

Concepts: citizenship, subjectivity and (neoliberal) governmentality
Citizenship is one of the oldest social and political institutions and one of the fundamental practices that structures human relations in modern societies. Citizenship is also a notoriously polyvalent and contested concept. Its complex and contested nature derives largely from the fact that citizenship is a relational concept. Citizenship articulates the relationship between the individual and the collective, between the citizens and the political community to which they belong. This articulation varies from place to place and from time to time. Indeed, citizenship is always and everywhere in a permanent process of construction and transformation. Yet for all its diversity and dynamism, there are three elements that are present in all conventional definitions of citizenship: membership, rights and duties.

Membership is about the 'who' of citizenship and reveals its relational character as well as one of its fundamental dynamics, namely, inclusion vs. exclusion. In the modern sense, citizenship "is about who belongs to the nation, who does not, and why" (Gorman, 2006, p. 1). From this point of view, citizenship can be defined as "an international filing system, a mechanism for allocating persons to states" (Brubaker, 1992, p. 31). However, citizenship as membership is far more complex and significant than the mere allocation of people to nation-states, or any other political community. Membership remits also to the sense of belonging and identity associated with being part of the political community. Indeed, citizenship is "a primary means through which societies assert, construct, and consecrate their sense of identity" (Gorman, 2006, p. 1).

Rights and duties are about the 'what' of citizenship. The specific rights and duties, the relative importance attributed to particular rights and duties, and the relative emphasis placed on rights and duties as a whole, have varied across time and space, but rights coexist with duties in all conceptions of citizenship. The relative weight and significance attached to each is a matter of emphasis, but emphasis matters. Indeed, the different emphasis given to rights and duties is one of the key aspects that differentiates the two classical theories of citizenship: liberal and republican. The first defines citizenship as a status, and is fundamentally a rights-based approach, which prioritises legal protection and individual freedom. The second defines citizenship as action, and is fundamentally a duties-based approach, which prioritises political participation and the common good. These two traditions have deep historical roots, have dominated the debate about citizenship, and remain the two mainstream theories of citizenship. The prevalence of each model at different times and places relates in no small part to one additional but crucial aspect, the education of citizens.

Education has been integral to citizenship since ancient times, both in theory and in practice. It is no accident that the best historical accounts of citizenship attribute significant importance and dedicate plenty of attention to the education of citizens (e.g. Heater, 2004). Not to mention that education features prominently in the work of some of the most influential theorists of citizenship, including Aristotle, Bodin, Locke, Rousseau and Marshall. The significance of the pedagogical dimension of citizenship is perfectly captured in this statement: "education for citizenship is not an optional extra, but an integral part of the concept" (Heater, 2004, p. 326). This reflects the fact that citizens are made, not born. In other words, we learn to be citizens. To be sure, most people obtain the legal status of citizens at birth, but that says little about what kind of citizen we will become (e.g. active, passive, green, etc.). Citizens need some degree of knowledge, skills and dispositions, as well as capabilities, for their rights and duties to be meaningful. In fact, who is a citizen and what kind of citizen one becomes is a highly manufactured process. The making of citizens is a long, complex and ongoing process that needs to be understood in the context of political socialisation, that is, the learning of norms and behaviours that allow individuals to become functioning members of a given political community.

The pedagogical dimension of citizenship invokes the notion of citizenship as subjectivity. Subjectivity refers to the construction of the self, that is, to the formation of subjects. The process of subject formation is understood here as a meditative process that involves the positioning of a subject in relation to something external. The traditional external referent of citizens as subjects (or citizens-subjects) has been the state (as the supreme political authority), as well as the other citizens. This relatively simple picture has been complicated in recent times with the emergence of corporations, both as (corporate) citizens and sources of (political) authority (Crane, Matten, & Moon 2008). The construction of the self is also a mediated process. The media influences the way we perceive and make sense of the world, which in turn impacts on how we act in that world. In other words, the construction of the self (in general) and the making of citizens (in particular) cannot be fully understood without adequate consideration of the role of the media in shaping the context in which we are socialised as subjects and citizens. This approach to citizenship as subjectivity requires that we examine the realms of the media and popular culture as "definitive parameters and promises of citizenship" (Canning, 2007, p. 139).

Consuming Environmental Citizenship

The pedagogical dimension of citizenship invokes also the notion of citizenship as governmentality. Governmentality refers to a form of indirect and subtle ruling that shapes human behaviour in ways that mask the mechanics of power and thus achieves seemingly free and consensual compliance but without conscious and public deliberation. The term derives from the work of Michel Foucault, the French philosopher who popularised the idea that 'power is everywhere', diffused and embodied in discourse, knowledge and 'regimes of truth' (Rabinow, 1991). Foucault used the term to shift the focus of political analysis from formal laws and institutions to the technologies of power that shape, direct and regulate our individual beliefs, desires, lifestyles and actions. He argued that coercion and regulation are not the only means used to produce ordered, predictable, manageable behaviour in modern societies (Foucault, 1991). Instead, modern political power tends to operate through more subtle and diffuse mechanisms designed to instil in each individual techniques of self-control (or self-regulation). In essence, governmentality refers to "the conduct of conduct", and ranges from "the governing of others" to "the governing of the self" (Mitchell, 2006, p. 389).

Governmentality, as a technology of government, has become increasingly associated with neoliberalism. Indeed, governmentality has become the preferred technology of neoliberal authorities. This is hardly surprising given the centrality of self-regulation in neoliberal thought. Under this form of governing, citizens are expected to "examine and govern themselves so as to improve their lives in ways that benefit themselves, their community and the state" (Bevir, 2011, p. 466). Political authorities still exist, but govern in a different way, *through* citizens rather than *over* citizens, shaping human conduct through the formation of will, ultimately inducing self-government. Neoliberalism, as a form of governmentality, works by "installing a concept of the human subject as an autonomous, individualized, self-directing agent at the heart of policy-making" (Bondi, 2005, p. 499). In other words, it works by producing individuals who "discipline themselves to use their freedom to make responsible choices" (Bevir, 2011, p. 466). These choices are to be made according to a neoliberal economic rationality – a cost-benefit analysis informed by the values and norms of a free market economy.

The articulation of citizenship as subjectivity and governmentality is particularly useful to elucidate the manufacturing of neoliberal green citizens and the role they perform in the governing of the environment. But before we explore some of the ways in which environmental citizens are being produced as neoliberal green citizens, it is important to understand how neoliberalism is transforming the traditional (i.e. political) conception of citizenship, and how this in turn impacts on the emerging concept of environmental citizenship.

Transformations: neoliberalising (environmental) citizenship
The increasing awareness and preoccupation regarding the human impact on the environment is having a profound impact in contemporary societies, not least in relation to the concept and content of citizenship. Environmental concerns and ecological values are redefining citizenship in ways that resemble a revolution at work, with the potential to radically transform what it means to be a citizen in the twenty-first century. This idea is neatly captured in the cover of Andrew Dobson's seminal book, *Citizenship and the Environment* (2003). The cover is a variation on the iconic painting of the French Revolution, Eugène Delacroix's *Liberty Leading the People* (1830). The variation is simple but highly effective: instead of the French national flag, Liberty leads the people holding a tree branch. The cover suggests that citizenship is undergoing another revolutionary transformation, as significant as the one that marked the birth of modern citizenship, this time informed by environmental concerns and ecological values.

Consuming Environmental Citizenship

The extent to which we can speak of a revolution at work is a question for debate, but there is little doubt that the environment and citizenship are converging in many and significant ways. Governments around the world are recognising environmental rights, activists refer to our duties to the environment, corporations present themselves as good environmental citizens, children are taught to be mindful of their ecological footprint, the media tell us repeatedly to reduce, reuse and recycle, and theorists have begun to consider all this under a new field of study called environmental citizenship. The diversity and complexity of this convergence has been mapped in my own exploration of the field, most recently in *Environment and Citizenship* (2015). However, there is another important, and arguably more profound revolution transforming citizenship in general, and environmental citizenship in particular, the neoliberal revolution. This revolution is shifting the focus from the citizen to the consumer and from the state to the corporation (as agents of citizenship), and from politics to markets (as the sphere of citizenship).

The neoliberalisation of citizenship is the product of the neoliberal ascendancy that followed the collapse of the Bretton Woods system in the early 1970s and the coming to power of the 'new right' in the United Kingdom and the United States. Neoliberalism, as a political and economic project characterised by privatisation, deregulation, and a frontal attack against the welfare state, rose to prominence in the 1980s, during the governments of Margaret Thatcher and Ronald Reagan (Harvey, 2005). The neoliberal paradigm has since expanded its global reach, in the form of 'neoliberal globalisation' (Kuisma, 2008), through international organisations such as the International Monetary Fund (IMF), the World Bank and the World Trade Organization (WTO).

The neoliberal turn has signalled a profound shift from the state to the market as the locus of wealth production and distribution. But its impact goes way beyond social policy and the economy. Neoliberalism operates as a totalising discourse, extending market values and market rules to all spheres of life, from health, education and political participation, to family life and personal relations (Brown, 2005). The extension of market rules to social and political relations has led some authors to argue that we are moving from being societies with a market economy to becoming market societies, particularly in the affluent West (Sandel, 2012). In this context, it should not be too surprising to find out that neoliberalism poses the most profound challenge to traditional (i.e. political) notions of citizenship. This challenge relates both to the 'who' and the 'what' of citizenship (membership, rights and duties), and has materialised into the formulation of different articulations (and subsets) of neoliberal citizenship, most notably corporate citizenship and consumer citizenship.

The neoliberal ascendancy has translated into the addition of a new member to the club: corporations. In recent years, corporations have emerged as powerful players in the sphere of citizenship. Their involvement derives in part from their influence over governments and their policies. However, what makes corporations particularly significant is their status of legal persons – a status that has enabled them to claim the status of citizens in their own right. The inclusion of corporations as citizens represents a profound shift in the conception of citizenship, from the traditional dyad (individual–government) to the neoliberal triad (individual–government–corporation). Indeed, given the emphasis neoliberalism places on minimising government and shifting relations to the market sphere, there is potential for a new, neoliberal dyad to emerge as central to the future of citizenship: individual–corporation.

The impact of neoliberalism has also been felt in the redefinition of the traditional citizen, the individual. Market theories of political exchange reduce the citizen to a 'consumer' or 'customer'. In essence, neoliberal citizenship shifts the focus from the individual as a political being (*zoon politikon*) towards the individual as an economic being (*homo economicus*). The extent and significance of this transformation are matters of contention. On the one hand, the consumer-citizen can be seen as a citizen with additional power, i.e. consumer power. However, that shift can also be interpreted as the displacement of one type of member (the citizen) for another (the consumer), making membership and the exercise of citizenship contingent upon wealth and the capacity to consume, and ultimately reducing citizenship to consumption.

The neoliberal turn has also had a profound impact on the content of citizenship. Neoliberalism redraws the picture of rights, revitalising some classic rights (most notably property rights), dismantling others (in particular social rights), and enabling the creation of new ones (mainly consumer rights). Neoliberalism also redraws the picture of duties, redefining some social rights as duties (particularly the right to work), shifting the emphasis from political to economic participation, and promoting the individualisation of responsibility. Neoliberal citizenship also includes the rights and duties of its new member, corporations. Traditionally, corporations have enjoyed commercial rights (as economic entities), but in recent times corporations have been able to claim and exercise civil and political rights – most notably, the right to free speech and the right to participate in political campaigns (in both cases, in the United States). In general, the neoliberal portrait of rights and duties shifts citizenship from the political arena to the economic terrain and, to some extent, transforms citizenship from a political into an economic activity.

This transformation is particularly noticeable in the way in which consumption is becoming part of a deeper transformation to the meaning and practice of citizenship – one that encourages citizens to exercise their political agency as consumers, voting with our wallet. This idea is rooted in classical market theory. Early in the nineteenth century, Austrian economist Frank Fetter wrote: "The market is a democracy where every penny gives the right to vote" (Quoted in Dickinson & Carsky, 2005, p. 25). The popularity of this idea has increased greatly with the rise of neoliberal governance since the late twentieth century.

The neoliberal ascendancy has translated into concepts and articulations of environmental citizenship that incorporate the environment into the notions of corporate citizenship and consumer citizenship – the latter being the focus of this chapter. The neoliberal discourse states that the most effective way in which citizens can (and should) exercise environmental citizenship is through their power as consumers, that is, embracing sustainable consumption. In essence, neoliberal environmental citizenship recasts the green citizen as a green consumer. The neoliberal articulation of environmental citizenship is becoming increasingly widespread, driven by corporations and embraced by governments as a form of governing the environment through citizens. The expansion of neoliberal environmental citizenship relies on the production of neoliberal green citizens. This requires pedagogies that emphasise self-reliance and the individualisation of responsibility. The rest of this chapter explores three illustrations of the production of neoliberal green citizens, and their role in governing the environment.

Campaigns: governing through consumer-citizens

Governments have become acutely aware of the need to address environmental concerns. Their specific policies and programmes vary significantly from country to country, but across the world governments are adopting the language of citizenship to frame their response to environmental issues. This has taken several forms, but the hegemony of the neoliberal mentality, with its aversion to government regulation, has translated into the adoption of more indirect and diffuse techniques for the governing of the environment. There is a noticeable shift from governing through direct regulation to governing through citizens by means of pedagogical and psychological techniques. This form of governing the environment involves "the use of social-engineering techniques to get the attention of the population to focus on specific environmental issues and to instil – in a non-openly coercive manner – new environmental conducts" (Darier, 1996, p. 594). This approach has been defined as "environmental governmentality" (Darier, 1996) or "environmentality" (Agrawal, 2005).

The convergence of neoliberal governmentality and environmental citizenship is closely related to the emergence of sustainable consumption as a fundamental articulation of environmental citizenship. This is done primarily through the production of consumer-citizens. Governments participate in this process, first and foremost, through the design of campaigns and policies that interpellate citizens as consumers – that is, as economic rather than political agents. This trend is particularly pronounced in affluent countries, but is being extended across the planet by global agencies such as the United Nations Environment Programme (UNEP). In the next few pages, we take a look at the manufacturing of neoliberal green citizens across three political spaces and levels of government: the national (United Kingdom), the regional (European Union) and the global (UNEP).

This approach to governing the environment through green consumers (or consumer-citizens) has been embraced prominently in the United Kingdom. The most recent illustration is the Green Deal, a government initiative launched in 2012 that provided loans for energy-saving home upgrades. Consumers would borrow the money to make the upgrades, and pay back the loan through their energy bills. The policy was based on market-driven, public-private approaches in line with the government's policy of relying on markets as the mechanism for delivering environmental policies and outcomes. The scheme lasted barely three years. In July 2015, the British government announced that there would be no more Green Deal cashback or loans, citing low take up and poor standards of workmanship (Palmer, 2015). The government is devising a replacement scheme to make a million more homes efficient by 2020. The Green Deal is the latest in a history of government initiatives centred on changing individual behaviour rather than making structural reforms when it comes to promoting sustainability in the United Kingdom.

Since the early 1990s, the British government has developed four major campaigns designed to change behaviour towards the environment: 'Helping the Earth Begins at Home' (1991), 'Going for Green' (1995), 'Are You Doing Your Bit?' (1999), and 'Together We Can' (2005). The campaigns have shifted progresssively from a centralised top-down approach, based on the assumption that people would comply with government advice once they became aware of the issues and of what to do, to a distributed 'bottom-up' approach that tries to encourage citizens to get involved and propose their own green initiatives (Barr, 2008). However, despite some concessions to notions of community in recent years, the campaigns are invariably aimed at altering individual behaviour, and engage the citizen as a consumer. The campaigns place individual and household consumption, and economic rationality, at the heart of environmental sustainability, equating saving energy with saving money, and promote market forces and self-regulation as the preferred road towards sustainability. The net effect of these campaigns is the creation of a consumer-citizen through which the government can conduct the governing of the environment.

The governing of the environment through consumer-citizens is also noticeable at the level of the European Union. This approach is particularly well illustrated by the 2006 campaign against climate change entitled: 'You Control Climate Change'

(European Commission, 2007). The campaign tells consumers to 'Turn down. Switch off. Recycle. Walk'. The objective is to get citizens to make small changes in their daily routines to reduce greenhouse gas emissions and tackle global warming. The campaign, with its tips, greenhouse gas calculators, games and information, effectively creates a 'climate citizen' in the European Union. This citizen is defined as an individual – or, at most, a household – that performs small, private-sphere activities in order to reduce greenhouse emissions. The focus is on individual action, with the great majority of the advice and tips regarding patterns of private behaviour, most of them related to the home (e.g. recycling and switching off lights) and/or home-related matters (e.g. walking to the local store and taking own bags to go shopping). The campaign also targets students, who are encouraged to sign a pledge to reduce their carbon dioxide emissions. This notion of individuals making a public commitment to reducing greenhouse gas emissions has since extended to different locations (Upham, 2012).

Whilst such changes in personal behaviour are laudable in and of themselves, the emphasis on small-scale initiatives and individual behaviour occludes large-scale structural issues underlying climate change (e.g. emissions from coal-based electricity production). In addition, this approach diverts attention from matters of environmental justice, such as climate debt, that would require addressing the disproportionate historical contributions to the current problem of climate change by the countries of the global North and those of the global South. Moreover, in a context where the wider causes of climate change are felt to be beyond individual control, the individualisation of responsibility can lead to resignation and acceptance rather than action, effectively resulting in "deresponsibilisation" (Butler, 2010, p. 183). Significantly, there are no tips or advice given to citizens about engaging in climate politics. In other words, there is no representation or interpellation of the citizen as a political actor, only as an economic being.

The governmental push to promote green consumer-citizens has become part of the global environmental strategy of the UNEP, as illustrated by its campaign 'Shopping for a Better World' (UNEP, 2003). The project focusses on marketing sustainable lifestyles as attractive, desirable and fashionable, as the key to selling environmentally friendly products. In the words of UNEP Executive Director, Klaus Toepfer: "what can be more modern, more fashionable, than caring about our planet" (UNEP, 2003). The programme targets forms of inappropriate consumption, not overconsumption. "Sustainable consumption – reads the press release – is not about consuming less, it is about consuming differently, consuming efficiently, and having an improved quality of life" (UNEP, 2003). Citizens (as consumers) are expected to exercise self-control regarding what and how they consume, not how much they consume (Rumpala, 2011). Once again, the focus on individual consumer behaviour diverts attention from unjust and environmentally unsustainable structural patterns of consumption, particularly between the global North and the global South. The same logic informs a recent scheme that explicitly invokes the language of citizenship and is designed to "encourage demand for sustainable tourism products and services": the Green Passport (UNEP, 2014).

The environmental citizen produced by these and similar governmental initiatives is someone who has internalised information about environmental problems, creating a sense of personal responsibility that is then expressed mainly through consumption. These campaigns not only shift the space of citizenship from the political to the economic sphere, but they also shift the emphasis from consumer rights to consumer duties, thus placing the burden of action on citizens (as consumers) rather than on governments and/or corporations and businesses. This disciplining of private citizens into green consumer practices that do not challenge consumer capitalism illustrates neoliberal environmentality at work. These schemes operate by deeply inscribing self-monitoring and self-control into citizens that – in the absence of inclusive and transparent deliberations – perpetuate social control and reinscribe hierarchies into the seemingly democratic operations of government (Davies, 2012). The production of neoliberal green citizens, and the trend to govern through green citizens at the expense of government regulation and structural reforms, is also promoted by ecological footprint calculators.

Calculators: individualising environmental responsibility
The main pedagogical tool in the manufacturing of green citizens is the ecological footprint calculator. The concept of the ecological footprint has been used widely in education, public policy and awareness campaigns, with an estimated six million people from over 45 countries accessing online personal footprint calculators each year (Cordero, Todd, & Abellera, 2008). The personal calculator asks a series of simple questions about shelter, food and transport, and then calculates the area of land required to support your lifestyle. The calculator typically produces a double score: the size of your ecological footprint on global hectares (gha), and the number of planets required if everybody lived like you. The current individual allocation of land per person is 1.8 gha. This means that if your footprint is larger than 1.8 gha your current lifestyle is unsustainable – and you owe an 'ecological debt' to those who are currently using less than their allocation, mostly people in the countries of the global South.

The ecological footprint calculator is an excellent tool to get a sense of the general sustainability of individual lifestyles and to identify which aspects contribute more to our ecological footprint. Studies show that environmental education for sustainability based on the use of the ecological footprint "enable students to evaluate, understand and examine the connection between personal and local lifestyle and the influence on ecological systems that support life on the global level" (Gottlieb, Vigoda-Gadot, Haim, & Kissinger, 2012, p. 197). In particular, personal calculators illustrate the significance of eating habits, which typically amount to around half of the total individual footprint. The importance of food in personal ecological footprints has been reflected in the recent UN-led campaign 'Think, Eat, Save: Reduce Your Foodprint'. The ecological foodprint is impacted by a range of elements, but the main variable is the consumption of animal products, especially meat. However, containing the ecological impact of animal products is also a matter of production. The burden of industrial livestock or the 'grain-oilseed-livestock complex' on the environment has been captured in the concept of 'ecological hoofprint' developed by Weis (2013). In any case, ecological footprint calculators indicate that a change in eating habits (especially if we are frequent meat-eaters) can make a significant difference to the size of our ecological footprint.

However, not everyone agrees on the pedagogical effectiveness of ecological footprint calculators. Their impact seems to rely on the way in which they are used. In and of themselves, these calculators can have the opposite of the intended effect and discourage individuals from improving their behaviour. This is largely to do with the fact that, because most people in developed countries live environmentally unsustainable lifestyles, the scores the calculators produce and the feedback they provide are almost invariably negative. The websites where the calculators are located typically assume the scenario of overshoot (i.e. unsustainability) and dedicate a considerable space to provide tips to reduce personal footprints, such as: changing eating habits, driving and flying less, reducing water consumption (e.g. taking fewer or shorter showers, installing water tanks), reducing energy consumption (e.g. switching off lights and avoiding standby mode), installing energy efficient appliances, shopping with care (e.g. taking your own bags, choosing products with minimal packaging, buying local products, growing your own fruit and vegetables), and learning from others (e.g. checking case studies online).

The assumption seems to be that negative scores will inspire people to change their lifestyles in order to reduce their footprint. However, people can react to negative feedback in a variety of ways, including unproductive ones, such as:

> feeling overwhelmed, feeling that sustainability is impossible, giving up, justifying their unsustainable behaviour, blaming other people for environmental problems, trivializing the impact of their own behaviour, deciding that environmental problems are not important, or discounting the accuracy of the footprint feedback itself. (Brook, 2011, p. 114).

Brook even notes that one possible reaction is that people may respond by changing their environmental views to match their behaviour. Her study suggests that negative feedback can increase or decrease sustainable behaviour depending on pre-existing commitment to environmentalism. Thus, whilst negative feedback might inspire additional efforts from people with a strong environmental commitment, it can discourage those lacking such disposition from making significant efforts or even lead them to give up on their efforts altogether. This is particularly problematic when we consider that "for the majority of available calculators, even when the most environmentally friendly options are adopted, one still exceeds the planet's biocapacity levels" (Franz & Papyrakis, 2011, p. 395). These consistently negative scores can render ecological footprint calculators into "a doom-saying, off-putting instrument" that promotes the syndrome that the problem is "so big nothing can be done" (Franz & Papyrakis, 2011, p. 395).

The main reason personal footprints in the global North are almost impossible to bring under 1.8 gha are the structural issues that escape our control as individuals, let alone as consumers. Individuals cannot change the transport system, the urban layout and the service infrastructure through consumption habits. Similarly, individual consumers have no control over large-scale industrial systems, such as food production, waste disposal and energy generation. In addition, affordability often means that we cannot decide where we live, how to travel between home and work, what types of houses we can buy, and we might even have little choice on what kind of food to purchase (e.g. if all we have access to is one or two large supermarkets). This tells us that, without significantly altering social structures, physical infrastructure and industrial processes, individual changes and actions, whilst important, have a limited impact. In turn, this suggests that "collective political action, not simply individual consumer action, is necessary to bring about the institutional changes that will be needed to achieve sustainability" (Obach, 2009, p. 298). In other words, 'shrinking ecological footprints' must be complemented with 'expanding political ones' (May, 2009).

However, ecological footprint calculators have no place for collective or political action. These instruments focus solely on individual behaviour, and in doing so contribute to manufacturing neoliberal citizens and promoting neoliberal environmental governmentality. Individuals are made responsible for their own choices, irrespective of how many structural constraints may actually factor into the organisation of their lives. The calculators provide no way to visualise the impact that structural changes would have on individual footprints, nor do they factor the effect that political activism and other forms of environmental action can have on our collective ecological footprints. The only relevant profile is that of the citizen as consumer. This approach to measuring the impact of our

Consuming Environmental Citizenship

actions on the environment ignores the political dimension of citizenship, effectively reducing citizenship to the act of sustainable consumption.

The ecological footprint also fails to adequately account for the past, that is, it cannot calculate ecological debt incurred through centuries of exploitation and appropriation of the environment, most notably by the global North. This could imply that people in the global North should reduce their ecological footprint below 1.8 gha, to pay our ecological debt and provide additional ecological space to those in the global South to develop – assuming that development is a desirable goal, and that it necessitates, at least temporarily, going over 1.8 gha per capita. But even if we were to ignore the past, present statistics are profoundly disturbing. For instance, if everyone on the planet were to enjoy the lifestyle of the average US citizen, the aspirational model for much of the developing world, we would require four Earths. This means that to sustain their large ecological footprints the countries of the global North run large ecological deficits with the global South. The global rebalance demands profound changes in the lifestyle habits of most people in the global North.

The issues raised by ecological footprint calculators should not discourage their use, especially not in educational settings. The key, however, is to make sense of the findings in ways that account for contextual and structural issues and thus enable a critical interpretation of the results. Indeed, ecological footprint calculators are an ideal instrument to illustrate both the construction of the neoliberal environmental citizen (who acts on the environment as a consumer) and the limits of that conception of citizenship to address current environmental issues (as noted above). In other words, the extent to which ecological footprint calculators contribute to manufacturing neoliberal green citizens or other forms of environmental citizens (e.g. ecological citizens) depends largely on how users in general and educators in particular frame and interpret the results. But these interpretations do not take place in a vacuum. Instead, they take place in a context shaped by popular culture and media representations. The final section of this chapter provides a brief analysis of such representations.

Representations: mediating environmental citizenship
The media provide both context and content when it comes to shaping our conceptions of environmental citizenship. The dominant portrait of green citizens in the current media is that of the green consumer, the sensible and sustainable consumer-citizen. This image has come to replace the focus on green activists. Green consumer-citizens do not get involved in politics, not even electoral politics. Instead, they embrace the ideal of sustainability and take up the challenge through sustainable consumption, changing consumer practices and habits in small and reasonable ways, voluntarily and without making a point of displaying or advocating particular lifestyles. This image of the green consumer can be found across news stories, documentaries and newspaper supplements dedicated to promoting green products and technologies (e.g. e-bikes, hybrid cars, solar panels, etc.) and providing tips on how to save energy and reduce waste. The narrative of sustainable consumption works in much the same way as that of corporate social responsibility. They are both presented as win-win scenarios, that is, practices that save money whilst helping to 'save the planet'. This neoliberal conception of environmental citizenship has come to prevail across all media platforms, including public service television in countries like Germany and the United Kingdom (Inthorn & Reder, 2011).

The neoliberal approach to environmental citizenship is best illustrated by programmes dedicated to encouraging audiences to make changes in their lifestyles and patterns of consumption. The most famous example is arguably Laura Gabbert and Justin Schein's documentary *No Impact Man* (2009).

Consuming Environmental Citizenship

The film follows Colin Beavan and his family during their year-long project to live with zero environmental impact. The experiment results in the family adopting a frugal way of life that includes deprivations such as foregoing takeout food and toilet paper, avoiding out-of-season produce, reducing the consumption of coffee, foregoing most modes of transportation including elevators, and eventually going without electricity altogether. The message is clear and simple: 'saving the planet one family at a time' (Beavan, 2009).

The concept of sustainable households has also been taken to television in Australia, where the public multicultural broadcaster SBS produced the series *Eco House Challenge* (2007). The objective of the series is similar to that behind *No Impact Man*, that is, to teach households ways to minimise their ecological footprint through sustainable consumption and the reduction of wasteful consumption. The programme results in a series of "experiments in environmental citizenship" that illustrate how "the management of populations in late liberal societies is increasingly occurring at the level of everyday life and consumption through a focus on the conduct and lifestyles of individuals" (Lewis, 2012, p. 324). These media texts are part of a trend to adopt the reality television format as a pedagogical tool to promote Do-It-Yourself (DIY) citizenship (Ouellette & Hay, 2008). The extent to which these and similar programmes deepen neoliberal citizenship or can emancipate citizens is still an open question, but in the overall climate it seems to fit neatly with the neoliberal agenda, and echoes the signature call of 'Captain Planet: The Power is Yours!'

The television series *Captain Planet and the Planeteers* is the most well-known and far-reaching pedagogical environmental animation. The series, created in 1990 by Ted Turner for his cable network TBS, screened a total of 117 episodes between 1990 and 1996. The cartoon still exists in syndication and continues to be shown regularly on US cable network Bloomberg, and around the world. The series won multiple awards, including two US environmental awards in 1993 and 1994. The influence of the series derives not just from its popularity but also from the Captain Planet Foundation, established in 1992, and the Planeteer Movement, launched in 2010. The movement was established so that fans can continue to connect to the show and apply its messages to their lives as real-life Planeteers.

The basic premise of the series is that Gaia (the spirit of planet Earth) calls upon five teenagers from around the world to lead battle against the eco-villains wreaking havoc on the planet. Each of the Planeteers is given a magic ring that enables them to control one element of nature (Earth, Fire, Water, Wind) and one extra element, Heart. The five can join their forces to summon Captain Planet, the environmental superhero. Each episode ends with Captain Planet declaring to the audience: 'The Power is Yours!' The series is overtly pedagogical and environmental – all the episodes end with hints and tips for children, and viewers in general, to look after the environment. But, once again, these tips articulate a concept of environmental citizenship that is synonymous with sustainable consumption. This is also the representation of environmental citizenship that dominates children's animated films – a genre shaped largely by the cultural hegemony of Hollywood.

The past few decades have seen an explosion of environmental films directed at children, including: *FernGully* (1992), *Free Willy* (1993), *Finding Nemo* (2003), *Happy Feet* (2006), *Wall-E* (2008), and *The Lorax* (2012). These and similar texts invite children (and parents) to care for and act on behalf of the environment. These films typically combine a dystopian vision of the future, associated with our present unsustainable lifestyles, with exhortations to do the right thing for nature and for future generations. The dominant narrative presents virtuous individuals as the key to solving the environmental predicament that has produced, or is driving the world towards, a dystopian future. The films portray corporate greed as a central part of the problem, but exclude governments from any significant role in addressing environmental problems. Instead, it is left to the individual consumer-citizen to challenge the power of the corporations – and transform them into good corporate citizens. Indeed, the relevant agents are citizens (as individual consumers) and corporations. The films ignore collective action and government regulation as part of the solution to our environmental predicament. This individualised response to environmental degradation denies any need to change institutional structures that drive or enable the consumerism these films sometimes overtly criticise. In fact, most of these films promote a culture of consumption through the relentless production and advertising of toys and other film-related merchandise.

Conclusion: environmental citizenshop
The environment is posing significant challenges to our understanding of citizenship. However, the neoliberal context in which environmental concerns and the renewed interest in citizenship have converged has profoundly shaped our current understanding of environmental citizenship. The neoliberal turn has translated into a rapid shift towards the language of individual and corporate responsibility through self-regulation, and a shift towards economics in general (e.g. market rules and values) and consumption in particular (e.g. sustainable consumption) in the dominant articulations of environmental citizenship. To be sure, sustainable consumption might be compatible with notions of environmental citizenship, especially if citizens are supported by institutional and political changes that create the appropriate social context. However, this requires governments to shift social values, set an example by developing green infrastructure, and force corporations to change their behaviour rather than rely on self-regulation. Whilst this is possible (and even desirable), in the present

economic and political context, dominated by a rampant neoliberal paradigm, the opposite seems to be happening. Citizenship is being consumed by market values, and active citizenship is often synonymous with shopping. In this context, environmental citizenship – understood as sustainable consumption – might best be termed environmental citizenshop.

References
Agrawal, A. (2005). *Environmentality: Technologies of government and the making of subjects*. Durham, NC; London, United Kingdom: Duke University Press.
Barr, S. (2008). *Environment and society: Sustainability, policy and the citizen*. Aldershot, United Kingdom: Ashgate.
Beavan, C. (2009). *No impact man: Saving the planet one family at a time*. London, United Kingdom: Piatkus.
Bevir, M. (2011). Governance and governmentality after neoliberalism. *Policy and Politics, 39*(4), 457–471.
Bondi, L. (2005). Working the spaces of neoliberal subjectivity: Psychotherapeutic technologies, professionalization and counselling. *Antipode, 37*(3), 497–514.
Brook, A. (2011). Ecological footprint feedback: Motivating or discouraging? *Social Influence, 6*(2), 113–128.
Brown, W. (2005). *Edgework: Critical essays on knowledge and politics*. Princeton, NJ: Princeton University Press.
Brubaker, R. (1992). *Citizenship and nationhood in France and Germany*. Cambridge, MA: Harvard University Press.
Butler, C. (2010). Morality and climate change: Is leaving your TV on standby a risky behaviour? *Environmental Values, 19*(2), 169–192.
Canning, K. (2007). The order of terms: Class, citizenship, and welfare state in German gender history. In K. Hagemann & J. H. Quataert (Eds.), *Gendering modern German history: Rewriting historiography* (pp. 128–146). New York, NY; Oxford, United Kingdom: Berghahn Books.
Cao, B. (2015). *Environment and citizenship*. London, United Kingdom; New York, NY: Routledge.

Cordero, E. C., Todd, A. M., & Abellera, D. (2008). Climate change education and the ecological footprint. *Bulletin of the American Meteorological Society, 89*(6), 865–872.

Crane, A., Matten, D., & Moon, J. (2008). *Corporations and citizenship.* Cambridge, United Kingdom: Cambridge University Press.

Darier, E. (1996). Environmental governmentality: The case of Canada's Green Plan. *Environmental Politics, 5*(4), 585–606.

Davies, J. S. (2012). Network governance theory: A Gramscian critique. *Environment and Planning A, 44*(11), 2687–2704.

Dickinson, R. & Carsky, M. (2005). The consumer as economic voter. In R. Harrison, T. Newholm, & D. Shaw (Eds.), *The ethical consumer* (pp. 25–36). Thousand Oaks, CA: SAGE.

Dobson, A. (2003). *Citizenship and the environment.* Oxford, United Kingdom: Oxford University Press.

European Commission (2007). *You control climate change.* Luxembourg: Office for Official Publications of the European Communities. Retrieved from https://ec.europa.eu/clima/sites/campaign/pdf/toolkit_en.pdf

Foucault, M. (1991). *Discipline and punish: The birth of the prison.* London, United Kingdom: Penguin.

Franz, J. & Papyrakis, E. (2011). Online calculators of ecological footprint: Do they promote or dissuade sustainable behaviour? *Sustainable Development, 19,* 391–401.

Gorman, D. (2006). *Imperial citizenship: Empire and the question of belonging.* Manchester, United Kingdom: Manchester University Press.

Gottlieb, D., Vigoda-Gadot, E., Haim, A., & Kissinger, M. (2012). The ecological footprint as an educational tool for sustainability: A case study analysis in an Israeli public high school. *International Journal of Educational Development, 32*(3), 193–200.

Harvey, D. (2005). *A brief history of neoliberalism.* Oxford, United Kingdom: Oxford University Press.

Heater, D. (2004). *Citizenship: The civic ideal in world history, politics and education.* Manchester, United Kingdom; New York, NY: Manchester University Press.

Inthorn, S. & Reder, M. (2011). Discourses of environmental citizenship: How television teaches us to be green. *International Journal of Media and Cultural Politics, 7*(1), 37–54.

Kuisma, M. (2008). Rights or privilege? The challenge of globalization to the values of citizenship. *Citizenship Studies, 12*(6), 613–627.

Lewis, T. (2012). 'There grows the neighborhood': Green citizenship, creativity and life politics on eco-TV. *International Journal of Cultural Studies, 15*(3), 315–326.

May, E. (2009). A practical environmental education: Shrinking ecological footprints, expanding political ones. *Our Schools/Our Selves, 19*(1), 17–24.

Mitchell, K. (2006). Neoliberal governmentality in the European Union: Education, training, and technologies of citizenship. *Environment and Planning D: Society and Space, 24*(3), 389–407.

Obach, B. (2009). Consumption, ecological footprints and global inequality: A lesson in individual and structural components of environmental problems. *Teaching Sociology, 37*(3), 294–300.

Ouellette, L. & Hay, J. (2008). *Better living through reality TV: Television and post-welfare citizenship.* Malden, MA: Blackwell Publishing.

Palmer, K. (2015, 23 July). Green Deal funding axed: What it means for assessments and unused vouchers, *The Telegraph.* Retrieved from http://www.telegraph.co.uk/finance/personalfinance/energy-bills/11758777/Green-Deal-funding-axed-what-it-means-for-assessments-and-unused-vouchers.html

Rabinow, P. (Ed.). (1991). *The Foucault reader: An introduction to Foucault's thought.* London, United Kingdom: Penguin.

Rumpala, Y. (2011). 'Sustainable consumption' as a new phase in a governmentalization of consumption. *Theory and Society, 40*(6), 669–699.

Sandel, M. (2012). *What money can't buy: The moral limits of markets.* London, United Kingdom: Allen Lane.

UNEP (2003, 2 June). Shopping for a better world. Retrieved from http://www.unep.org/Documents.Multilingual/Default.asp?DocumentID=321&ArticleID=4019 [Accessed 3 March 2016]

UNEP (2014). Green passport. Retrieved from http://www.unep.org/resourceefficiency/Business/SectoralActivities/Tourism/Activities/GreenPassport/tabid/78823/Default.aspx [Accessed 3 March 2016]

Upham, P. (2012). Environmental citizens: Climate pledger attitudes and micro-generation installation. *Local Environment, 17*(1), 75–91.

Weis, T. (2013). The meat of the global food crisis. *The Journal of Peasant Studies, 40*(1), 65–85.

CHAPTER TWO

'EMPOWERED GIRLS' IN NEOLIBERAL TIMES:
MALALA AS THE *EFFECT* OF HETEROGENEOUS
DISCOURSES

Shenila Khoja-Moolji

Introduction
In 2012, Malala Yousafzai, a Pakistani girl then 15 years old, was shot in the head by a member of the Taliban, a transnational Islamist group. Malala was returning home from school. While she recovered shortly thereafter, this incident has since then received significant attention from transnational educational development and aid organisations, as well as heads of states in the global north. They have rallied around the symbol of Malala to express support, not only for her but also for the education of girls more broadly in Pakistan and in the global south. For instance, Gordon Brown, the current United Nations Special Envoy for Global Education, issued a petition entitled 'I am Malala' to promote universal access to primary schooling for girls (Brown, 2012a); and the United Nations Educational, Scientific and Cultural Organization launched an advocacy campaign entitled 'Stand Up For Malala', seeking to raise awareness about the rights of Pakistani girls to get an education (n.d.). Malala, thus, functions as a *floating signifier* – she is taken up by different institutions to articulate wide-ranging, and sometimes contradictory, desires, fears and investments in and about muslim[1] girls. What makes Malala so *productive*? What gives her such appeal and reach? What does she promise and to whom? How does Malala come into being?

Images of empowered girls like Malala do not exist in isolation. They become meaningful and take their force within a discursive structure, where particular discourses are maintained

'Empowered Girls' in Neoliberal Times

in dialogue with, and against, other discourses and organised around practices of exclusion (Mills, 1997, p. 11-13). Foucault (1978) notes that this "tactical polyvalence of discourses" (p. 100) is intended to produce specific effects and subjects, and consequently directs us to think about discourse as "practices that systematically form the objects of which they speak" (p. 49). To understand the production and operation of empowered girls then, we have to inquire into the multiple discourses that interact to produce this concept and the subjects signified by it. In this chapter, I explore the discursive structure within which Malala in particular, and empowered girls in general, are situated. Through a close reading of Malala's representation across multiple platforms – from policy reports, newspaper articles and interviews to advertisements for fundraising campaigns books – this chapter seeks to uncover the discourses that make Malala and her activism meaningful. I focus on the distribution of these discourses and attempt to reconstruct their connections to understand the overall strategy and effect. In doing so, I seek to take away the coherence with which empowered girls are presented and show that they are put together contingently out of heterogeneous discourses, ideas and knowledges. More broadly, I explore the kinds of ideological, political and pedagogical work that the binary of empowered/ dis-empowered girls are made to do. I ask: what pedagogical work do images of empowered girls like Malala – and their correlative dis-empowered girls – do? Who takes on the position of dis-empowered girls? What kinds of subjectivities are made recognisable and which ones are left as unthinkable?

I propose that Malala's story sits at the nexus of at least three distinct discourses: discourse on neoliberal governmentality; discourse on girl power; and discourse on adolescent sexuality. Specifically, I argue that: Malala is aligned with norms of neoliberal governmentality that place responsibility for addressing social problems on the individual; her figure is taken up to make available enactments of girl power through partaking in consumer culture for a particular group of girls, who can be classified by their socio-economic class, alignment with liberal feminism, and, sometimes, race; and finally, her calls for formal education are positioned as the only viable life choice for adolescents and put forth a particular thinking about adolescent sexuality that is played out against practices of child marriage that may be prevalent in some parts of the global south. I argue that these discourses come together to set up a new binary – one that pits muslim girls against empowered girls. Malala is made to tell a particular story about people in the global south. She is represented as the girl who defied cultural logics operative in Pakistan, and who now embodies a transnational, secular modernity exemplified by her emphasis on the autonomous self, enactment of choice, advocacy for freedom, and arguments for gender equality. Instead of destabilising the trope of the 'oppressed muslim girl', Malala's image is deployed to reinforce it – she is made into an *exception,* which excludes other muslim girls from partaking in the kind of empowered subjectivity that she performs. As an empowered girl, she puts forth a theory of culture as tradition, where culture is understood to be something that people in the global south have, and empowered girls, who take up neoliberal subject positions, are marked as modern and presumably acultural. In this new binary then, the space of empowered girls is expansive in that many individuals can stake a claim to it through particularised practices; however, the subject position of muslim girls is homogenised and appears as the absolute 'other', and does not confer the kind of heterogeneity that is exhibited by empowered girls. I conclude with providing some reflections about girls' education in Pakistan as a counter-discourse to the kind of normativities that are set up through the image of Malala. To be sure, this chapter is not against Malala. In fact, like others, I, too, enormously respect her courage, commitments, and activism. I am more concerned about how Malala – as an empowered girl – is made to tell a story about muslim girls, and the broader political and ideological work that is done in and through particular readings and presentations of her story. This chapter, thus, nourishes counter-discourses (Brown, 2008) that feature power and politics, which are often displaced in calls for girls' empowerment through education.

Desiring empowered girls: playing out the normative Liberal (feminist) discourse

In this section, I play out the assumptions and arguments that stoke our desires for, and hold out the possibility of, empowered girls. I also reflect on the implications of these for bringing into effect some subject positions and marking others as inhabitable. I consider three interconnected areas: the emancipatory promise of education, enactments of success in today's transnational neoliberal societies, and the incitement to help 'third world' women.

Liberal humanist philosophy sees every individual as born equal, free and rational, and seeks to disrupt barriers to the exercise of individual freedom (Mehta, 1997). In this context, education is believed to be the right of every individual as it provides an increased awareness about this freedom as well as the modes of exercising it. In addition, education is also positioned to provide functional and material benefits by enabling individuals to increase their productivity and enhance their competitiveness in the global market. Generally, it is believed that education produces citizens who can make a meaningful contribution to their own, as well as their families', communities' and nations' well-being. For instance, UNICEF USA's website for education opens with this promise:

> Every child has the right to learn. Education transforms lives and breaks the cycle of poverty that traps so many children. Education for girls is particularly important – an educated

mother will make sure her own children go to, and stay in, school. (www.unicefusa.org)

Accordingly, in the context of the global south, where access to formal schooling especially for girls is limited in some areas, it is believed that increasing access will lead to the production of an enlightened citizenry that can overcome problems as wide-ranging as poverty, corruption, crime, terrorism, environmental degradation, etc. International development organisations, transnational aid agencies and local governments have, therefore, come together to promote education in the global south. The United Nations, for instance, has placed universal primary education as one of its top eight priorities for the Millennium Development Goals to be achieved by 2015 (www.un.org), and organisations such as the United States Agency for International Development (USAID), the Canadian International Development Agency (CIDA) and Oxfam International are called upon to provide financial and policy support, serve as content experts, and monitor and evaluate the progress.

More broadly, education is believed to facilitate the eradication of remnants of pre-modern sensibilities. Instances of child marriage, practices of female genital mutilation, restrictions on women's movements and participation in the public sphere, domestic violence, etc., are all considered everyday realities for the women and girls in the global south. It is hoped that education can enhance the recognition of human rights and engender the qualities of self-determination, self-enterprise, freedom of expression and leadership in the populace. Thus, a range of informal educational projects that focus on leadership, empowerment and advocacy are sponsored by transnational organisations (consider *G(irls)20 Summit*, a collaboration of several corporate organisations (www.girls20summit.com); Nike Foundation's *Girl Effect* campaign (www.girleffect.org); or United Nations' *Girl Up* campaign (www.girlup.org), which seek to transform girls into 'leaders' or 'change agents' capable of producing change for themselves and in their communities. Instead of relying on others or even the state, it is believed that girls should take personal responsibility for identifying, speaking up and addressing their social problems. Taking ownership of one's own development is considered a certain means of success in today's risk societies. Thus, access to both formal (such as primary schooling) and specialised (such as human rights) education is assumed to be critical for individuals and nations in the global south if they are to make economic, social, or cultural progress.

The project of empowerment is predicated on the condition of disempowerment. There is, hence, an impetus to produce an 'other' who not only legitimises one's empowerment but also becomes an object of one's enactment of this empowerment. It is in this context that we can read the heavy focus of empowerment projects in the global north to help dis-empowered women in the global south. However, Mohanty (2006) sees this "Third World woman" who is in need of empowerment as a western construct (p. 22). Here, the third world woman:

> leads an essentially truncated life based on her gender (read: sexually constrained) and being 'Third World' (read: ignorant, poor, uneducated, tradition-bound, domestic, family-oriented, victimised, etc.). This … is in contrast to the (implicit) self-representation of Western women as educated, as modern, as having control over their own bodies and sexualities and the freedom to make their own decisions. (Mohanty, 2006, p. 22)

Histories of orientalist and colonial writings have produced a sturdy trope of the 'oppressed muslim woman', which is re-articulated today in the context of the war on terror (see Abu-Lughod, 2013; Shehabuddin, 2011). Through these articulations muslim women/girls are portrayed as oppressed by islam, muslim men and/or patriarchal cultures. Popular media displays the myriad ways in which muslim girls are oppressed:

they are compelled to wear the hijab, are married at a young age without their consent, do not have access to formal schooling, and have limited rights with respect to divorce or inheritance within their families (for an example see Mona Eltahawy's (2012) article entitled, 'Why do they hate us? The real war on women in the Middle East', in *Foreign Policy* magazine). Confessional stories by muslim women who have been subjected to violence corroborate these views (see Hirsi Ali, 2007; Manji, 2003). The possibilities for muslim women are assumed to be worse in African and Asian states where democratic governance has failed to take root; failed state institutions and intense religious sentiments in countries such as Pakistan, Afghanistan and Nigeria are often cited as the rationale for military interventions in these countries (see Bush, 2001; Dockterman, 2014). Against this background, muslim girls emerge as the primary sites of concern for, to use Ticktin's (2011) phrase, "humanitarian regimes of care". Girls' education campaigns such as Nike Foundation's the *Girl Effect* often propose that one of the reasons black and brown girls continue to be oppressed is their lack of access to formal schooling. Drawing on assumptions about the emancipatory promise of education, noted earlier in the chapter, the logic seems that if muslim girls could only get an education they would be able to break the cycle of oppression and along with it poverty, crime, violence and a plethora of other issues plaguing the lives of people in developing countries. Thus, a direct link and causality is established between education and ending the oppression of muslim women. Empowerment projects position education as an instrument to end muslim women's oppression and propose schooling as the alternate pathway.

Furthermore, it is believed that sustainable change requires altering social and cultural attitudes towards women in the third world and as a result development agencies focus on raising awareness around certain key issues. For instance, the

'Empowered Girls' in Neoliberal Times

United Nations Children's Fund and the United Nations Population Fund have embarked on campaigns against child marriages, a custom prevalent in some countries of the global south. They argue that marrying girls at a young age leads to disruption in their educational and emotional development, is harmful for their health, and constitutes a violation of their human rights. Similarly, USAID has spent approximately $20 million dollars on its Gender Equity Programs in Pakistan (www.transition.usaid.gov). This effort makes small grants in the hopes to "facilitate behavioral change in society by enabling women to access information, resources, and institutions and improving public attitudes towards women's rights issues" (www.transition.usaid.gov). Significantly, international organisations try to partner with local women's rights agencies in order to ensure that their work is contextually relevant.

The emancipatory promise of education and desire to help an oppressed 'other' come together to position formal schooling as the panacea for society's problem and saving muslim girls, an honourable enactment of empowerment. In this context, Malala becomes an ideal signifier, and can be taken by both actors on the Right and Left to connote different meanings. In the following section, I attempt to uncover the culturally specific discourses of neoliberal governmentality, girl power, and adolescent sexuality that produce the figure of Malala, and argue that the deployment and mobilisation of Malala as signifier, while superficially aimed at re-articulating the normative assumptions noted above, in fact, also circulates particular conceptions of personhood, girlhood and sexuality that are presented as universal.

Malala: the effect of heterogeneous discourses

In this section, I reflect on three discourses – neoliberal governmentality, girl power and adolescent sexuality – that come together in meaningful ways to produce the discursive figure of Malala as an empowered girl. These discourse centres emerged rhizomatically (Deleuze & Guattari, 1987) for me, wherein particular conceptual lines supported, reinforced and/or contested others to make the image of Malala, and campaigns for girls' empowerment, meaningful. In highlighting some discourses over others, however, I do not intend to fossilise them. Indeed, discourses are constantly changing and fluid (Mills, 1997, p. 49). My hope is to enact what Massumi (1987) calls *nomad thought*, which seeks to synthesise "a multiplicity of elements without effacing their heterogeneity or hindering their potential for future rearranging" (p. xiii). I draw attention to the assemblage of ideas, knowledges, and concepts that makes the discourse on empowered girls possible. I also note the ways in which different kinds of girls – such as Malala, Shiza Shahid (CEO of The Malala Fund) as well as western girls and women who as consumers engage in advocacy on behalf of Malala – are able to take up the subject position of empowered girl. However, this subjectivity is also based on foreclosures, which I will reflect on later in the chapter.

Foucault's (2000a) work on governmentality directs us to consider the ways in which discourses, knowledges, and practices work together to enable the government of subjects. Governmentality, as "the conduct of conduct" (Foucault, 2000b, p. 341), includes practices that "constitute, define, organise and instrumentalise the strategies that individuals in their freedom can use in dealing with each other" (Foucault, 1984, p. 300). Individuals take up particular knowledges, practices and behaviours from within a field of possibilities, and the "art of governing" (Foucault, 2007), then, entails guiding individuals towards desired knowledges and practices that make them simultaneously more obedient and productive. In today's western context, neoliberal economic, political and social assumptions form the dominant rationality of self-governance. Here, citizens are individualised and expected to choose rationally between options to maximise their life trajectories. Social services are increasingly privatised, with heightening pressure for a limited role for the state. Neoliberal governmentality, hence, can be understood as the prioritisation of neoliberal logistics in the self-governance of citizens.

If we were to read the common attributes associated with empowered girls – self-enterprising, self-determining, prioritising education and career – as a *"set of relations* rather than as the natural qualities" (Lesko, 2012, p. 106, emphasis in original), then we might be able to make visible the processes of knowledge production and consumption that underlie them. I contend that, as an empowered girl, Malala is taken up to portray a specific kind of empowerment – one that is grounded in assumptions of neoliberal governmentality. Her calls for universal education take their meaning from, and make sense within, the discourse on neoliberal governmentality that relies on self-governance to solve social problems and is structured by market sensibilities. Other actors in her story – such as the CEO of The Malala Fund: Shiza Shahid, and the western girl who is asked to support Pakistani girls by participating in consumption culture (see Barneys New York campaign for The Malala Fund) – too, enact different components of empowered girlhood grounded in neoliberal rationalities.

Malala performs a subjectivity that promises to solve social problems "by waging a social revolution, not against capitalism, racism and inequality, but against the order of the self and the way we govern our selves [*sic*]" (Cruikshank, 1996, p. 231). She is taken up by transnational organisations that in and through her image and words urge children to obtain an education, girls to learn about human rights, and Pakistanis to participate in the elections, all by way of addressing wider social and political issues of poverty, violence against women, and corruption, respectively. Malala inaugurates what Rose (1996) calls the "new regime of the actively responsible self", where "individuals are to fulfil their national obligations not through their relations of dependency and obligation to one another, but through seeking to fulfil themselves within a variety of micro-moral domains or 'communities'" (p. 57). Lemke (2001) notes that the "withdrawal of the state" via the empowerment of the individual citizen can be read as a technique of neoliberal governmentality, which puts the onus of solving social problems on the individual through acquiring appropriate knowledges, managing the self, speaking up, etc. (pp. 201–202). The individual citizen is made responsible for achieving social justice.

Furthermore, to be empowered within this regime means to be able to fully and proficiently partake in it. Given that neoliberal regimes are structured by "the rationalities of competition, accountability and consumer demand" (Rose, 1996, p. 41), Malala's demand for formal schooling make sense because it gives girls an opportunity to work on themselves and build specific capabilities, skills and knowledges that are valued in the neoliberal order. Elsewhere (Khoja-Moolji, 2015), drawing on the work of Murphy (2012/2013), I have argued that such approaches to empowerment enrol girls in neoliberal economic projects of wage-based labour and devalue their reproductive labour. They also mark lives led outside the formal workforce as deviant or in need of reform. Elias (2014) has made a similar argument in her critique of the United Kingdom government's approach to international development, with its heavy focus on issues of child marriage and female genital mutilation. Elias (2014) goes further and questions the motivations of the UK government's development endeavours by pointing to its reluctance in addressing women's land rights. She notes that advancing such rights entails critiquing the land-grabbing practices of multinational corporations, with which the UK government is not willing to engage; campaigns against child marriage and female genital mutilation, however, do not often entail similar critiques of big business. Elias's (2014) insights can be broadened to include other developed countries as well. A report by the World Development Movement, for instance, shows that the G8's (includes Canada, France, Germany, Italy, Japan, Russia, UK and USA) New Alliance for Food Security and Nutrition launched in 2012 provides aid money to countries in Africa in return for making changes in land, seed and trade rules that benefit foreign investment in the agricultural sector (World Development Movement). Hence, calls for girls' education that articulate particular modes of living and working are intricately connected with modes of being that can thrive in neoliberal economic and political orders. Malala's calls for universal education are an enactment of a reconstituted subjectivity, one that is self-enterprising and self-determining and takes the onus of solving social problems on itself. What we observe here is a conflation of the responsible moral individual with the economic actor – a congruence that, according to Lemke (2001), is critical for neoliberal governmentality (p. 201). Hence, Malala seems to be produced by a discourse on neoliberal governmentality that posits responsibilisation and marketisation of the self as vital for addressing social issues. However, this depoliticises issues, such as educational access, poverty, unemployment and violence, which need broader structural solutions. It presents these complicated issues as ahistorical and apolitical, making invisible the complicity of a range of different actors – including transnational organisations – in the current status of education in Pakistan. Wendy Brown (2008, p. 15) observes that,

> Depoliticization involves construing inequality, subordination, marginalization, and social conflict, which all require political analysis and political solutions, as personal and individual, on the one hand, or as natural, religious, or cultural on the other. ... Depoliticization involves removing a political phenomenon from comprehension of its *historical*

emergence and from a recognition of the powers that produce and contour it. No matter its particular form and mechanics, depoliticization always eschews power and history in the representation of its subject. (original emphasis)

What we find is that complex social issues, which are effects of local as well as transnational economic, political and social practices, are abstracted from the domain of politics and history, and re-articulated through the language of personal responsibility, human rights or girl power. What is critical to note here is not that complex arguments are not being presented; in fact, in her speech to the United Nations, after re-articulating the normative discourse of education's promise and the right of every child to have an education, Malala made an astute observation about security in everyday life that is necessary for formal schooling to produce any substantial improvement in the quality of life of people. She noted:

> peace is necessary for education. In many parts of the world especially Pakistan and Afghanistan; terrorism, wars and conflicts stop children to go to their schools. We are really tired of these wars. Women and children are suffering in many parts of the world in many ways. (Yousafzai, 2013)

And, after meeting with the President of the USA and the First Lady in 2013, Malala explicitly mentioned the negative consequences of American drone strikes in Pakistan during a public statement: "I also expressed [to the President] my concerns that drone attacks are fueling terrorism. Innocent victims are killed in these acts, and they lead to resentment among the Pakistani people" (Rucker, 2013). That this statement was followed by "If we refocus efforts on education it will make a big impact" (Rucker, 2013), which again proposes education as a solution, is unfortunate. However, it should not distract us from the glimpses of complexity, interconnectedness of the global north and global south, and political commitment that is required to improve the lives of girls in Pakistan. Such critiques, though, require more material and ideational investment and are often sidelined in favour of simplistic solutions: universal access to primary education for girls.

Malala's figure is not only operative for girls in the global south; she makes available opportunities for enactments of 'girl power' for girls in the global north as well. Consider the collaboration between The Malala Fund and Barneys New York, a large fashion outlet. According to the partnership, designer Maria Cornejo and Barneys plan to donate 10% of in-store and online sales from Maria's collection to The Malala Fund (www.thewindow.barneys.com/girl-power-shiza-shahid-malala-fund/). The title page of the website directs attention to the CEO of the fund: 'Girl Power: Shiza Shahid of The Malala Fund'. Aimed at young women of a particular socio-economic class and racial background, the Barneys campaign fulfils these women's desires of 'helping' muslim girls at their convenience, via the swipe of a credit card, as they adorn their favourite designer fashion articles. These empowered women enact 'girl power' through their purchasing power.

The concept of 'girl power' in western contexts is linked to third wave feminism (see Driscoll, 2008). Having become popular since the 1990s, it now has global currency and takes on different meanings as it travels, from resistive practices to an unapologetic enactment of traditional femininity. Yet, as varied as its enactments are, it can be read as grounded within the rationalities of neoliberal subjectivity, where girls are seen as having the freedom to choose their life trajectories and engage in self-expression; it is assumed that they have already achieved the first and second wave feminist movements' demands for gender equality. Aapola, Gonick, and Harris (2005) have theorised the emergence of 'girl power' in western contexts as an expression of individualisation within the context of neoliberalism. They note that calls for self-invention or self-determination via breaking loose from gender identities and relations, an essential aspect of girl power, in fact assists in the reproduction of neoliberal subjecthood: "embedded in this concept is a sense that a life of success and happiness is within reach of girls who learn the skills and/or have the characteristics necessary for continual self-invention" (Aapola et al., 2005, p. 39).

In the context of greater opportunities for young women to participate in the economy in western countries, consumption has emerged as one of the prominent spaces where girls can participate in self-invention, enact a unique personality and highlight their individuality. Commercial interests have capitalised on the new purchasing power that young women now have, and expressly target them. Here, girls are encouraged to express themselves through fashion and enact their right to choose. Harris (2004), however, notes that, as a commodity, girl power allows girls to perform a feminist identity – such as via purchases of clothing or music that reproduce feminist rhetoric – but does not require an investment in social change. Hence, girls are incited to buy Barneys' products and feel that they are enacting feminist ideas of solidarity with Pakistani girls but their engagement with feminism halts there; they are not expected to think about the ways in which their consumption practices are entangled with, and productive of, global economic inequalities – perhaps the very articles of clothing that they are purchasing were produced by young girls in factories in Pakistan. Instead, it is the practice of consumption, and not critique, which becomes synonymous with social action.

Yet, it is also Shiza Shahid, the CEO of The Malala Fund and a Pakistani American, who is centred in the Barneys campaign. It is Shiza who seems to symbolise girl power. Below is an excerpt from the website:

> In 2009, Shiza Shahid, then a sophomore at Stanford University, watched a YouTube video of Pakistani teen activist Malala Yousafzai taking a powerful stand on behalf of girls'

'Empowered Girls' in Neoliberal Times

right to education. "She had just started speaking out and she came from an area about three hours north of the city where I'm from," said Shiza of her immediate connection to Malala. "In her area, the Taliban had taken over the region and were trying to ban female education." No one was talking about the situation, and Shiza felt moved to make a connection. She reached out to the young girl's father to ask how she could help. That summer, Shiza planned a camp for Malala and her friends, giving them the tools and resources to become more effective activists.

Shiza, too, is made to tell the story of an empowered girl. However, it is a different kind of narrative where Shiza, who is muslim and has connections to Pakistan, migrated to the United States early enough to embody a neoliberal empowered subjectivity. In this short excerpt, we can see an enactment of a girlhood that marks Pakistani girls as helpless and in need of western intervention. Shiza is the highly educated, Pakistani-but-American girl who decides to take initiative; she is self-enterprising in that she sets forth to address this social violation through personal action without relying on the state; she identifies an issue that "no one was talking about"; and eventually sets up a Fund that can allow western feminists to partake in the project of emancipating muslim girls. In the process, however, a long, local tradition of women's activism in Pakistan, more broadly, and in Khyber-Pukhtunkhwa – Malala and Shiza's province – in particular, is erased. For instance, in Malala Yousafzai's own co-authored autobiography, *I am Malala* (2013), we learn about strong Pashtun women and their activism. We are made to believe that it was not until Shiza Shahid's intervention that Pakistani women had the tools or capacity to engage in a sustained critique of local manifestations of patriarchy in relation to the Taliban. This, of course, is not true and, undoubtedly, both Malala and Shiza would disagree with the narrative. However, it is precisely this that is being said, in unstated terms. What is critical here is to pay attention to the discursive strategies in and through which empowered girls are deployed by commercial organisations to tell a story, not only about these specific girls but more broadly, and often implicitly, about people in the global south.

Drawing on Goldman's (1991) work on 'commodity feminism', which explicates the ways in which commercial interests have taken up and popularised particular icons and forms of feminism, McRobbie (2008) suggests that we unpack the uptake of commodity feminism by inquiring into the class and ethnic composition of the girls that it targets. What is at stake when individuals like Malala and Shiza are marked as empowered girls enacting girl power? Aapola et al. (2005) worry about consequences for girls from different socio-economic, political and racial backgrounds when "values of self-determination and individuality become the new cultural ideal of femininity" (p. 37), and Griffin (2001) argues that "the subject position of the consuming girl is not of equivalent relevance for all girls and young women: it is profoundly shaped by class, ethnicity, sexuality and disability" (as cited in Harris, 2004, p. 91). What kinds of subject positions are then available for girls in Pakistan? Which ones are marked as abnormal or deviations? McRobbie (2009) has observed that the appropriation of the site of girlhood by commercial interests has the effect of 'undoing' feminism and of discouraging its renewal. She cautions us about the dangers that arise "when a selection of feminist values and ideals appear to be inscribed within a more profound and determined attempt, undertaken by an array of political and cultural forces, to reshape notions of womanhood so that they fit with new or emerging (neoliberalised) social and economic arrangements" (McRobbie, 2009, p. 57). In this case, not only is the feminism of Pakistanis undone but a limited range of practices and knowledges are made available to enact an empowered girlhood (see Khoja-Moolji & Niccolini, 2016, for postfeminist performances of muslim girlhood). Indeed, it is a profoundly raced and classed proposition, unavailable to many girls.

Discourses on adolescent sexuality: avoiding precocity and promoting slow development
In addition to the educational campaigns such as 'I am Malala' and 'Stand up for Malala', (United Nations Educational, Scientific and Cultural Organization, n.d.), The Office of Gordon and Sarah Brown (2012b), United Nations Children's Fund (2001; 2005) and United Nations Population Fund (2012) have also embarked on campaigns against child marriages. Similarly, Elias (2014) notes that the United Kingdom Department for International Development's (DFID) agenda in relation to girls entails a focus on girls' sexual health, including attention to child marriage and female genital mutilation. These two issues were also the focus of DFID's Girl Summit held in July 2014 (Elias, 2014). That organisations that focus on girls' education also invest resources in campaigns against child marriage and female genital mutilation is not surprising and it is not coincidental. These campaigns are situated within the same discursive field and are informed by a system of reasoning about adolescent sexuality; that is, they are referential. A particular kind of productive life is valorised in and through these campaigns, marking other ways of living and being as abnormal, deviant, or unproductive.

In order to promote formal education as the only viable, developmentally appropriate avenue for adolescents, all other life scripts must be marked as inappropriate. The discourse on child marriage, in practice, then supports the discourse on girls' education. Underlying these discourses is an anxiety linked with adolescent sexuality, the desire to avoid precocity and promote slow development of adolescents. Lesko (2012) defines precocity as the exhibition of "any adultlike behaviors or proclivities, especially passion or self-assertiveness" (p. 53). She notes that, at the turn of the century, fears around such behaviours of adolescents led to the production of organisational and institutional mechanisms, including mass schooling, aimed at prolonging dependency (Lesko, 2012). Sexual practices of adolescents came under scrutiny, and precocity was linked to pathology or degeneracy. Any movement away from the normative script of slow development or any acknowledgement of the sexual desires of adolescents was marked as a deviation. Viewed through this lens, we can read campaigns against child marriage as aiming to prevent precocity; they argue that muslim adolescent girls should be in schools, and not get married, become sexually active, or engage in reproductive labour. What informs these campaigns are preoccupations and anxieties around the sexual activity of girls (who are racialised) *and* sturdy divisions between productive/waged vs. reproductive/unwaged labour.

Yet, the discourse on sexuality produces different subjectivities for girls in western societies. While sexually active young girls in the West – such as the racialised figure of the 'teen mother' – are also chastised and marked as 'at-risk' (Harris, 2004), particular strands of liberal feminism provide resources for (often white) girls to affirm their sexual desires, enact sexual assertiveness, and claim ownership of their bodies. Variously called 'sex positive', 'pro-sex' or 'sex-radical' feminism, the rise of these strands of feminisms in the United States can be traced to the 1980s, and more recently has been termed as postfeminism (see McRobbie, 2009; Ringrose, 2012). Here, white, middle-class girls assert ownership of their bodies and view sexual freedom as a key component of women's freedom. They position themselves against the patriarchal control of female sexuality and argue against legal or social norms that seek to control sexual activity. This discourse provides space for girls from a particular socio-economic class and race to enact agentic subject positions involving sexual assertiveness, a kind of agency not available to girls from the global south who are the

'Empowered Girls' in Neoliberal Times

object of the discourses on child marriage. This, too, is due to their socio-economic and racial positioning; it precludes them from enacting agentic sexual subjectivities reserved only for white, middle-class girls from the global north. As mentioned earlier, I acknowledge that sex-positive feminism is raced and classed, and can be deployed to hinder freedom for women. Indeed, Driscoll (2008) highlights the complicated implications of sex-positive feminism by noting that, "while 'sex positive' images of girls can be performed in ways which support girls' presumed destiny and completion in heterosexual romance, the same images can be construed as dangerous when performed or 'cited' differently" (p. 24). What is at stake here, however, is how, for what purposes, and to what effects does girls' sexuality become a site in and through which particular subject positions are made (un)available for girls in the global south, and, how this discourse sustains the logic of empowering girls through education and waged labour. Thus, Malala as signifier, inaugurates conversations about the ideal de-sexualised figure of the 'school girl', which participates in disciplining brown and black girls' sexuality.

Setting up a new binary: empowered girl vs. muslim girl

> What I can be quite literally is constrained in advance by a regime of truth which decides in advance what will and will not be a recognisable form of being ... this does not mean that a given regime of truth sets the invariable framework for recognition; it means only that it is in relation to this framework that recognition takes place or the norms that govern recognition are challenged or transformed. (Butler, 2005, p. 22)

Within the framework of empowered/disempowered girls, who is made 'recognisable'? Who is made 'unthinkable'? How might the norms of recognition be challenged and transformed?

The concept of *empowered girls* is based on a foreclosure: there must be subjectivities outside it for it to make sense; there must be some subject positions that cannot be assimilated into it (Butler, 2000, p. 340). This concept is made meaningful against the trope of the 'oppressed muslim girl', who is portrayed perennially as the other (see Said, 1978), the victimised subject, and the primary focus of our humanitarian concern. The oppressed muslim girl performs a subjectivity in relation to which the notion of empowered girl is sustained. In this context, for a muslim girl such as Malala to lay claim to aspects of an empowered subjectivity – such as speaking up against the drone attacks by the United States military in her native province – is considered a threat. The very concept of empowered girl is brought into question by this "spectral invocation" (Butler, 2000, p. 340). The discourse of empowered girl is made to rearticulate itself. And, it does so by assimilating and dissimulating Malala into itself. That is, she moves from the subject position of 'oppressed muslim girl' to an 'empowered girl' and in this way comes to tell the story about both positions when needed (Khoja-Moolji, 2017).

The discourse on empowered girls reactivates itself through individualising and abstracting Malala. Malala is not represented as a symbol of the courage of muslims and Pakistanis to stand up against local forms of violence. Instead, she is shown to be an *exception*. Through extensive media coverage and uptake of her image by international organisations, she is individualised in her courage and successful performance of an empowered subjectivity. She is presented as succeeding against all odds; as a hero; or, as *TIME* magazine calls her, the "*champion* for girls everywhere" (Clinton, 2013). She is made into an exception by practices such as declaring the day when she was shot as 'Malala Day', receiving a nomination for the Nobel Peace Prize, and book deals worth millions of dollars. Even the title of her book, *I am Malala: The Girl Who Stood Up for Education and Was Shot by the Taliban* (2013), centres her person, emphasising her uniqueness. Popular writing and blogs make

'Empowered Girls' in Neoliberal Times

very little mention of Malala's father, who is also an activist, or the two other girls who were shot alongside her. The discourse on empowered girls re-articulates Malala in its own terms, and distances her from other muslim girls. She is made to *simultaneously* stand in for, represent and symbolise the oppressed muslim girls, and is positioned as the empowered girl who is not one of them.

Producing Malala as the exception is a technique of power. Exception proceeds by individualising and abstracting her from the local environment and cultures, and connecting her positive attributes to another source, such as her formal education, desire for success and ambition. Her courage is, then, not read as grounded in local cultural practices that valorise social justice. Instead, she is positioned as a singular force against local customs and cultural elements. Ong (2006) conceptualises exception as "an extraordinary departure ... that can be deployed to include as well as to exclude" (p. 5). She goes on to note that, "the politics of exception in an era of globalisation has disquieting ethical-political implications for those who are included as well those who are excluded in shifting technologies of governing and of demarcation" (Ong, 2006, p. 5). Marking Malala as the exception sustains the trope of the 'oppressed muslim girls' against which the concept of 'empowered girls' is maintained. It denies other muslim girls similar forms of empowered subjectivities, and sustains the façade of islam as an oppressive religion, making interventions – such as through universal education of girls, or empowerment projects – necessary and even ethically imperative.

We observe a new binary emerging, where empowered girls are pitted against muslim girls. While we can see a diversity of figures – Malala, Shiza, young women in New York who shop at Barneys, high school girls who host bake sales for Malala – take up the subject position of empowered girls, the 'other' of empowered girls in the particular story of Malala is often presented as the homogenous, oppressed muslim girl. There is no variation within this 'other' – 'they' are seen as living similar lives, under uniform patriarchal pressures, and with identical lack of avenues to resist their subjection. This is a particular feature of the muslim 'other' and cannot be assimilated into the broader binary of empowered vs. disempowered girls or Anita Harris's (2004) can-do vs. at-risk girl, where the latter category is expansive enough to create particularised subject positions for girls from different socio-economic class, race and immigrant backgrounds. At-risk girls, for instance, can be teenage girls who get pregnant, welfare mothers, or girls who do drugs, etc. However, this same proliferation of subject positions does not hold true for the binary of empowered vs. muslim girls. Here, the latter is a fairly restrictive framework within which muslim girls should recognise themselves; the discourse does not take into account the everyday realities of muslim girls across racial, class, ethnic, national, sexual and ability lines. The homogenous oppressed muslim girl facilitates the creation, and legitimisation, of charitable, educational, economic and political interventions in the lives of people in the global south. Sensoy and Marshall (2010) observe that, "'Third World girls' in crisis are created for the consumption, education, and empowerment of youth in the West" (p. 301). It is this muslim girl's story that serves the pedagogical purpose to inform western audiences of what uncivilised, traditional, backward femininity and cultures look like, and helps position western, liberal ways of being as superior.

This discourse on empowered girls vs. muslim girls proposes a particular theory of culture. Here, muslim girls are marked as oppressed because somehow they are more entangled with their cultural traditions and customs when compared to empowered girls, who seem to be enacting an acultural identity. It is culture that is blamed for the mistreatment of women in the global south. In this context, human rights advocacy campaigns (such as Stand Up for Malala) or Barneys' Girl Power campaign, are viewed as modern, apolitical, and acultural. However, scholars have identified the liberal values embedded in transnational discourses on human rights and girl power, which have been one of the major sites for re-citing Malala (see Asad, 2003; Lila Abu-Lughod, 2013; Brown, 2008). For instance, critiquing discourses of girl power, Sensoy and Marshall (2010) argue that, "discourses rooted in a humanitarian project framed as completely altruistic function to universalise a particular Western girlhood, rather than to participate in the self-actualisation of Muslim girls" (p. 301). The discourse on empowered girls is not a value-neutral proposition. It brings with itself particular conceptions of personhood, family, community, role of the state, capacity of individuals and a vision for good life. Hence, what is needed is a different kind of project – one that pays attention to the material realities of girls in their everyday lives and views them as entangled in transnational politics, economics and culture, including ideologies of empowerment. Indeed, a more nuanced theory of culture, which sees it as a fluid, contested formation that is always in flux, might enable us to better excavate recourses for social change for girls.

De-stabilising the homogenised muslim girl

As Judith Butler (1990) notes, "the very subject of women is no longer understood in stable or abiding terms" (p. 1). I, too, argue the same for the subject position of muslim girls. During the past several decades, works by scholars and practitioners have highlighted the many different ways of being 'muslim' and 'woman'. Consider, the diversity of women in Pakistan itself. During my own work as a human rights educator (which I later critiqued – see Khoja-Moolji, 2014) in rural and city communities in the province of Sindh, I found that it was not so much access to schooling but the public/private divide in schooling – with its differential quality of teaching – and opportunities for employment that were the topics of discussion and debate. Participants in my project critiqued the liberal promise of education by consistently pointing to the many individuals with Master's degrees in their villages who were unemployed. They argued for gendered division of labour, especially when it provided them safety and security in the harsh economic realities of rural Sindh, and pointed to the depression their brothers and fathers had to experience when unable to ensure safety and economic independence for their families. This kind of analysis is much more complicated and nuanced than the simple proposition that education might improve the lives of girls. Similarly, in her ethnographic fieldwork with low-income female teachers in Pakistan, Ayesha Khurshid (2012) contests the linear readings of women's empowerment. She notes that the "modern educated subjecttivity of Pakistani women from low-income communities is informed by a complex movement between the globally circulating 'empowerment through individual rights' discourse and their desire to establish and maintain strong family and community ties" (Khurshid, 2012, p. 236). Participants in her study constructed their identities through notions and practices of 'wisdom', allowing them to bring coherence to discourses of human rights and honour, often pitted as oppositional (Khurshid, 2012).

What should we, then, make of the transnational calls for girls' access to education? What kind of education would lead to the emancipation that is promised? Or more pointedly, what else has to be done within the realm of education – in terms of quality, teacher education, curriculum development – and more broadly in the social, economic and political spheres to improve the lives of girls? The 'access to education' argument is simple; it reduces the complicated, historical and political ways in which women's empowerment is/can be enacted.

'Empowered Girls' in Neoliberal Times

Conclusion

In a letter to Malala, Adnan Rasheed, a member of the Taliban, points out the simplicity of the proposition that Taliban are against education,

> please mind that Taliban never attacked you because of going to school or you were education lover, also please mind that *Taliban or Mujahideen are not against the education of any men or women or girl*. Taliban believe that you were intentionally writing against them and running a smearing campaign to malign their efforts to establish Islamic system in Swat and your writings were provocative. (emphasis mine, cited in Khan, 2013)

He goes on further to point to the local circumstances (such as drone strikes) that worry people like him by asking, "if you were shot [by] Americans in a drone attack, would [the] world have ever heard updates on your medical status? Would the media make a fuss about you?" (Khan, 2013). This grounded critique, however, is quickly dismissed by Gordon Brown, the United Nations special envoy on global education: "Nobody will believe a word the Taliban say about the right of girls like Malala to go to school until they stop burning down schools and stop massacring pupils" (Imtiaz, 2013). Why not take into account the material realities of girls, their families, and their communities? Why depoliticise education when it clearly seems to be entangled in local, national and transnational politics? We need a denser account of Pakistani girls' lives and an understanding of how schools are entangled in politics and in intersections of the local with the global (and vice-versa).

This chapter interrupts the unproblematic celebration of empowered girls through a close reading of representations of Malala Yousafzai and by revealing the discursive structures that bring her into effect. I reconstruct elements of discourses on neoliberal governmentality, girl power and adolescent sexuality to show how they come together contingently to produce, and give effect to, Malala. More broadly, I observe the emergence of a new kind of binary, where empowered girls are read as such in relation to muslim girls. This construct, however, presents muslim girls as a monolithic, homogenous 'other', and depoliticises issues such as education, which require political analysis and political solutions.

Note
1. Throughout this chapter, I do not capitalise islam and muslim to signal that there are many different ways of being muslim and many different understandings about the religion of islam, which are betrayed by practices of capitalisation (for more see Khoja-Moolji, 2015. Similarly, terms such as 'other', third world, south, western and white are not capitalised.

References
Aapola, S., Gonick, M., & Harris, A. (2005). *Young femininities. Girlhood, power and social change.* Basingstoke, United Kingdom: Palgrave Macmillan.
Abu-Lughod, L. (2013). *Do Muslim women need saving?* Cambridge, MA: Harvard University Press.
Ahmad, A. (2012, 11 November). 'I am Malala': TIME's Person Of The Year? *Huffington Post.* Retrieved from http://www.huffingtonpost.com/alayna-ahmad/i-am-malala-times-person-_b_2221517.html
Anonymous. (2013, 5 April). Malala Yousafzai foundation makes first grant. *The Guardian.* Retrieved from http://www.guardian.co.uk/world/2013/apr/05/malala-yousafzai-girls-schooling-fund
Asad, T. (2003). *Formations of the secular: Christianity, Islam, modernity.* Redwood City, CA: Stanford University Press.
Brown, G. (2012a, 25 October). Malala Yousafzai's courage can start new movement for global education. *The Guardian.* Retrieved from https://www.theguardian.com/global-development/poverty-matters/2012/oct/25/malala-yousafzai-courage-global-education

Brown, G. (2012b). *Out of wedlock, into school: Combating child marriage through education.* Retrieved from http://gordonandsarah brown.com/wp-content/uploads/2012/03/Child-Marriage-FINAL-for-Print.pdf

Brown, W. (2008). *Regulating aversion: Tolerance in the age of identity and empire.* Princeton, NJ: Princeton University Press.

Bush, L. (2001, 17 November). Radio address by Mrs. Bush. Retrieved from http://www.presidency.ucsb.edu/ws/?pid=24992

Butler, J. (2000). Interview with Gary A. Olson and Lynn Worsham. In S. Salih (Ed.), *The Judith Butler reader* (pp. 727–765). Oxford, United Kingdom: Blackwell Publishing.

Butler, J. (2005). *Giving an account of oneself.* New York, NY: Fordham University Press.

Clinton, C. (2013, 18 April). Malala Yousafzai. *TIME Magazine.* Retrieved from http://time100.time.com/2013/04/18/time-100/slide/malala-yousafzai/

Cruikshank, B. (1996). Revolutions within: Self-government and self-esteem. In A. Barry, T. Osborne, & N. Rose (Eds.), *Foucault and political reason: Liberalism, neo-liberalism, and rationalities of government* (pp. 231–251). Chicago, IL: University of Chicago Press.

Deleuze, G. & Guattari, F. (Eds.) (1987). *A thousand plateaus: Capitalism and schizophrenia.* Minneapolis, MN: University of Minnesota Press.

Dockterman, E. (2014, 24 September). After Boko Haram: Hillary Clinton promises education for 14 million girls. *TIME.* Retrieved from http://time.com/3425011/hillary-clinton-education-boko-haram-julia-gillard/

Driscoll, C. (2008). Girls today. Girls, girl culture and girl studies. *Girlhood Studies, 1*(1), 13–32.

Elias, R. (2014, May 18). 'The girl effect' and what it obscures. *Politics reconsidered.* Retrieved from http://politicsreconsidered.net/2014/05/18/the-girl-effect/

Eltahawy, M. (2012, April 23). Why do they hate us? The real war on women in the Middle East. *Foreign Policy.* Retrieved from http://www.foreignpolicy.com/articles/2012/04/23/why_do_they_hate_us

Foucault, M. (1978). *The history of sexuality*. New York, NY: Vintage Books.
Foucault, M. (1984). The ethics of the concern of the self as a practice of freedom. In P. Rabinow (Ed.), *Essential works of Foucault, 1954-1984, Vol. 1. Ethics* (pp. 281–301). New York, NY: The New Press.
Foucault, M. (2000a). Governmentality (R. Hurley et al. Trans.). In J. D. Faubion (Ed.), *Michel Foucault: Power* (pp. 201–222). New York, NY: The New Press.
Foucault, M. (2000b). The subject and power (R. Hurley et al., Trans.). In J. D. Faubion (Ed.). *Michel Foucault: Power* (pp. 326–348). New York, NY: The New Press.
Foucault, M. (2007). *Security, territory, population: Lectures at the Collège de France 1977-1978* (G. Burchell, Trans). M. Senellart (Ed). Basingstoke, United Kingdom; New York, NY: Palgrave Macmillan.
Goldman, R. (1991). Commodity feminism. *Critical Studies in Mass Communication, 8*(3), 333–351.
Harris, A. (2004). *Future girl: Young women in the 21st century*. London, United Kingdom; New York, NY: Routledge.
Hirsi Ali, A. (2007). *Infidel*. New York, NY: Free Press.
Imtiaz, S. (2013, 17 July). Taliban's letter to Malala Yousafzai: This is why we tried to kill you. *The Guardian*. Retrieved from http://www.theguardian.com/world/2013/jul/17/taliban-letter-malala-yousafzai
Khan, T. (2013, 17 July). Taliban leader advises Malala to return, join madrassa. *The Express Tribune*. Retrieved from http://tribune.com.pk/story/578128/taliban-leader-advises-malala-to-return-join-madrassa/
Khoja-Moolji, S. (2014). Producing neoliberal citizens: Critical reflections on human rights education in Pakistan. *Gender and Education*. London, United Kingdom: Taylor & Francis.
Khoja-Moolji, S. (2015). Suturing together girls and education: An investigation into the social (re)production of girls' education as a hegemonic ideology. *Diaspora, Indigenous, and Minority Education, 9*(2), 87–107.
Khoja-Moolji, S. (2015). Poststructuralist approaches to teaching about gender, Islam, and Muslim societies. *Feminist Teacher, 24*(3), 169–183.

Khoja-Moolji, S. & Niccolini, A. (2016). Watch me speak: Muslim girls' narratives and postfeminist pleasures of surveillance. In R. Heyman & E. Van der Meulen, *Expanding the gaze. Gender and the politics of surveillance* (pp. 84–102). Toronto, Canada: University of Toronto Press.

Khoja-Moolji, S. (2017). The making of 'humans' and their others in/through human rights advocacy. *Signs: Journal of Women in Culture and Society*, 42(2), 377–402.

Khurshid, A. (2012). A transnational community of Pakistani Muslim women: Narratives of rights, honor, and wisdom in a women's education project. *Anthropology & Education Quarterly*, 43, 235–252.

Lemke, T. (2001). The birth of bio-politics: Michel Foucault's lecture at the Collège de France on neo-liberal governmentality. *Economy and Society*, 30, 190–207.

Lesko, N. (2012). *Act your age!: A cultural construction of adolescence.* London, United Kingdom; New York, NY: Routledge.

Manji, I. (2003). *The trouble with Islam: A Muslim's call for reform in her faith.* Toronto, Canada: Random House.

Massumi, B. (1987). Translator's foreword: Pleasures of philosophy & notes on the translation and acknowledgements. In G. Deleuze & F. Guattari (Eds.). *A thousand plateaus: Capitalism and schizophrenia* (pp. ix–xix). Minneapolis, MN: University of Minnesota Press.

McRobbie, A. (2008). Young women and consumer culture. *Cultural Studies*, 22(5), 531–550.

McRobbie, A. (2009). *The aftermath of feminism. Gender, culture and social change.* London, United Kingdom: SAGE.

Mehta, U. S. (1997). Liberal strategies of exclusion. In F. Cooper & A. L. Stoler, *Tensions of empire: Colonial cultures in a bourgeois world.* (pp. 59–86). Oakland, CA: University of California Press.

Mills, S. (1997). *Discourse.* New York, NY: Routledge.

Mohanty, C. T. (2002). 'Under Western eyes' revisited: Feminist solidarity through anticapitalist struggles. *Signs: Journal of Women in Culture and Society*, 28, 499–535.

Mohanty, C. T. (2006). *Feminism without borders: Decolonizing theory, practicing solidarity* (6th ed.). Durham, NC; London, United Kingdom: Duke University Press.

Murphy, M. (2012/2013). The girl: Mergers of feminism and finance in neoliberal times. *The Scholar and Feminist Online, 11*(1–2), Retrieved from http://sfonline.barnard.edu/gender-justice-and-neoliberal-transformations/the-girl-mergers-of-feminism-and-finance-in-neoliberal-times/

Ong, A. (2006). *Neoliberalism as exception: Mutations in citizenship and sovereignty.* Durham, NC; London, United Kingdom: Duke University Press.

Quinn, B. (2013, 20 March). Taliban victim Malala Yousafzai starts school in UK. *The Guardian.* Retrieved from http://www.guardian.co.uk/world/2013/mar/20/taliban-victim-malala-yousafzai-school

Ringrose, J. (2012). *Postfeminist education? Girls and the sexual politics of school.* London, United Kingdom: Routledge.

Rose, N. (1996). Governing 'advanced' liberal democracies. In A. Barry, T. Osborne, & N. Rose (Eds.), *Foucault and political reason: Liberalism, neo-liberalism, and rationalities of government* (pp. 37–64). Chicago, IL: University of Chicago Press.

Rucker, P. (2013, 11 October). Malala Yousafzai meets with the Obamas in the Oval Office. *The Washington Post.* Retrieved from http://www.washingtonpost.com/blogs/post-politics/wp/2013/10/11/malala-yousafzai-meets-with-the-obamas-in-the-oval-office/

Rudisill, E. (2014). *Girl power: Shiza Shahid of the Malala Fund.* Retrieved from http://thewindow.barneys.com/girl-power-shiza-shahid-malala-fund/

Said, E. W. (1978). *Orientalism.* New York, NY: Pantheon.

Sensoy, C. & Marshall, E. (2010). Missionary girl power: Saving the 'Third World' one girl at a time. *Gender and Education, 22*(3), 295–311.

Shehabuddin, E. (2011). Gender and the figure of the 'Moderate Muslim': Feminism in the 21st century. In J. Butler & E. Weed (Eds.), *The Question of gender: Joan W. Scott's critical feminism* (pp. 102–142). Bloomington, IN: Indiana University Press.

Ticktin, M. (2011). *Casualties of care. Immigration and the politics of humanitarianism in France.* Berkeley, CA; Los Angeles, CA: University of California Press.

'Empowered Girls' in Neoliberal Times

United Nations Children's Fund. (2001). *Child marriages must stop.* Florence, Italy: United Nations Children's Fund.

United Nations Children's Fund. (2005). *Early marriage. A harmful traditional practice: a statistical exploration.* New York, NY: United Nations Children's Fund.

United Nations Educational, Scientific and Cultural Organization. (n.d.). *High-level advocacy event: Stand up for Malala – girls' education is a right!* Retrieved from http://www.unesco.org/new/en/education/themes/leading-the-international-agenda/gender-and-education/about-us/stand-up-for-malala-girls-education-is-a-right/

United Nations Educational, Scientific and Cultural Organization. (n.d.). *Malala: Symbolizing the right of girls to education.* Retrieved from http://www.unesco.org/new/en/unesco/resources/malala-symbolizing-the-right-of-girls-to-education/

United Nations Population Fund. (2012). *Marrying too young: End child marriage.* New York, NY: UNFPA.

World Development Movement (n.d.). Official website. Retrieved from http://www.wdm.org.uk/

Yousafzai, M. (2013). Speech at the United Nations. Retrieved from https://secure.aworldatschool.org/page/content/the-text-of-malala-yousafzais-speech-at-the-united-nations/

Yousafzai, M. & Lamb, C. (2013). *I am Malala: The girl who stood up for education and was shot by the Taliban.* London, United Kingdom: Little, Brown and Company.

CHAPTER THREE

OUR BORDERS: NEOLIBERALISM, IDENTITY AND ASYLUM SEEKER POLICY IN AUSTRALIA, 2001-2013

Ben Revi

Introduction
Despite Australia's history as a migrant nation, the arrival of asylum seekers by boat has attracted public controversy and harsh policy responses. Boat arrivals have been linked to broader economic and cultural issues, reflecting neoliberal reforms undertaken in Australia since the 1980s. Accordingly, 'protecting our borders' has been constructed as a test of Australia's ability to maintain sovereignty in the context of international openness. This phenomenon has been labelled the 'liberal paradox' - opening borders to trade while closing borders to people (McNevin, 2007). This chapter argues asylum seeker policy under Australian Labor Party (ALP) governments, between 2007 and 2013, presents a 'social democratic paradox', where 'fairness' in domestic politics provokes harshness towards migration. Changes in asylum policy during this time illustrate the difficulty in advancing international human rights discourses in a political context captured by neoliberalism, which constructs asylum seekers as an existential risk to the neoliberal state. After more than a decade of policy change, the Australian government finally sought to neutralise this 'risk' by restricting the resettlement of refugees arriving by boat to zero.

The profound impact of neoliberalism on Australian identity has constrained the capacity for social-democratic governments to act to restore collective welfare. Advocates for a more open approach to refugee processing must find ways to overcome this restrictive discourse, and redefine what it is to be, and to deserve to be, 'Australian'.

The timeframe chosen here reflects a particular history of policy and discourse change in the treatment of asylum seekers in Australia. In 2001, the government of Prime Minister John Howard elevated the plight of 'asylum seekers' to a highly visible feature of an election campaign. Between 2007 and 2013, the Australian Labor Party in government gradually hardened its policy to match the existing hegemonic neoliberal discourse, exposing this social democratic paradox. This chapter will situate this policy change into the context of Australia's longer history of immigration, and a broader global history of neoliberalism and identity. It will also show that the overlapping timeframes between the emergence of neoliberalism and patterns of migration policy tell a story about the appropriation of neoliberal identity politics by various governments over time.

The 'neoliberal state', hegemony and paradox

Neoliberalism is a political project that elevates the free operation of markets to a status of moral importance. It differs from classical liberalism in both discourse and practice. Classical liberalism promoted limited state interference in the life of the individual on the principle of freedom from harm; in the work of Mill, for example, 'small government' reflects a desire to ensure power does not concentrate in the hands of the few, but such a vision of liberalism does not preclude the possibility of state-funded education as a way to ensure citizens are fully trained to exercise their liberty (Mill, 1848; Miller, 2003). This is consistent with the modernist embrace of positivism, viewing liberalism as a utilitarian approach to benefit to the many, without any presumed moral character. Starting with Hayek (1944), neoliberalism recasts this project as a means to free citizens from all forms of compulsion, and takes on an implicit moral objective (against the perceived immorality of socialism, the 'road to serfdom'). By the 1970s, neoliberal activists such as Milton Friedman (2002) were arguing that the only morally consistent role for public policy is to shrink the state through privatisation or eradication of public services, to develop an entrepreneurial citizenship. Yet neoliberalism emerges itself as a flexible project, malleable enough to adapt to, and transform, local conditions, and although neoliberalism is different everywhere, it is nonetheless recognisable everywhere. In many developed countries neoliberalism has close to a 'hegemonic' force in the Gramscian (1971) sense, in that it rules by the consent of the led and defeats political argument through its discursive position as 'common sense'. Government by open markets, balanced budgets and free trade agreements have become a political norm. Differences between classes or states are constructed as mere politics, a superficial sport practised underneath the great singular weight of economics – only, of course, in its neoliberal form – which can be understood as a science, not subject to debate.

There are many competing narratives to explain the shift in liberalism to its 'neo' form, including the 'failure' of Keynesian policy to ameliorate 1970s downturns (O'Connor, 2001); changes in the focus of the economics discipline generally, and personnel changes in major global institutions (Harvey, 2007); and a broader hegemonic shift from growth to profit (Gill & Law, 1989). There is likely to be some truth in all these explanations, yet neither explains one particular contradiction in actual neoliberalism – how the promotion of free movement in capital has, in so many cases, been accompanied by the demonisation of free movement in people. The 'liberal paradox' refers in the first instance to neoliberalism in practice rather than theory: why does freedom stop at the refugee camp or detention centre? Can this be explained through inconsistencies in neoliberal theory, or are there other forces at play?

Our Borders

The neoliberal state is a series of institutions which implement and maintain neoliberal discourse and practice. Such a definition accepts the broad Gramscian view that the state is more than just a governmental apparatus controlled at different times by specific political actors – the state is a social relation, incorporating civil and political society. Power and ideology, dispersed throughout these superstructural layers of society, forms the whole of the state. While adopting a governmentality perspective, this chapter acknowledges Jessop and Oosterlynck's (2008) critique that where governmentality studies concentrate on micro-level instances of neoliberal power, they often fail to address neoliberal hegemony at the level of the state. While it is possible to see neoliberalism manifest in innumerable social interactions throughout civil and political society, it is at the borders of the broadly defined state where paradoxes in liberalism, and social democracy, emerge.

In Australia, neoliberal reforms at the state level began under 'social democratic', ALP rule, starting in 1983. At this time, Australia reduced tariffs, floated the dollar, deregulated the finance industry and privatised a number of public companies. Similar examples of social democrats adopting neoliberalism, such as François Mitterrand in France, show this was in keeping with the contemporary international climate (see Bell, 2005). While liberal and conservative parties in the neoliberal state are forced into a paradox providing border 'security' while removing barriers to trade, so too are social democratic parties forced into a paradox promoting 'fairness' in both the domestic and global spheres.

Discursively, neoliberalism rests on a specific reading of freedom. As Harvey (2007, p. 16) writes, "the freedoms it embodies reflect the interests of private property owners, businesses, multicultural corporations, and financial capital". The ideal neoliberal citizen is, first and foremost, an *economic* citizen. This individual has no *a priori* interest in collective activity besides that which may be of direct benefit. Citizens are to express their preferences not by public service, work, or social integration, but by consumer choices. Government must therefore not impede the citizen's ability to influence the state through consumption. The neoliberal state, broadly conceived, delivers the conditions to support these interests. The ALP has responded to these circumstances by diluting its historical discourses of equality, instead promising 'fairness', 'spreading the benefits' gained by liberal reforms (Swan, 2012). It is not clear what might happen if the interests of the people, expressed both through their consumer choices (withdrawing consumer spending, for example) and electoral choices, express a preference out of line with neoliberal doctrines. The paradox of popular angst over migration within the neoliberal state plays out against this context.

It is McNevin (2007), following Hollifield (2004), who argued that the treatment of migrants in Australia, particularly asylum seekers and refugees, can be seen as a 'liberal paradox'. Although some migrant labour – particularly 'skilled' migration, under strict rules and restricted to migrants carrying specific nationalities – is needed to support profitable industry, borders are closed to asylum seekers as a "performance [providing] a politically soothing contrast to Australia's projection into the global marketplace, which had instilled insecurity amongst sectors of the population" (McNevin, 2007, pp. 625–626).

Governmentality, neoliberalism and asylum

Governmentality is the term Foucault used to describe 'government rationality' (Gordon, 1991), the dominant discourse and practice of government in the modern era. Whereas classical political tracts aimed to establish and maintain sovereign power for an individual or a 'general will', modern political discourse is focussed on governance: "the welfare of the population, the improvement of its condition, the increase of its wealth, longevity, health, etc." (Foucault, 1991,

p. 100). Government becomes "the conduct of conduct" (Rose, 1999, p. 3; Dean, 1999, p. 6), the range of techniques which work upon the population to deliver governance of the individual as subject.

Governmentality predates neoliberalism, and indeed, techniques associated with governmentality underpinned the governing rationality of welfare states during the Keynesian era. Certainly, the targets Foucault outlined – welfare, longevity, health – are consistent with 'welfare state' approaches (note too that Foucault's lectures on governmentality were given in 1978, one year prior to the era of Thatcher and Reagan). The impact of neoliberalism on governmentality, therefore, is a contested field. Is there a distinct neoliberal rationality, or does a generic, apolitical governmentality adapt to serve the interests of the neoliberal state?

The governmentality approach has in recent times been accused of leading toward descriptive or technical accounts of neoliberal activity, ignoring the role of the political (Lemke, 2013; Jessop & Oosterlynck, 2008). A Foucauldian view sees liberal governmentality as a regime of truth which allowed statements about government to be constructed as not political, but 'true' (Oksala, 2013). Political debate, in this framework, can be seen as power struggles over regimes of truth. Yet the emergence of neoliberalism reflects the success of a political campaign, which involved activists, intellectuals, and institutions, as well as discourse. The coexistence of the technical and the political here offers a theoretical problem. In order to resolve this, we can begin with Lemke's argument that governmentality is not an overarching theory, but an approach to studying the intricacies of liberal government (Lemke, 2013), which can be partnered with a more expansive idea of the political. While acknowledging that Foucault broke with Marxist approaches, it should be possible to pair a Foucauldian analysis with a wider Gramscian framework to argue that neoliberalism operates as a hegemonic force, which functions according to a specific governing rationality across civil society at the level of individual subjects. Asylum seeker policy exists at the margins of this fusion of governmentality and hegemony, the boundaries of the neoliberal state – since asylum seekers, located beyond the state cannot be made into neoliberal subjects – they can be constructed as an existential risk.

There are a number of specific governing rationalities observed during the neoliberal era which help to clarify the relationship between neoliberalism, governance and asylum. As noted above, liberal governmentality is constructed as 'apolitical', a function of economic science, conceived by experts (such as independent reserve banks, committees and advisors) whose recommendations determine appropriate social behaviours and methods to encourage their practice (Dean, 1999, pp. 22–26). Politicians are judged not on their skill in delivering agreement and compromise, but rather on their skill at delivering balanced budgets and economic growth. Neoliberal techniques, using expert advice and research, "appear to act technically rather than morally" (O'Malley, 1996, p. 191). Policy is then constructed as existing outside the scope of public debate. Discourse, in the Foucauldian manner of 'regimes of truth', is dominant among the techniques of governing rationality in the neoliberal state.

Large-scale state government intervention within the neoliberal state is couched in the actuarial discourse of insurance against risk. Governmentality scholars do not argue with Beck (1992) that the development of a 'risk society' represents an epochal shift in the construction of an ideology of risk (O'Malley, 2004). Rather, risk is merely one of the many discursive techniques that spread neoliberal rationality throughout civil and political society, and while this discourse may seem more prominent in contemporary politics (risk against immigration leading to social breakdown, for example), the concept of insurance against the risks of 'want, disease, ignorance, squalor and idleness' dominated the Beveridge report (Beveridge, 1942). Neoliberal governmentality simply redefines risk, away from the impact of social structure upon the individual, towards the individual's own potential failings. This leaves little actual work for government, except to insure against the risk of external threats. This last objective is so pronounced it can overcome the need for balanced budgets, otherwise the defining theoretical objective of neoliberalism. As Dean (2010, p. 469) points out, neoliberal states were quick to fund large military and security projects in the wake of the increased terrorist threat after 2001:

> this is clearly 'too much government' ... [yet] once it is accepted that zero risk is the only acceptable level of risk in a given situation or space, then a critique of too much government in terms of economic costs can no longer be successful.

The Australian Government's offshore detention policies, with an annual cost of more than $1 billion in 2014 (Whyte, 2015), can be seen in this light. Asylum seekers, like terrorists, are seen as such a threat that "zero risk is the only acceptable level of risk" (Dean, 2010, p. 469).

The objectification of asylum seekers is set against the subjectification of citizens within the neoliberal state. Neoliberal rationality develops its citizens as they become entrepreneurial, individualistic and market-driven subjects, encouraging "people to see themselves as individualised and active subjects responsible for enhancing their own well-being" (Larner, 2000, p. 13). This neoliberal citizen is defined not only against the welfare dependent, but also the asylum seeker, who has failed to develop as an entrepreneurial subject yet has requested entry into the neoliberal state. If "the central contention is that poor people have something more wrong with them than their poverty" (Dean, 1999, p. 62), there may be an additional contention that asylum seekers must have something more wrong with them than their persecution. This tension can help to explain the dominance of the asylum seeker as a construction within political debate in Australia. Internationally, this malaise in migration debates takes distinct forms; in the United Kingdom, it is not asylum seekers, but European migrants who are seen as a threat to neoliberal citizenship. In both cases, the migrant is seen as taking advantage of institutional rules – human rights declarations for asylum seekers, free movement treaties for European migrants – which offer 'unfair' access to the neoliberal state by those who are yet to prove themselves as subjects. In both cases, public debate about the arrival and treatment of migrants has become immersed in a discourse of risk to neoliberal citizens, articulated economically and socially but not politically, reflecting the neoliberal identity of 'individualised and active' subjects at its core.

Neoliberalism, identity and asylum seekers in Australia

The emergence of the neoliberal state is not an epochal shift, but a gradual process, which adopts various discourses and techniques of government over time. Neoliberalism's form evolves over time, while its function – the development of a profitable, entrepreneurial population – remains static. During the early 1980s, Australian neoliberalism suggested an openness to migration, evidenced by the acceptance of Vietnamese and Lebanese refugees, material and discursive support for multiculturalism, reconciliation with Aboriginal and Torres Strait Islander peoples, and support for Asian integration and republicanism, pivoting Australia's foreign policy away from its historical ties to Britain towards its new trading partners. If this discourse aimed to enmesh neoliberalism by creating an 'open' Australian identity, it failed, overcome by the competing discourses of risk. This held Australia at risk of losing its British heritage, at risk of losing its sovereignty to globalisation.

Our Borders

Migration issues have been contentious since European settlement. In 1901, a system informally known as the 'White Australia Policy' restricted migration to desirable nationalities. In the aftermath of World War II, a 'populate or perish' policy saw Australia receive migrants from southern Europe, which caused anxieties – or constructed risks – among sections of the existing population (McMaster, 2002). The nation's first 'boat people' arrived only in 1976, fleeing the aftermath of the Vietnam War. At this time, Australia chose to resettle all 2,059 who arrived by boat (Betts, 2001, p. 34), along with more than 80,000 others throughout the 1980s (Jupp, 2002, p. 185). Yet when Cambodian asylum seekers began to arrive by boat in 1989, then Prime Minister Bob Hawke referred to them as "queue jumpers" and "economic refugees" (Tazreiter, 2010, p. 205), terms that have since become enshrined in public debate. Cambodian 'boat people' were the first to be detained while their applications for asylum were processed. In 1992, the Keating Government made detention mandatory (Betts, 2001, p. 34; Tazreiter, 2010, p. 205), despite Australia being a founding signatory of the 1951 United Nations Convention Relating to the Status of Refugees. Yet this policy merely formed part of the apolitical governing techniques of the Australian state, and was scarcely remarked upon until 1999, when numbers of 'boat people' grew in one year, from 200 to 3,740 (Betts, 2001). By this time, neoliberal rationality had shifted, and an acceptance of neoliberal openness in trade and skilled migration was matched with a harsh reassertion of Australia's colonial cultural sovereignty. Australian integration into Asian markets was to be tempered by a reinforcement of Western cultural heritage and recent migrants were to adhere to Western cultural norms (Clark, 2002; Johnson, 2007).

Independent MP Pauline Hanson conflated the cultural with the economic, arguing "immigration must be halted in the short term so that our dole queues are not added to by, in many cases, unskilled migrants not fluent in the English language" (Commonwealth of Australia, House of Representatives, 10 September, 1996, p. 3859). Yet in order to reduce those 'queues', Australia restricted immigration under its humanitarian and family reunion categories, while allowing employers to sponsor migrant employees for long-term temporary stays, and encouraging overseas students graduating with in-demand degrees to apply for permanent residency (Betts, 2003; Hawthorne, 2005). The broad effect was to redefine Australia's migration programme in economic rather than cultural terms, of 'deserving' and 'undeserving' migrants. In this way, neoliberalism has appropriated a discourse familiar to many ears, echoing arguments around the 'deserving' poor observed during the nineteenth century. Again, the neoliberal state shows its flexibility, appropriating a diverse range of institutional and discursive techniques, as 'regimes of truth', in support of its interests. This discursive space offered little support when, during the late 1990s, displaced people began arriving in Australia to seek asylum in larger numbers.

It is worthwhile here to present an all-too-short summary of the main arguments used to delegitimise asylum seekers. To describe asylum seekers as 'queue jumpers' assumes the existence of an orderly queue, which is not assured, especially to Afghan refugees who have no access to Australian consulates. To criticise asylum seekers about the cost of their journey is to make a false link between wealth and persecution (Pedersen, Attwell, & Heveli, 2005, p. 152). To argue asylum seekers are choosing to seek asylum in Australia rather than their nearer neighbours for economic reasons overstates the protection offered by 'transit countries' such as Indonesia. As Taylor and Rafferty-Brown explain,

> recognized refugees find themselves in a state of limbo ... in which children are deprived of effective access to education

and adults are deprived of the meaning given to life by gainful employment. (Taylor & Rafferty-Brown, 2010, p. 561)

Neoliberalism, identity and asylum seekers in Australia, 2001–2013

Australian policy towards asylum seekers gained increased visibility between 2001 and 2013. The issue is, at time of writing, still a major point of political contention in Australia, and could well develop further. An analysis of policy change over these 12 years shows that, just as there is a paradox of 'freedom' in liberal discourse preventing the free movement of peoples in order to 'insure' local populations against risk, so too there is a paradox of 'fairness' in social democratic discourse, which prevents fair movement of people in order to ensure local populations are treated according to a strictly economic meaning of 'fairness'.

Some historical context will help defend this argument. In the lead-up to the 2001 election, the Norwegian freighter *MV Tampa* rescued asylum seekers from a smaller boat, the *Palapa*, which had experienced distress at sea. The Howard Government refused to let the *Tampa* enter Australian territory, in order to refuse access to the asylum seekers on board (Marr, Wilkinson, & Ware, 2003). This developed into the 'children overboard' scandal, where Defence Minister Peter Reith claimed asylum seekers were throwing children into the ocean to encourage Australian naval rescues. These claims turned out to be false. However, the anecdote was used to make wider claims about the character of asylum seekers. Immigration Minister Phillip Ruddock described the "act" as "disturbing and premeditated" (Henderson, Saunders, Roberts, & Egan, 2001, p. 1), while Howard himself said on radio, "I certainly don't want people like that coming here, I really don't" (Mares, 2002, p. 105; Saxton, 2003, p. 117). Ruddock also argued that research showed that poor English and low education led to 'criminal activity', which "highlights the importance of selecting migrants" (Leech

& Haslem, 2001, p. 5). Claims to a shared human identity were, for Ruddock, less important than the capacity to perform as an individualised neoliberal subject.

Howard's justification for refusing access to the *Tampa* was, famously, that "we decide who comes to this country and the circumstances in which they come" (Philpott, 2002, p. 65). This is a stark turn of phrase. It rejects the basis of the UN convention which calls for refugees to be resettled without discrimination. Howard's stance is a determined effort to accept only those migrants who fulfil the criteria of neoliberal citizenship. This fits with the Howard government's broader philosophy of conservative neoliberalism. As Anthony Burke argues, "security has functioned, particularly in the rhetoric of the Howard governments, as a drive for historic, strategic and ontological *certitude*" (Burke, 2008, p. 184). Asylum policy was integrated with social, historical, strategic and economic values; it was articulated as fundamental to Australia's sovereignty and identity.

The Howard Government embarked on the 'Pacific solution', offering aid to Pacific nations Nauru and Papua New Guinea in exchange for the establishment of detention centres 'offshore'. This move aimed to re-establish a sense of security about Australia's 'borders'. The policy came at a massive cost – $114 million in 2001–2002, with an extra $31 million promised in aid (Maclellan, 2002). The cost, of course, was justified in terms of the risk now associated with irregular migration. Of the 1,550 people held in detention on Pacific nations, 65.5% were 'resettled' (i.e. found to be genuine refugees), 58% of whom in Australia and 38% in New Zealand (Kneebone, 2006, p. 708). So, in the end, Australia accepted a large number of refugees in line with its international commitments. However, it did so only after a loud and costly performance of securing its sovereign borders against a series of alleged risks. This is the 'liberal paradox' in action – in Stuart Hall's words, "marching towards the future clad in the armour of the past" (Hall, 2011, p. 713).

The election of the Rudd Labor Government in 2007 reframed neoliberal discourse, arguing the role of government was to provide not equality but 'fairness' (Rudd, 2007). As a result of political action from social movements within and outside the ALP as an organisation, the party's stance on asylum seeker policy had changed, and this was implemented in government. The detention centres in Nauru and Papua New Guinea were closed, and onshore community detention was introduced (Millbank, 2009, p. 11). This is a good example of the continued existence of the political within neoliberal hegemony. Although governmentality studies can sideline the possibilities of organisation and resistance, it can be seen here that this resistance, over time, made a direct impact on institutional policy within the neoliberal state. However, it is clear in hindsight that this political activity led only to thin change – it modified particular actions, but not the overarching governing rationality. When from 2009, asylum seekers began again to travel to Australia on boats in larger numbers (Millbank, 2009, p. 13), policy discourses returned to a harsher tone. Discourse at the level of government promoted 'fairness' for 'hard-working families' (Deeming, 2013a; Deeming, 2013b). Now led by Prime Minister Julia Gillard, the government embraced a 'sustainable' population growth strategy, limiting immigration of all kinds to protect Australia's "clean beaches and precious open space" (Kelly, 2010). Gillard implied the policy change was not about the racial or cultural aspects of migration, but insurance against the economic risk of infrastructure incapacity, linking population growth with "long commutes, stuck in traffic" (Franklin & Fraser, 2010, p. 6). Gillard also reasserted the discourse of security from the risk of immigration as an existential threat, arguing "for people to say they're anxious about border security doesn't make them intolerant. It certainly doesn't make them a racist" (Maley & Maiden, 2010, p. 1).

Gillard adopted a number of strategies to insure against the risk now constructed of boat arrivals, including negotiations with Afghanistan to promise a safe return to Afghan asylum seekers (Maley & Maiden, 2010). The key plank, for some time, was a 'people-swap' deal with Malaysia, abandoned after it was declared invalid by the High Court of Australia (Lowes, 2012). Government discourse forcefully articulated the 'queue jumper' myth to establish public support for the Malaysia deal. In a joint press release, Gillard and Immigration Minister Chris Bowen advised asylum seekers that "if you arrive in Australian waters and are taken back to Malaysia you will go to the back of the queue" (Gillard & Bowen, 2011, p. 421). It was also constructed as insurance against the risk of people smuggler activity – a distortion, or corruption, of the market for people movement – which remained central to the ALP's construction of the issue (McKenzie & Hasmath, 2013). The ALP continued to situate the problem of boat arrivals at the undesirable decisions of individuals, and government intervention was intended only to reinforce a valid market for asylum.

With the Malaysia policy unavailable, the Gillard Government adopted one of the clearest techniques available to liberal governmentality – it devolved policymaking to a body of technical experts, whose deliberations could be implemented by the neoliberal state outside the scope of political debate. An 'expert panel' was commissioned to prepare a report to advise on an asylum policy (Expert Panel on Asylum Seekers, 2012) and, resulting from their report, offshore detention centres on Nauru and Papua New Guinea were reopened (Franklin, 2012). Furthermore, Australia adopted the report's recommendation to institute a 'no advantage' principle for boat arrivals, whereby asylum seekers arriving by boat would have their applications processed at the same slow speed as those remaining offshore.

Such a policy restates the myth of the 'queue'. The expert panel's recommendations were again underpinned by the hegemonic neoliberal discourse of individual choice in the market for movement and asylum. Interestingly, the government's response rested on a newly modified discourse – offshore detention would "deter people from endangering their lives by getting on unseaworthy vessels" (Commonwealth of Australia, House of Representatives, 25 June, 2013, p. 6939). The discourse of insurance against risk was now placed not only upon the local population, but on outsiders who sought access to asylum in Australia. The risk of death to asylum seekers, like the risk of their arrival, was too great not to attract government intervention. Of course, the risks asylum seekers experience when remaining in transit countries or in places of persecution were minimised, particularly by Foreign Minister Bob Carr, who claimed asylum seekers arriving by boat were "overwhelmingly not people fleeing persecution but economic migrants" (Probyn & Butterly, 2013, p. 14), recycling an older phrase.

During the 2013 election, both major parties settled on a policy whereby asylum seekers arriving by boat would "never be settled in Australia" (Hall, Swan, Hurst, & Allard, 2013, p. 1). At great public expense, this plan would detain all boat arrivals in offshore facilities, then resettle all those found to be genuine refugees in Papua New Guinea. The Australian public would no longer be exposed to any risk – economic, security or otherwise – posed by refugees sailing to the country on boats. 'Fairness', which had been the key discourse of the ALP in government, no longer held any space for fairness towards asylum seekers even when found to be refugees. The word had been redefined in terms of 'fair' access, by neoliberal citizens, to markets in goods and labour. Such an identity politics limits the capacity for the Australian Government to resettle asylum seekers, constructed to be incapable of performing as neoliberal citizens, into Australian social and economic life.

Conclusion

The logic of neoliberal citizenship holds every activity to be, first, an economic activity. The movement of displaced persons is seen not as an act of desperation made necessary by collective repression, but an economic choice made by individuals. Every component of an asylum seeker's journey – the cost, the route, the destination, the use of 'smugglers' – is seen as an avoidable choice. This logic marginalises aspects of reality for asylum seekers, in which those choices are restricted, information is scarce, and exploitation is rife. Furthermore, as the act of arriving in Australia to seek asylum is constructed as improper, going beyond the technical institutional rules set by the neoliberal state, asylum seekers are constructed as unfit for settlement. Even those legally found to be refugees in need of protection are considered a risk to existing residents, in terms of population growth, services, jobs, culture and identity.

The example shows the ability of neoliberalism to appropriate discourse more familiar to the social democratic tradition, such as 'fairness', to guide. It shows the power of individualism as a discourse that converts collective welfare into individual services, and presents a zero-sum view that constructs the welfare of others as antagonistic to the welfare of the self.

References

Beck, U. (1992). *Risk society: Towards a new modernity*. London, United Kingdom: SAGE.

Bell, D. S. (2005). *François Mitterrand*. Cambridge, United Kingdom: Polity.

Betts, K. (2001). Boatpeople and public opinion in Australia. *People and Place, 9*(4), 34–48.

Betts, K. (2003). Immigration policy under the Howard Government. *Australian Journal of Social Issues, 38*(2), 169–192.

Beveridge, W. (1942). *Social insurance and allied services*. London, United Kingdom: HMSO.

Burke, A. (2008). *In fear of security: Australia's invasion anxiety.* Melbourne, Australia: Cambridge University Press.

Clark, A. (2002). History in black and white: A critical analysis of the black armband debate. *Journal of Australian Studies, 26*(75), 1–11.

Commonwealth of Australia, House of Representatives (1996). Parliamentary debates. *Official Hansard.* Canberra, ACT: Australian Parliament.

Commonwealth of Australia, House of Representatives (2013). Parliamentary debates. *Official Hansard.* Canberra, ACT: Australian Parliament.

Dean, M. (1999). *Governmentality: Power and rule in modern society.* London, United Kingdom: SAGE.

Dean, M. (2010). Power at the heart of the present: Exception, risk and sovereignty. *European Journal of Cultural Studies, 13*(4), 459–475.

Deeming, C. (2013a). Regional issue: Social policy developments in Australia and New Zealand. *Social Policy & Administration, 47*(6), 668–691.

Deeming, C. (2013b). Social democracy and social policy in neoliberal times. *Journal of Sociology, 47,* 17–34.

Expert Panel on Asylum Seekers (2012). *Report of the Expert Panel on Asylum Seekers.* Canberra, ACT, Australia: Australian Government.

Foucault, M. (1991). Governmentality. In G. Burchell, C. Gordon, & P. Miller (Eds.), *The Foucault effect: Studies in governmentality* (pp. 87–104). Chicago, IL: University of Chicago Press.

Franklin, M. (2012, 14 August). At last, people put before politics. *The Australian,* p. 1.

Franklin, M. & Fraser, A. (2010, 9 July). Gillard stays out of planning but urges quality of life. *The Australian,* p. 6.

Friedman, M. (2002). *Capitalism and freedom.* Chicago, IL: University of Chicago Press.

Gill, S. R. & Law, D. (1989). Global hegemony and the structural power of capital. *International Studies Quarterly, 33*(4), 475–499.

Gillard, J. & Bowen, C. (2011). *The regional cooperation framework.* Canberra, ACT, Australia: Press Office of the Prime Minister of Australia.

Gordon, C. (1991). Government rationality: An introduction. In G. Burchell, C. Gordon, & P. Miller (Eds.), *The Foucault effect: Studies in governmentality* (pp. 1–52). Chicago: University of Chicago Press.

Gramsci, A. (1971). *Selections from the prison notebooks* (Trans. G. N. Smith & Q. Hoare). Southampton, United Kingdom: The Camelot Press Ltd.

Hall, B., Swan, J., Hurst, D., & Allard, T. (2013, 20 July). Rudd reveals his PNG solution. *The Sydney Morning Herald*, p. 1.

Hall, S. (2011). The neo-liberal revolution. *Cultural Studies, 25*(6), 705–728.

Harvey, D. (2007). *A brief history of neoliberalism*. Oxford, United Kingdom: Oxford University Press.

Hawthorne, L. (2005). 'Picking winners': The recent transformation of Australia's skilled migration policy. *International Migration Review, 39*(3), 663–696.

Hayek, F. A. (1944). *The Road to serfdom*. London, United Kingdom: Routledge.

Henderson, I., Saunders, M., Roberts, J., & Egan, C. (2001, 8 October). Boat children overboard – Howard hard line becomes poll focus. *The Australian*, p. 1.

Hollifield, J. F. (2004). The emerging migration state. *International Migration Review, 38*(3), 885–912.

Jessop, B. & Oosterlynck, S. (2008). Cultural political economy: On making the cultural turn without falling into soft economic sociology. *Geoforum, 39*(3), 1155–1169.

Johnson, C. (2007). John Howard's 'values' and Australian identity. *Australian Journal of Political Science, 42*(2), 195–209.

Jupp, J. (2002). *From White Australia to Woomera: The story of Australian immigration*. Cambridge, United Kingdom: Cambridge University Press.

Kelly, P. (2010, 21 July). Gillard first to pull population lever. *The Australian*.

Kneebone, S. (2006). The Pacific Plan: The provision of 'effective protection'? *International Journal of Refugee Law, 18*(3–4), 696–721.

Larner, W. (2000). Neo-liberalism: Policy, ideology, governmentality. *Studies in Political Economy, 63*, 5–22.

Leech, G. & Haslem, B. (2001, 11 September). Ruddock tries to stay a step ahead of smugglers. *The Australian.*
Lemke, T. (2013). Foucault, politics and failure. In J. Nilsson & S-O. Wallenstein (Eds.), *Foucault, biopolitics, and governmentality* (pp. 35–52). Stockholm, Sweden: Södertörn University.
Lowes, S. (2012). The legality of extraterritorial processing of asylum claims: The judgment of the High Court of Australia in the 'Malaysian Solution' Case. *Human Rights Law Review, 12*(1), 168–182.
Maclellan, N. (2002). The Pacific 'non solution'. *Pacific Journalism Review, 8*(1), 145–154.
Maley, P. & Maiden, S. (2010, 5 July). Julia Gillard to send back boatpeople. *The Australian.*
Mares, P. (2002). *Borderline: Australia's response to refugees and asylum seekers.* Sydney, Australia: UNSW Press.
Marr, D., Wilkinson, M., & Ware, R. (2003). *Dark victory.* Sydney, Australia: Allen & Unwin.
McKenzie, J. & Hasmath, R. (2013). Deterring the 'boat people': Explaining the Australian government's People Swap response to asylum seekers. *Australian Journal of Political Science, 48*(4), 417–430.
McMaster, D. (2002). Asylum-seekers and the insecurity of a nation. *Australian Journal of International Affairs, 56*(2), 279–290.
McNevin, A. (2007). The liberal paradox and the politics of asylum in Australia. *Australian Journal of Political Science, 42*(4), 611–630.
Mill, J. S. ([1848] 1965). *Principles of political economy with some of their applications to social philosophy* (Ed. J. M. Robson). Toronto, Canada; London, United Kingdom: University of Toronto Press; Routledge & Kegan Paul.
Millbank, A. (2009). Kind or cruel?: Labor's boat people policies. *People and Place, 17*(4), 8.
Miller, D. E. (2003). Mill's 'Socialism'. *Politics, Philosophy & Economics, 2*(2), 213–238.
O'Connor, J. (2001). *The fiscal crisis of the state.* Piscataway, NJ: Transaction Publishers.
O'Malley, P. (1996). Risk and responsibility. In A. Barry, T. Osborne, & N. Rose (Eds.), *Foucault and political reason* (pp. 189–208). Chicago, IL: University of Chicago Press.

O'Malley, P. (2004). *Risk, uncertainty and government*. London, United Kingdom: Glass House Press.

Oksala, J. (2013). Neoliberalism and biopolitical governmentality. In J. Nilsson & S.-O. Wallenstein (Eds.), *Foucault, biopolitics and governmentality* (pp. 53–72). Stockholm, Sweden: Södertörn University.

Pedersen, A., Attwell, J., & Heveli, D. (2005). Prediction of negative attitudes toward Australian asylum seekers: False beliefs, nationalism, and self-esteem. *Australian Journal of Psychology, 57*(3), 148–160.

Philpott, S. (2002). Protecting the borderline and minding the bottom line: Asylum seekers and politics in contemporary Australia. *Refuge: Canada's Journal on Refugees, 20*(4), 63–75.

Probyn, A. & Butterly, N. (2013, 26 June). Carr: Most boat people not refugees. *The West Australian*, p. 14.

Rose, N. (1999). *Powers of freedom*. Cambridge, United Kingdom: Cambridge University Press.

Rudd, K. (2007, 14 November). Election speech at Brisbane. Retrieved from http://electionspeeches.moadoph.gov.au/speeches/2007-kevin-rudd

Saxton, A. (2003). 'I certainly don't want people like that here': The discursive construction of 'asylum seekers'. *Media International Australia, Incorporating Culture & Policy, 109*, 109–120.

Swan, W. (2012, 4 March). Treasurer's economic note. Retrieved from http://ministers.treasury.gov.au/ministers/wms/content/eco nomicnotes/2012/attachments/016_Treasurer's_Economic_ Note.pdf

Taylor, S. & Rafferty-Brown, B. (2010). Waiting for life to begin: The plight of asylum seekers caught by Australia's Indonesian Solution. *International Journal of Refugee Law, 22*(4), 558–592.

Tazreiter, C. (2010, 5 February). Local to global activism: The movement to protect the rights of refugees and asylum seekers. *Social movement studies, 9*(2), 201–214. Retrieved from http://www.tandfonline.com/doi/abs/10.1080/147428310036 03349

Whyte, S. (2015, 5 February). Government spends $1.2 billion on offshore processing centres in one year. *Sydney Morning Herald.* Retrieved from http://www.smh.com.au/federal-politics/political-news/government-spends-12-billion-on-offshore-processing-centres-in-one-year-20150205-13708n.html

CHAPTER FOUR

"THE WAY YOU MAKE ME FEEL": SHAME AND THE NEOLIBERAL GOVERNANCE OF DISABILITY WELFARE SUBJECTIVITIES IN AUSTRALIA AND THE UK

Karen Soldatic and Hannah Morgan

Disability and neoliberal statistical panic

There has been a growing global statistical panic surrounding 'disability' over recent years. This disability anxiety has been couched around a discourse of *un*sustainability as governments use a particular set of disability statistics to argue that they can no longer afford disability welfare that is, one of fiscal doom and gloom, "looming in the horizon"(Woodward, 2009, p. 197). Such concerns have been occurring across most OECD countries, and these statistical discourses of disability fiscal panic have become normalised with the onset of austerity measures since the financial crash in late 2007. Global policy institutions such as the OECD, World Bank and the IMF have situated disability within economic discourses of global restructuring (Grover & Soldatic, 2013). Disability is thus now central to economic debates pertaining to the future 'health' of the nation that dominates debates of welfare retraction that aim to move people off welfare and into the world of work (Soldatic, 2013).

Disability's shift from the fringes to the epicentre of economic policy emerged in the mid-1990s (Soldatic & Chapman, 2010). Before this, disability was mostly positioned as a category of social welfare and medicine (Clear & Gleeson, 2001). This changed with the emergence of two specific forces: the disability rights movement and the rise of neoliberalism as a policy orthodoxy (Roulstone & Morgan, 2009). As French and Swain contend (2007), while these two movements have disparate aims for disabled people, their focal point around disabled people's enduring exclusion from the labour market and the resultant effects of entrenched poverty and dependence on welfare has, at times, led to a precarious position of convergence.

The timing of the disability rights movement's call for the 'right to work' emerges in concert with workfare. Peck (2001) suggests that workfare is the key domestic social project of neoliberal global restructuring as it seeks to re-regulate the relationship between the labour market and state welfare provisioning by making welfare supports dependent upon individualised economic contribution. This deepening of the market society via workfare regimes first surfaced in North America under the Reagan administration but came into full effect in the US during the Clinton Administration with the passage of the Personal Responsibility and Work Opportunity Reconciliation Act 1996 (Abramovitz, 2006, p. 339). Workfare is now part of an international project promoted through global policy institutes such as the OECD and IMF (Grover & Soldatic, 2013). In the last 10 years, most Western nation states have undertaken some form of welfare restructuring to reflect the institutional requirements of a workfare state (Soldatic, 2013). In the UK, the Blair Labour Government developed its 'making work pay' strategy and its *New Deal* policy (Peck, 2001) which have been further consolidated under the Cameron Conservative-led Coalition Government's radical withdrawal of any claim to citizenship entitlement, affecting a multitude of groups, and particularly disabled people (Roulstone & Morgan, 2014).

The hegemony of neoliberalism has redefined ideas of citizenship, social inclusion and social mobility. The liberal social contract of 'rights and entitlements' and 'roughly equal' has radically shifted to the coercive authoritarian neoliberal logic of 'responsibilities and obligations'; often pitched in the populist mantra of 'no rights without responsibilities' (Fiske & Briskman, 2007). This means that access to social entitlements is no longer based on need or necessity alone. The discursive panic created by statistical repetition of doom and gloom creates public consent for an authoritarian logic that requires citizens to *earn* their social entitlements through performance of market behaviours in exchange for welfare benefits and supports. Work, labour market attachment and subordination to the imperatives of the market are thus promoted as the highest form of citizen responsibility (Lister, 2001). Workfare is thus inherently contradictory, as it combines the imperative of market individualism of the New Right with the authoritarian obligations asserted by neo-conservatives.

Nearly all Western liberal democracies have undertaken large-scale disability policy restructuring in line with neoliberal welfare policy trends (Humpage, 2007). While there is a multiplicity of local variations and deviations, international analysis suggests that neoliberal disability policy converges around the restructuring of disability social security entitlements with the primary aim of steering disabled people off disability pensions and into the open labour market (Roulstone & Barnes, 2005; Grover & Soldatic, 2013). Consistent across Australia, Britain, Canada and the USA has been the large-scale implementation of numerous governance technologies to 'activate' disabled people's labour-market participation (OECD, 2009). These activation technologies concentrate on compelling disability social security recipients into a set of prescribed activity tests as a condition of maintaining access to benefits, such as individual compacts, participation plans, sanctioning regimes and in many instances, the straight denial of social security support (Grover & Piggott, 2013; Soldatic, 2013). These all aim to contain disability pension growth and curtail future fiscal outlays by making disabled people disappear from the welfare rolls (Grover & Soldatic, 2013).

While major scholars in welfare studies often interrogate neoliberal workfare governance in the key centres of global power, such as the USA and the UK (Jessop, 2002; Peck, 2001), as Grover and Soldatic (2013) illustrate, it has been Australia that has been the experimental 'hot bed' of neoliberal workfare restructuring, and, it has been the area of disability that has been central to its trialling of new forms of neoliberal governance under governments of either persuasion (Morris, Wilson, & Soldatic, 2015). In fact, in recent years we have seen the active global transfer of neoliberal disability welfare restructuring as the Australian political elite are increasingly invited to remind their global political counterparts of the benefits of Australian neoliberal restructuring (see Hockey, 2012). Thus, this interscalar transfer of neoliberal orthodoxy, spoken within intimate elite political networks, moves from the centre to the periphery and back again, in a continued dialogue of discursive privilege and power.

This global statistical panic, however, discloses little about the reproduction of neoliberal violence in the everyday experience of disability in a continually and rapidly changing polity where disability has become centre stage in economic policy deliberations (Soldatic & Pini, 2012). Rarely are the voices of disabled people heard in these critical public policy debates (Gibilisco, 2010) despite the impact of these policies on disabled people's subjectivities. Thus, there is the possibility of another reading of these statistics, a reading that critically focusses on the narratives of disabled people who have developed a range of strategies to sustain their emotional well-being to contend with the barrage of neoliberal workfare policies that shame them into compliance. In this chapter, we draw upon interviews conducted as part of two national studies in Australia and the UK with disabled people who have been experiencing at first hand the *affect effects* of neoliberal workfare. Despite the differing socio-spatial contexts, these people's narratives reveal an intimate convergence – a highly masculine able-bodied project that denies subjects care for themselves and others, whilst having to perform 'care for the nation' via the realm of work.

Emotions, disability and neoliberal governance

Emotions have had a contested and chequered history within scholarly research since the emergence of industrial capitalism. With the advance of neoliberal capitalism, they have become, once again, prominent in work that seeks to critically illustrate the regulatory role of emotions with capital's ebbs and flows. Authors such as Ahmed (2004), Skeggs (2004) and Tyler (2013) are documenting the emotionality of neoliberalism as it increasingly frames social citizenship via the emotional lens. This rich body of work identifies the ways in which emotions infuse the contested boundaries of the private and the public as an array of emotions are actively drawn upon by elite actors to socially shape new forms of neoliberal governance at the micro-scale of the 'self'. Emotions thus are not things that belong to an individual as a separate object, but are in fact, framed with moral meanings and sentiments that operate discursively at the macro-scale to create nascent forms of social control, which can become embodied as everyday practices of self-governance.

Disabled people have long been aware of the role of emotions in social regulating their daily lives (Marks, 1999). Emotions have historically been powerful mechanisms to maintain disabled people's confinement within the asylum, clear them from the streets, and to hide them away from the public gaze (Schweik, 2009). Latterly, Kolarova (2012) demonstrates how disabled people have had to take on "handicap, social stigma, dependence, isolation and economic disadvantage" in exchange for the status of being a "tolerated exception" from neoliberal requirements of citizenship (Stone, 1984, p. 4 cited in Kolarova 2012, p. 265). For disabled people, emotions are thus deeply political. This is both due to the direct and indirect affects it has on their lives, which are disabling, stigmatising and extremely painful. As Reeve (2012) contends, the emotional sphere of disability social regulation operates in the "'most mundane everyday words or deeds that exclude or invalidate' (Hughes, 2007, pp. 682)" a form of "ontological invalidation [that] undermines psycho-emotional well-being" (Reeve, pp. 79–80). Authors such as Ahmed (2004), Skeggs (2004) and Tyler (2013) are documenting the affect effects or emotionality of liberalism as it increasingly frames social citizenship via the emotional lens. The affect effects thus frame disabled people's intra-corporeal engagement, effectively reaffirming social processes of oppression as forms of internalised self-governance. Emotions for disabled people, are therefore, a key area of social life where they are required to manage other people's emotions, whilst simultaneously managing their own, all for the benefit of others.

Of all of the emotions, it is shame that dominates the everyday experience of disability. As Charlton (1998) notes, "shame and other manifestations of this process are devastating, for they prevent people with disabilities from knowing their real selves" (p. 27). To have an unruly corporeality is one of great shame, signifying to the public a rejected body (Wendell, 1996) and a corporeality that is in fact of "no social value" (Siebers, 2008, p. 162). This negative social devaluation re-positions disability as *the* human spectacle, the ongoing invalidating gaze forces disabled people to adopt, practice and perform a tightly controlled performance to avoid the shaming gaze of the able-bodied public (Soldatic, 2010). Most critically, for disabled people, the recurrent experience of shame, and the internalised practices of self-management to avoid public shaming, radically alters their own sense of self-dignity and self-respect (Reeve, 2012). With each external repetition, these underlying structures of internalised shame reaffirm an internal dialogue of self-disrespect, which are durable and enduring (Siebers, 2008).

For disabled people, these acts of shaming – through public depictions of disabled people in political or media discourse and representations coupled with the daily acts of staring they encounter in a multiplicity of spaces and places – are a form of violence (Garland-Thomas, 2009). This is captured in the burgeoning literature on disability 'hate crime' (Sherry, 2010; Roulstone & Mason-Bish 2013) where Sherry's apparently common-sense subtitle 'Does Anyone *Really* Hate Disabled People?' is in stark contrast to the level and intensity of everyday routinised violence that disabled people experience. This generates a heightened sense of fear for disabled people when navigating the world due to the frequency, irregularity and randomness of this violence (Roulstone & Morgan, 2014). These everyday forms of shaming experienced by disabled people are reflective of Young's (1990) definition of violence when she denotes that:

> Members of some groups of people live with the knowledge that they must fear random, unprovoked attacks on their person or property, which have no motive but to damage, humiliate or destroy the person. (Young, 1990, p. 61)

The long-lasting effects of such random attacks prohibit many disabled people from actively traversing and experiencing the outside world. As Roulstone and Morgan (2014) have argued, disabled people are frequently feeling this form of everyday routinised violence, directly and indirectly, as they are shamed by the political elite's attack on disability welfare with the ongoing intensification of neoliberal restructuring of welfare. It seems that, increasingly, disabled people are shamed not just because they are disabled, but because of their potential association with the welfare system that disability suggests (Soldatic, 2010). The implied profligate expansion of welfare provision that permitted too great a number of *exceptions* "from the requirements of conscientious citizenship and individual responsibility" (Kolarova, 2012, p. 265) is utilised as a way in which to "*justify* the channelling of public hostilities towards vulnerable and/or disadvantaged populations" (Tyler, 2013, p. 212). This reclassification of large numbers of disabled people from deserving to undeserving recipients of welfare provision transforms them into "symbolic and material scapegoats" (Tyler, 2013, p. 211) for the economic crises and resultant austerity.

Shame is the emotion that "makes you want to disappear, to hide away and to cover yourself" (Probyn, 2004, p. 329). Roulstone and Morgan (2014) argue that many disabled people are now remaining 'in place', stuck within their homes with their curtains closed to avoid the public shaming and rise of direct acts of violence that has coincided with the political construction of disabled people as neoliberal welfare scroungers. In fact, as Roulstone and Mason-Bish (2012) have documented there has been a massive increase of violent hate crime against disabled people with the advent of neoliberal political discourse to make them feel ashamed of their claim to social entitlements.

This everyday experience of internalising the affect effects of neoliberal shame both violates disabled people's sense of identity, and also their sense of security and safety when being 'out of place' (Soldatic, 2013). The structural collective shaming of disabled people thus becomes embodied in the reproduction of everyday life, where disabled people are shamed by the performance of the non-market self. Neoliberalism is thus extremely mobile. Moving from the structural, the political and the group through to navigating down to the individual who is required to perform the market individual in everyday life. Shame performs this inter-scalar labour on its behalf.

Nussbaum suggests that shame is *the* social emotion (Nussbaum, 2004). It is the emotion best known for keeping people *in their place* due to "its everyday dependence on the proximities of others, of place, of routine, of biography and history" (Probyn, 2004, p. 329). Primarily, its use as a subtle everyday mechanism to contain marginalised social groups, works to establish borders and boundaries around sets of bodies – dividing, sorting and classifying bodies and minds into a complex web of social regulating regimes (Sayer, 2005). Nussbaum (2004) refers to this process as stigmatised shame, where the role of shame in public moral discourse is to stigmatise the class of people towards which it is targeted as a form of group subordination. The resultant feelings of shame associated with this type of public shaming leaves members who identify with the stigmatised group feeling unworthy; a feeling that disabled people can readily corroborate.

Therefore, it is not surprising that shame has a long-standing association with violence (Scheff & Retzinger, 1991). Shame has been used throughout the establishment of modern liberal democracies to regulate the socio-spatial sphere (Nussbaum 2004) and yet, is most often exhibited as individual acts of violence in direct response to structural shame (Scheff & Retzinger, 1991). Shame's power is hence its ability to become embodied and internalised as individual moral failure, as it subtly oozes through a range of spaces and places to hide the structural effects of social inequality, exclusion and deprivation (Sayer, 2005). Shame is embedded in, and emerges from, our social existence and, therefore, it shapes, and is shaped by, the political sphere (Nussbaum, 2004). It is actively used to individualise structural deprivation to re-situate the place of blame and entails the reimagining of the 'rational individual' or of 'homo economicus' as an *emotional* being. This emotional being is *irrational, unruly* and *resistant* to market behaviours, logics and norms.

It is these individualising properties of shame and public acts of shaming that are incredibly significant in revealing the architecture of neoliberal workfare and the experience of neoliberal forms of everyday life. The targeting of individual behaviour as a moral public discourse has been prominent across Western liberal democracies implementing workfare strategies. For example, US President Reagan referred to single mothers on welfare as 'welfare queens' (Goodin, 2002) and Prime Minister Tony Blair insisted that disabled people were using disability benefits "as an excuse to never work again" (Lyall quoted in Galvin, 2004, p. 126). In Australia and the United Kingdom the 'welfare scrounger' has become a powerful moral signifier across successive governments (Soldatic, 2010; Roulstone & Morgan, 2014). Wilson and Turnbull (2001) argue that such strategies are a *"calculated political tactic"* of the New Right (p. 384, original emphasis), personified around a 'politics of blame' that discursively constructs, poor working subjects as the primary cause of the welfare and fiscal crises (Haylett, 2003). All of these efforts are thus designed to move public resentment away from neoliberal governments as growing numbers of their citizens are faced with a precarious existence, of high economic insecurity and of growing material deprivation with neoliberal global restructuring. Shame thus actively displaces political discontent, providing governments with a proxy to target one's anger for the downward spiral in social mobility experienced so much by the lower-middle classes (McRobbie, 2013).

Shaming of welfare recipients also encourages an active process of forgetting, forgetting past injustices, past inequalities and past structural exclusions, hiding such structural marginalisation through blaming and shaming. As Ranciere (2004) argues, this shifting political frame then creates a form of seeing of what was previously *un*seen. This key technique of neoliberal governance lays the grounds for the political elite to build a new moral consensus of social norms, dominated by new meanings of citizenship that are framed around precarious forms of work in low wage casualised labour markets as the 'new norm' of participation. The desired effects of shaming are thus twofold – to build public consensus for neoliberal workfare restructuring, and also to remove social entitlements as a right of citizenship and propel welfare recipients into the labour market.

As we illustrate throughout the next section, neoliberalism actively draws upon acts of shaming to force disabled people to comply with its coercive regulating regime (Bessant, Watts, Dalton, & Smyth, 2006). As legitimising discourses to advance the market logic of neoliberalism, the structural processes of neoliberal welfare restructuring not only individualise, but directly blame, disabled people suffering from structural disadvantage. Shame is used to articulate the lack of a job as a private moral failure. It is used to labour the inter-scalar moralisation of neoliberal intensification. Moralising structural disadvantage reinforces existing social divisions (Martin, 2007), whilst reconstituting new social hierarchies. Most significantly, shaming has become a calculated political tactic to re-imagine the disability landscape, creating new divisions to separate the deserving from the *un*deserving disabled welfare recipient (Grover & Piggott, 2013). With the emergence of a neoliberal workfare state, a new set of social norms is required; re-regulating and re-classifying disabled citizens into two classes – those so-called disabled people who are *un*deserving of social entitlements and plague the system by actively abdicating their responsibilities, and those *truly* deserving disabled citizens who are unable to contribute to the neoliberal project.

Repeated experience of shame within neoliberal workfare spaces undermined disabled people's sense of self and their ability to act in the world. The chapter combines two separate studies that occurred in Australia and the UK. The Australian study was part of Soldatic's PhD research that focussed upon Australian disability income reform with the onset of neoliberalism and its intensification with the 2004 re-election of a majority Conservative government (Soldatic, 2010). The second study, completed in the UK during 2012, drew upon the findings of Soldatic's Australian study, working in collaboration with researchers from Lancaster University. While the temporal moment of each set of interviews does not occur simultaneously, the structural transformations with the intensification of neoliberalism as policy hegemony are directly comparable (Grover & Soldatic, 2013). The comparative analysis of the interviews confirms the global literature on the policy mobility of neoliberal welfare to work measures, that despite local contingencies, illustrates the transfer of international learnings, processes and practices to build consensus within the polity to achieve the structural, institutional and regulatory transformations that neoliberalism demands.

The interview transcripts reveal that the dominant experience of disabled people in Australia and the UK with neoliberal intensification is that of public shaming, through a diverse range of political discourses. The constant barrage of shame promoted an internalisation of the violation and disrespect embedded in institutionalised practices of shame. Public discourses and symbolic representations to promote neoliberal governance not only misrecognised disabled people's structural disadvantage, but actively worked to further stigmatise disabled people as a group in order to assure their compliance with the new workfare norms of neoliberal governance. Shame labours on neoliberalism's behalf, traversing the inter-scalar relations between the citizen and the state, transforming disabled people's subjectivity through everyday forms of violence. These everyday practices of violence become internalised, and yet, remain abstract and distinct critical components of the affect effects of shame. The discursive power of statistical panic moves from the parliament, the financial market and the press, and is then lived and negotiated in everyday life.

Neoliberalism and disabled people's songs of shame
Shaming employs multiple strategies. Some acts of shaming are subtle, while others are deliberately overt, intended to signify to a group the set of power relations in which they are embedded (Barbalet, 1998). Shaming occurs at all levels, from the macro-structural scale to the micro-spaces and places (Sayer, 2005).

Edges of Identity

Disabled people from Australia and the UK participating in these studies clearly understood neoliberal acts of shaming to reflect their marginalised position of power in workfare governance. Most significantly, they actively internalised the public shame of being unemployed and on welfare as a moral evaluation of the self. We were first alerted to this with Beatrice,[1] a young women with a vision impairment living with her mother in Perth, Australia. Even though Beatrice has made multiple attempts to find work, actively seeking the support from workfare services, she repeatedly disclosed the feelings of inferiority experienced when making her best efforts to join a neoliberal labour market that has historically excluded disabled women. At the end of the interview, Beatrice told how she no longer had the energy to pursue employment as "I was feeling I wasn't worth it, even though I had skills I thought I wasn't good enough anymore". All the disabled people in the UK and Australia participating in these two studies expressed these individualised feelings of internalised shame. While Beatrice's shame is commonly expressed as a form of low-lying shame, revealed as ongoing feelings of inferiority, others expressed more overt forms of shame. In fact, it appeared that as neoliberal workfare intensified across the two countries, the everyday experience of shame was heightened for the research participants with their failure to gain employment, even though they actively worked hard to gain employment of any kind. To us, as researchers, it appeared that as the research participants intensified their efforts to gain employment, so did their experiences of internalised shame and feelings of unworthiness intensify. The internalisation of social forms of shaming had a transformative effect. For Beatrice she no longer wanted to "go out to try for another job" and, therefore, she largely remained 'in place', isolated in her home with her mother. However, for others these effects were more direct and violent.

"The Way You Make Me Feel"

Rachel, a woman with cerebral palsy, reveals the extreme forms of hiding that disabled people may need to practise to escape neoliberal workfare strategies that aim to 'activate' disabled people's labour market participation. Rachel was forced to see a workfare employment provider and meet regularly with a case management to manage her transition to employment and off welfare. Eventually a job was found, however, this job was within a local library that was unpaid. The local library had stairs and no lift. Rachel was a wheelchair user. Additionally, this unpaid job would force Rachel to spend money from her disability payment to get to and from work, which she could ill afford. Even though Rachel explained this situation to the case worker, Rachel was forced to 'go to work'. Eventually, Rachel decided to actively exclude herself from the barrage of daily shaming that was experienced with having to work for free in an inaccessible workplace. In fact, Rachel took to hiding from the workfare case worker she was assigned, which in turn left her isolated from communicating with the rest of her world. To escape workfare governance, she needed to disconnect herself from her primary form of communication – the telephone: "so I was at the point she had me so terrified, haranguing and bullying me, I took the phone off the hook, and all but hid under the bed".

Rachel's experiences and practices of resistance, along with Beatrice's experiences of unworthiness, also demonstrate the contradictory nature of workfare governance, which combines the New Right agenda of market activity with neo-conservative authoritarian logic of obligation. Neo-conservatives such as Mead (1986) have long argued that these necessarily coercive strategies promote active engagement with the labour market and society, but in fact, these practices of shaming disabled workfare conscripts into compliance, as experienced by Rachel and Beatrice, did not encourage or enable them to seek employment; rather, it ensured that they used *active practices of exclusion* to protect themselves from further injury by a violent and punitive system. These findings reinforce Sayer's (2005) argument on shame wherein he states that it leaves people "feeling inadequate and hid[ing] from the gaze of others" (p. 153). Rather than wanting to participate and collaborate with workfare services, Rachel adopted a range of practices to remove herself as far as possible from the workfare spaces, even at risk of losing access to their entitlements. Hiding at home appeared as a central mechanism for Australian disabled people on welfare to hide one's shame from the world of being a disabled welfare recipient, and also to hide from further possible shaming from neoliberal activation strategies.

In the UK, however, the home no longer represented the possibility of hiding from the public shaming that neoliberal workfare advances. The research participants from the UK were clearly able to articulate how neoliberal workfare brought shame to their home via the brown envelope. Its distinct brownness and typography clearly demarcate it from other official correspondence. Thus, the envelope was readily identifiable as coming from social security to both the postman – the deliverer, and the disabled people at home – the receiver (Reeve, 2012). It is understood by disabled people as a key mechanism of neoliberal governance of inter-scalar relations, that brings the authority of administrative bureaucracy down to the intimacy of the home. The contents contained within the brown envelope summoned disabled welfare recipients to disability re-assessments, a process that either verified or refuted their disability identity which, in turn, had material ramifications via the disability support payment system. Sarah, a young women with multiple sclerosis living with her parents on a disability welfare payment, stated that the confluence of media reporting, political speak, and general gossip within one's friendship group about neoliberal welfare retraction brought shame to disabled people's homes on two fronts. First, the brown envelope publicly identifies your status as someone on welfare who is potentially 'scrounging'. It also represented the fear of potentially losing one's disability status and hence, access to the disability social security system. Thus, for disabled people in the UK, hiding at home was not safe from the external world that drew upon shame to force disabled people to participate in neoliberal workfare. The inter-scalar labour of neoliberal shame asserts its authority over everyday life, where disabled individualised shame brings stigmatisation to one's most intimate spaces, to keep disabled people in their place. In fact, this inter-scalar labour of shame created its own risks and fear, which threw its recipients into whirlwinds of despair as they were required to manage their internalised shame, hiding from their communities, their families and even themselves:

> Sarah: Yeah, I have a general brown envelope fear. ... I know that brown envelopes are from the DWP [Department of Work and Pensions]. I've actually got one upstairs that's been there for three days and I haven't yet opened it. I will open it, just it takes me a couple of days to pluck up the courage. So yeah, I knew it was from, brown envelopes are generally from the DWP so ...

Thus, the invasion of safety within the home with the distinct brown envelope brought new fears and risks for all of the participants that were interviewed in the UK. Moreover, Sarah's hiding of the envelope in her home until she built up her courage to review the letter unfortunately, puts her at greater risk of losing access to benefits, as disabled people were expected to respond to these notifications within 10 working days of receipt. If not, disability support payments were discontinued.

These experiences of shaming reiterate Young's (1990) understanding of violence. In these instances, these are felt as random attacks on the person and reveal the importance of disclosing the association of shame with violence in workfare governance. Michael, a young married Australian man with a physical disability, describes the constant fear, shame and violence that many disabled people live with on a daily basis, particularly in having to try to comply with a highly coercive and unpredictable system that has total control over one's material resources. As Michael's experience suggests, while neoliberal states are highly efficient in delivering, via mail, the set of instructions that aim to refute one's claim to disability entitlements, when state workfare agencies withdraw these entitlements mistakenly, disabled people experience the added shame of not being informed of the error via mail:

> Like when they make the mistake when they cut me off disability. They made the mistake and they sent me no apology. You could imagine how I felt when I got a letter saying ... sorry you've been cut from disability ... you know your income is gone ... shh ... and that took a whole month to send out a letter. They cut disability, didn't notify me until a month later. So I was without payment for a whole month ... It was really quite a shock as we complied with all of their rules and things and they never told us why they did it.

Thus, for disabled people both in Australia and the UK, feeling ashamed of oneself and one's body was coupled with the personal indignity of the material implications of randomly losing access to, and thus control of, one's income. The structural intent of such everyday experiences is to deepen the regulatory logic of the market society so that it becomes internalised and hence, naturalised. The shame of individualised market failure normalises the everyday forms of neoliberal structural violence, appearing abstract and intangible (Tyler, 2013). Shame, as it labours on behalf of neoliberalism, maintains people in their place.

Shame, however, was highly mobile. In fact, it travelled from the home to the place of disability verification. This was particularly acute within the UK, where respondents highlighted the ways in which one's disability was verified by one's ability to navigate travel between spaces and places, as they travelled from their homes to the disability testing centres to have your status verified or refuted. Katherine, a women who acquired a disability less than two years prior to interview, illustrates how the disabled subjectivities are regulated across varying spaces, and how this navigation is tested with a high degree of suspicion:

> You go in there completely honest and open and yet the first question is "how did you get here?" As if, if you've got there by yourself then you have absolutely no right to be here and I just kind of looked at her. "A friend gave me a lift." "Well where did she drop you off?" It's like the Spanish Inquisition over something as –. And then the stairs and the lift obviously and how did you negotiate the entrance, did you use the stairs or did you use the lift? How long did it take you to get from –? And I just was stunned.

Thus, Katherine's description of the assessment process identifies how disability becomes spatially regulated. To get her assessment for a disability support payment Katherine needed to navigate an upstairs isolated room, hidden from the main entrance of the room. As Katherine describes, this spatial location of the disability assessment office becomes pivotal to the process of jointly assessing disability and shaming disabled people for claiming a disabled subjectivity. As Katherine outlines, the neoliberal disability assessment actively questions her spatial orientation, where the navigation of space and, the movement from place to place is embedded within the assessment to mark out the 'really disabled' and the 'welfare scroungers'. In the UK, this was repeated in nearly all of the interviews, where disabled people were strongly aware how they were watched as they navigated inaccessible assessment sites.

Edges of Identity

In Australia, suspicion was not built into all of the dynamics of the assessment process, and generally, disabled people initially felt more confident in their initial navigation of workfare spaces. However, suspicion was embedded throughout the system, and was even extended to individuals who were 'marked' in the system as disabled, but may have been seeking additional entitlements that were associated with their lawful disability status. Paul, a man with a mental illness, supports a number of peers in a voluntary role in dealing with the Australian neoliberal workfare agency – Centrelink. Paul describes how shaming, mistrust, and randomised attacks on the person's integrity results in individuals withdrawing from the system:

> The stress it caused her was just unbelievable, because they were making out that she is a liar, like, you know. "This person is telling lies. She is trying to cheat the system." You know, like, she is trying to get mobility. It was only a few dollars.

Such practices and their random application, even when unprovoked, reaffirms Young's (1990) definition of systemic violence. Disabled people who took part in this study disclosed that their experiences of a neoliberal workfare state resulted in both a collective and personal injury. Their feelings of shame, and their ongoing experience of fear, demonstrate the continued role of violence in state institutional practice. With the state's transformation to a neoliberal workfare state, its governing institutions have developed a number of shaming strategies to meet this end.

The participants' experiences of neoliberal workfare governance demonstrate the importance of shame as a state tool to produce rigid conformity to a highly punitive system. Further, research participants' experiences in both Australia and the UK of the workfare system signify the level of personal shame and humiliation that violate disabled people's dignity, through the randomisation and unpredictability of their access to material

"The Way You Make Me Feel"

resources – previously a recognised entitlement of disability citizenship. Personal feelings of failure are a direct result of state coercive practices of shaming, which are reaffirmed by the constant material insecurity and negotiation of minimal resources to maintain a basic standard of living. Thus, the structural reproduction of shame, in turn, reinforces individual feelings of personal failure. As Bourdieu (1996) has noted, those who experience failure through no fault of their own are still likely to feel shame, which Sayer (2005) argues is a "structurally generated effect" (p. 154).

Disabled people must both comply with and reproduce the medicalised classifying regime of their bodies, and in fact participate in a game of shaming themselves in order to gain access to the required resources to support their effective participation in workfare governance. This balancing act of negotiating the lived bodily space of severe material deprivation, rigid state regulatory compliance and the moralisation of their bodies can fall at any time. For some, such as Emma, a young single mother living in Melbourne, Australia, who has had a number of encounters with state child welfare agencies, the intensity of shame she has been made to feel about herself, her material deprivation and her mothering have led to Scheff and Retzinger's (1991) shame-rage spiral. Emma describes below a recent 'run-in' that she has had with state workfare authorities and the police:

> It's bad when you've got a family. I remember one week I was supposed to get paid but I didn't get paid. I got so mad at them. I said "if you don't pay me I'm going to rob your place". They got scared, then thought I was going to rob them so they said "Ok we will pay you next week". I'm like "I need the money now because I have to pay my son's childcare." They said "we are so sorry we can't give you your money today as your money doesn't go in until next week." I said, "this week is my pay day and I want my money now" and I made a smart remark that I'm going to rob the [...] Bank and the police came

and thought that I was really going to rob the bank and arrested me that day.

Emma's case demonstrates the extreme levels of state violence that underpin neoliberal authoritarian workfare governance. The state, as Emma's description above reveals, will use extensive measures to bring shame on disabled people to ensure compliance with its neoliberal authoritarian workfare governance. Rather than seek to redress the harmful injustices that Emma has experienced, the state uses its full force to ensure compliance with a system that has forced Emma to this position. Of course, Emma may have had other choices, but the material destitution of her real life, her commitment to caring for her young son and the constant shame she has endured under workfare governing institutions rendered almost all other options futile. As Sayer (2005) argues, the shame that is caused by severe structural deprivation and stigmatisation often results in individual acts of violence. Unfortunately for Emma, the consequences of highly individualised acts of violence, result in state aggression and further violence, and the state is more than willing to use disabled women on workfare, such as Emma, as public examples to produce and reproduce violent, authoritarian neoliberal workfare regimes.

Concluding thoughts

In this chapter we have explored the way in which the implementation of workfare-based welfare reform in Australia and the UK has utilised shame as a form of neoliberal governance. The chapter illustrates the ways non-market actors signify significant fiscal risk for the future health of the nation. The penetration in the public imagination of statistical doom and gloom associated with disabled people on welfare aims to deepen and normalise regulatory regimes that advance the neoliberal market society. Disabled people, a particularly targeted group, are being subjected to activation technologies that are frequently re-classifying them (often without any accompanying change in their condition) as insufficiently or inadequately disabled to remain as *exceptions* to the demands of a neoliberal citizenship that is premised upon able-bodied, masculine notions of contribution and individual responsibility. The experiences of our respondents reaffirm that, despite the development of the disability rights movement with its emphasis on a collective identity based on pride with claims couched in the language of rights, "fundamentally disability is defined by public policy. In other words, disability is whatever policy says it is" (Hahn, 1985, p. 94). In this chapter we have provided an alternative reading of the statistical disability panic employed to drive neoliberal welfare reform. Through the narratives of the disabled people in our study we have illustrated the central role shame plays in classifying and (self) regulating the behaviour and emotions of welfare recipients.

While shame has long held a position of close proximity to disability, with the onset of neoliberalism and its latter intensification vis-à-vis, austerity, the experience of shame for disabled people takes on a qualitative new form. Shame and its attachment to disability has now reached new political heights; no longer are disabled people discursively positioned as the deserving poor. The crafting of neoliberal political discourse to legitimise disability retraction pervades historical discourses of charity and pity. Moralising discourses of charity and pity were historically situated to keep disabled people in place, contained within the walls of the institution, removed from the streetscape. Neoliberal political discourses of shame aim to mobilise disabled bodies as active members of the precarious low wage labour market, compelling them to compete with few labour protections and regulations. Contradictorily, as many of the participants reveal, ongoing public shaming often resulted in a counter response – to hide from the world and the violence that it entails with neoliberal intensification – to escape from the qualitatively new risks created for disabled people at the scale of the everyday.

Processes of neoliberal reclassification undermine the well-being of disabled people subjecting them to damaging forms of psycho-emotional disablism. Disabled people are forced into highly precarious positions as they negotiate the labouring affect effects of neoliberal shame. Insecure and low wage employment or, the random and unexplained withdrawal of benefit income become the everyday, mundane effects of neoliberal inter-scalar violence. Moreover, the manner in which the reforms of disability-based entitlement to welfare benefits have been framed demonstrates the ways in which stigmatisation is employed as a form of governance to legitimise the dominant mantra of 'there is no alternative' to either welfare reform or the shaming of disabled people. The misrecognition of the structural disadvantage experienced by disabled people enables popular discourse to vilify disabled people, either as a result of their reclassification as 'faux' disabled people (Roulstone & Morgan, 2014) or their continued failure to achieve the neoliberal imperative of self-sufficiency.

Thus through this stigmatising, shaming and shameful reclassification disabled people are "mobilised to do the ideological dirty work of neoliberalism" (Tyler, 2013, p. 211) accepting the blame and resultant shame that accompanies this. This re-focussing of an invalidating gaze through the lens of shame exacerbates the exclusion of disabled people. More overt forms of socio-spatial segregation such as the residential institution or day centre, have given way to more nuanced and complex forms of exclusion and regulation. The isolation of disabled people in their own homes serves to individualise the political nature of emotions, which are to be endured away from opportunities for collective opportunities to resist and subvert the affects of shame. The affect effect is to keep disabled people in place.

Acknowledgements
We would like to acknowledge the support of the Fogarty Foundation for funding the interviews conducted in Australia (2006–2009) and the British Academy for their support for the UK study (2012).

Note
1. All the names used in this chapter are pseudonyms.

References
Abramovitz, M. (2006). Welfare reform in the United States: Gender, race and class matter, *Critical Social Policy, 26*(2), 336–364.
Ahmed, S. (2004). *The cultural politics of emotion*. London, United Kingdom: Routledge.
Barbalet, J. (1998). *Emotion, social theory, and social structure: A macrosociological approach*. Cambridge, United Kingdom: Cambridge University Press.
Bessant, J., Watts, R., Dalton, T., & Smyth, P. (2006). *Talking policy: How social policy is made*. Sydney, Australia: Allen and Unwin.
Bourdieu, P. (1986). The forms of capital. In J. G. Rochardson (Ed.), *Handbook of theory and research for the sociology of emotion* (pp. 241–258). London, United Kingdom: Greenwood Press.
Braedley, S. & Luxton, M. (2010). Competing philosophies. Neoliberalism and challenges of everyday life. In S. Braedley & M. Luxton (Eds.), *Neoliberalism and everyday life* (pp. 184–201). Montreal, Canada: McGill-Queen's University Press.
Charlton, J. (1998). *Nothing about us without us: Disability oppression and empowerment*. Berkeley, CA: University of California Press.
Clear, M. & Gleeson, B. (2001). Disability and materialist embodiment, *Journal of Australian Political Economy, 49*(1), 34–55.
Fiske, L. & Briskman, L. (2007). Rights and responsibilities: Reclaiming human rights in political discourse. *Just Policy, 43*, 50–54.
French, S. & Swain, J. (2007). User involvement in services for disabled people. In R. Jones & F. Jenkins (Eds.), *Management, leadership and development in the allied health professions: An introduction* (pp. 249–266). Abingdon, United Kingdom: Radcliffe Publishing.

Galvin, R. (2004). Can welfare reform make disability disappear? *Australian Journal of Social Issues, 39*(3), 343-353.
Garland-Thomson, R. (2009). *Staring: How we look.* New York, NY: Oxford University Press.
Gibilisco, P. (2010). *Politics, disability and social inclusion: People with different abilities in the 21st century.* Saabrücken, Germany: VDM Verlag Dr. Müller.
Goodin, R. (2002). Structures of mutual obligation. *Journal of Social Policy, 31*(4), 579-596.
Grover, C. & Piggott, L. (2013). A right not to work and disabled people. *Social and Public Policy Review, 7*(1), 25-39.
Grover, C. & Soldatic, K. (2013). Neoliberal restructuring, disabled people and social (in)security in Australia and Britain. *Scandinavian Journal of Disability Research, 15*(3), 216-232.
Hahn, H. (1985). Toward a politics of disability: Definitions disciplines, and policies. *The Social Science Journal, 22*(4), 87-105.
Haylett, C. (2003). Remaking labour imaginaries: Social reproduction and the internationalising project of welfare reform. *Political Geography, 22,* 765-788.
Hockey, J. (2012, 17 April). *The age of the end of entitlement.* Address to the Institute of Economic Affairs, London. Retrieved from https://iea.org.uk/in-the-media/press-release/the-age-of-entitlement
Humpage, L. (2007). Models of disability, work and welfare in Australia, *Social Policy & Administration, 41*(3), 215-231.
Jessop, B. (2002). *The future of the capitalist state.* Cambridge, United Kingdom: Polity Press.
Kolarova, K. (2012). Affective politics of disability shame in the times of neoliberal exceptionalism. In S. Mesquita, M. K. Wiedlack, & K. Lasthofer (Eds.), *Import-export-transport. Queer theory, Queer critique and activism in motion* (pp. 261-279). Vienna, Austria: Zaglossus.
Lister, R. (2001). Towards a citizens' welfare state: The 3 + 2 'R's of welfare reform. *Theory, Culture & Society, 18,* 91-111.
Marks, D. (1999). *Disability: Controversial debates and psychosocial perspectives.* London, United Kingdom: Routledge.

Martin, S. (2007). *Welfare reform, the underclass thesis and the process of legitimising social divisions.* http://library.bsl.org.au/jspui/bitstream/1/919/1/Welfare%20reform,%20the%20underclass%20thesis%20martin.pdf

McRobbie, A. (2013). Feminisim, the family and the new 'mediated' maternalism. *New formations: a journal of culture/theory/ politics, 80-81*, 119-137.

Mead, L. M. (1986). *Beyond entitlement: The social obligations of citizenship.* New York, NY: Free Press.

Morris, A., Wilson, S., & Soldatic, K. (2015). Doing the 'hard yakka': Implications of Australia's workfare policies for disabled people. In C. Grover & L. Piggott (Eds.), *Disabled people, work and welfare: Is employment really the answer?* (pp. 43-64). Bristol, United Kingdom: Policy Press.

Nussbaum, M. (2004). *Hiding from humanity: Disgust, shame and the law.* Princeton, NJ: Princeton University Press.

OECD (Organisation for Economic Co-operation and Development). (2009). *Sickness, disability and work: Keeping on track in the economic downturn.* London, United Kingdom: OECD Directorate for Employment, Labour and Social Affairs.

Peck, J. (2001). *Workfare states.* New York, NY: Guilford Press.

Probyn, S. (2004). Everyday shame, *Cultural Studies, 18*(2/3), 328-349.

Ranciere, J. (2004). *The politics of aesthetics: The distribution of the sensible* (Trans. G. Rockhill). London, United Kingdom; New York, NY: Continuum.

Reeve, D. (2012). Psycho-emotional disablism: The missing link? In N. Watson, A. Roulstone, & C. Thomas (Eds.), *Routledge Handbook of Disability Studies* (pp. 78-92). London, United Kingdom: Routledge.

Roulstone, A. & Barnes, C. (Eds.). (2005). *Working futures: Disabled people, policy and social inclusion.* Bristol, United Kingdom: Policy Press.

Roulstone, A. & Mason-Bish, H. (Eds.). (2012). *Disability hate crime and violence.* London, United Kingdom: Routledge.

Roulstone, A. & Morgan, H. (2009). Neo-liberal individualism or self-directed support: Are we all speaking the same language on modernising adult social care? *Social Policy and Society, 8*(3), 333-345.

Roulstone, A. & Morgan, H. (2014). Accessible public space for the 'not obviously disabled': Jeopardized selfhood in an era of welfare retraction. In K. Soldatic, H. Morgan, & A. Roulstone (Eds.), *Disability – Spaces and Places of Policy Exclusion* (pp. 64–79). London, United Kingdom: Routledge.

Sayer, A. (2005). *The moral significance of class.* Oxford, United Kingdom: Oxford University Press.

Scheff, T. & Retzinger, S. (1991). *Emotions and violence: Shame and rage in destructive conflicts.* Lexington, MA: Lexington Books.

Schweik, S. (2009). *The ugly laws: Disability in public.* New York, NY; London, United Kingdom: New York University Press.

Sherry, M. (2010). *Disability hate crimes: Does anyone really hate disabled people?* Farnham, United Kingdom: Ashgate.

Siebers, T. (2008). *Disability Theory.* Ann Arbor, MI: University of Michigan Press.

Skeggs, B. (2004). *Class, self, culture.* London, United Kingdom: Routledge.

Soldatic, K. (2010). *Disability and the Australian neoliberal workfare state (1996–2006)* (Unpublished doctoral thesis). University of Western Australia, Crawley, Western Australia. Retrieved from http://research-repository.uwa.edu.au/files/3225070/ Soldatic _Karen_2009.pdf

Soldatic K. (2013). Appointment time: Disability and neoliberal temporalities, *Critical Sociology, 39*(3), 405–419.

Soldatic, K. & Chapman, A. (2010). Surviving the assault? The Australian disability movement and the neoliberal workfare state. *Social Movement Studies,* (special issue on Australian social movements), *9*(2), 136–154.

Soldatic, K. & Pini, B. (2012). Continuity or change? Disability policy and the Rudd Government. *Social Policy and Society, 11*(2), 183–196.

Springer, S. (2010). *Cambodia's neoliberal order: Violence, authoritarianism and the contestation of public space.* Abingdon, United Kingdom: Routledge.

Tyler, I. (2013). *Revolting subjects. Social abjection and resistance in neoliberal Britain.* London, United Kingdom: Zed.

Wendell, S. (1996). *The rejected body: Feminist philosophical reflections on disability,* New York, NY: Routledge.

Wilson, S. & Turnbull, N. (2001). Wedge politics and welfare reform in Australia. *Australian Journal of Politics and History*, 47(3), 384–402.

Woodward, K. (2009). *Statistical panic.* Durham, NC: Duke University Press.

Young, I. (1990). *Justice and the politics of difference.* Princeton, NJ: Princeton University Press.

CHAPTER FIVE

SUBJECTS OR SUBJECTED? THE PUZZLE
OF IDENTITY IN NEOLIBERAL TIMES

Tom Brock and Mark Carrigan

What concerns us here is how to make best sense of the proliferation of subjectivities under neoliberal circumstances in a way that recognises the role of agency without falling into the trap of voluntarism. This is what we see as the puzzle of identity in neoliberal times. As Gill (2008) has pointed out, those studying neoliberalism have a rich array of conceptual tools available for minutely dissecting cultural forms and, yet, there "is very little understanding of how culture relates to subjectivity, identity or lived embodied experiences of selfhood" (p. 433). Our chapter represents a modest attempt to address this gap in the literature by offering an account of social identity which draws on Margaret Archer's (2007) work on biography and reflexivity but also incorporating Foucauldian concerns into the picture so as to conceptualise the production of subjectivities in terms of the iterative unfolding of agency and power over the life course. We elaborate this perspective through a brief case study of the asexual community, drawing out some of its implications for other areas of research and arguing that it offers useful resources for making sense of contemporary subjectivities in a way that avoids both voluntarism and determinism.

To offer such an account, we must first attempt a theoretical reconciliation between two traditions of thought that are commonly seen as antithetical,[1] incorporating certain insights from Foucault into a realist account of the emergence of social identity. Our motivation for this arises from the belief that while there are problematic aspects to Foucault's "concept of individual

Subjects or Subjected?

subjectivities as the passive product of micro technologies of power" (Mouzelis, 1995, p. 45), this analytical approach nonetheless delineates modalities through which power operates. We feel that these are, at best, under-theorised within critical realism and, at worst, entirely ignored. Through a critical reading of some of Foucault's work in the area,[2] we develop an account of *coming to assume an identity* that sees subjection and subjectivity as two moments of a biographical process. We then use the example of the asexual community to concretise what is an unavoidably abstract discussion, illustrating how the analytical process we have advocated offers purchase upon the state of *being* asexual and the process of *becoming* asexual, avoiding the all too common tendency to foreground one at the expense of the other.

Finally, we consider the relationship that this process of *coming to identify* as asexual has with neoliberalism and the construction of neoliberal subjectivities. Writers have drawn attention to the ways in which neoliberalism operates as a mode of 'governmentality' that shapes the self in paradoxical ways (Rose, 1990). This is particularly apparent in discussions of 'abjection' (Tyler, 2013) and the so-called 'entrepreneurial self' (Scharff, 2014), where is it argued that the political and economic rationalities of contemporary society now govern to create subjects who internalise the values of autonomy and competition but at the cost of cognitively disassociating from those regarded as insufficiently ambitious. In other words, under the auspices of advanced liberalism, exclusionary politics has become based on governmentalities of 'failure' (Tyler, 2010), which construct subjectivities through a synergy of political and economic rationalities that incite entrepreneurism. Following Barnett, Clarke, Cloke, and Malpass (2008), we use our case study to critically engage with this position, and show that governance does not necessarily transform people's subjectivities in a "strong sense" (pp. 648–649). Rather, in exploring the relationship between governing actions (through norms) and the formation of subjective dispositions, we show how a consideration of narrative conceptions of the self and of personhood can expose the recursive and reflexive relations that exist between people's habitual practices and their capacity to deliberate reasonably.

Unpacking social identity

To clarify what the puzzle of identity is, we must first unpack it, focussing on those two aspects that are critical to explaining its constitution: *power* and *normativity*. It is to this end that Foucault (2002) proves particularly salutary, for he identifies that the "subject" is not just one 'thing':

> There are two meanings of the word "subject": subject to someone else by control and dependence, and tied to his own identity by a conscience or self-knowledge. Both meanings suggest a form of power that subjugates and makes subject to. (Foucault, 2002, p. 331)

It was in identifying these two meanings of the word "subject" that Foucault placed relations of power at the centre of his understanding of processes of "subjectivation": how it is that the subject both constitutes itself but is also something to be constituted. This argument is traced particularly well within *Technologies of the Self*, where Foucault (2000a, p. 223) argues that it is people's practices which splice forms of power with the processes of self-constitution. Subjectivity, it is suggested, is uncovered as one examines those specific techniques that people use to understand themselves within "certain kinds of interdictions" – specific historical contexts of knowledge (or discourse) that provided the conditions of possibility for such understandings to be chosen (Foucault, 2000a, p. 224). It is this sense of choice which characterises the dual-nature of the "subject", for Foucault, and, for us, it brings to bear the puzzle of identity, which cannot be understood simply as something which is *directed* upon someone by a kind of coercive power but,

Subjects or Subjected?

rather, as something that is intricately bound to our practices. In other words, the subject can constitute itself through those practices which are available to it but that these practices are themselves informed by the historical contexts of knowledge and forms of power that reside within them. In one sense, for Foucault (2000a), these may be considered prohibitive forms of power that exist *outside* of the subject's control insofar as they are entwined with the various kinds of scientific and ethical knowledge which informs such practices in the first instance (p. 224). While criticisms can certainly be made of Foucault's historiography, particularly a tendency towards over-generalisation and vagueness (Mouzelis, 1995), this attentiveness to historical specificity, at least *in principle,* retains an immense value for making sense of identity formation (see Weeks, 1977).

Foucault (2000a) talks of these "technologies" of the self as matrices of reason for action (p. 225). Subjectivity is constituted through each of these matrices, "each [implying] certain modes of training and modification ... in the obvious sense of acquiring certain skills but also acquiring certain attitudes". The implication of this is that subjectivity is not a "given" but is made through a tangled network of interpenetrating social practices,

> [Subjectivity] is not a *substance*. It is a *form*. It is a form, and this form is not primarily or always identical to itself. You do not have the same type of relationship to yourself when you constitute yourself as a political subject who goes to vote or speaks at a meeting and when you are seeking to fulfill your desires in a sexual relationship ... In each case, one plays, one establishes a different type of relationship to oneself. (Foucault, 2000a, p. 290; emphasis added)

Rather than men making history, then, Foucault saw history as a contingent intersection of practices, each irreducible to the goals of the actors in question. His focus was on the practices through which subjects became constituted and on the different viewpoints of power that manufactured them. Thus, what resides in Foucault's unpacking of identity is a necessary distinction between "subjectivation" and "subjection"; two points from which to view the relations of power that shape social identities. Subjectivation leaves us with a sense of how subjects are creating themselves in and around relations of power; subjection, alternatively, brackets everything off *but* the influence of power in manufacturing the subject. The implication of this bracketing exercise, which is purely methodological, is to "give oneself as the object of analysis *power relations* ... that are distinct from objective capacities ... [but] can be grasped in the diversity of their linkages" (Foucault, 2002, p. 338; also see Kelly, 2013).

It is in his 1973–1975 Collège de France lectures that Foucault ties the norm to what he calls, broadly, *disciplinary power*. It is this kind of power (and its relations) that is of interest to us because, for Foucault, disciplinary power manifests itself through techniques that target individual bodies in order to train subjects to be simultaneously efficient and obedient. In *Psychiatric Power*, Foucault (2008) argues that within a disciplinary context, the norm functions as the universal prescription for all disciplinary subjects. The following year, in *Abnormal*, Foucault (2004) identifies the norm as the 'element' upon which a certain exercise of power is founded and legitimised. Thus, he elaborates on precisely *how* the norm functions, within a disciplinary context, to recognise that the norm brings with it a principle of qualification *and* correction. In other words, the norm's function is not to exclude and reject; on the contrary, it is always linked to a positive technique of intervention and transformation.

This leaves us with a sense of the 'Janus-faced' nature of normativity, as it provides the evaluative grounds for our social practices and, therefore, is spliced, in Foucault's (2002) own words, with "a form of power that subjugates and makes subject to" (p. 331). As such, the explanation to our puzzle rests on an analysis of power relations that can help us make sense of how it is that such evaluative claims materialise. This is the aim of the next section.

Problematization and identity construction

What is the process by which a norm comes to *be*? How it is that evaluative claims emerge in the first instance? Once again, we turn to Foucault for insight, whose theoretical concept, 'problematization', allows us to open up the process of normalisation to consider its affective and evaluative dimensions (also see Cresswell & Brock, 2017).

Foucault deployed the concept of problematization in two ways; first, he used it to describe his analytical method, which involves one examining the terms of reference within which any given issue is cast. The problematization is a point of analysis, Foucault (2000b) suggests, "in which one tries to see how the different solutions to a problem have been constructed" (p. 118). To examine how a phenomenon is problematized, then, is to assess how it is has been questioned, classified and managed over time. That one thinks problematically about these terms of references, then, leads Foucault to ask "how and why [do] certain things (behaviour, phenomena, processes) become a problem" (Foucault, 1985, p. 115, cited in Bacchi, 2012).

Foucault best concretises this abstraction in *The History of Sexuality, Vol. 1*. Here, he questions the functioning of 'sexuality' as an analytics of power that is related to the emergence of a science of sexuality (Foucault, 1998). It is in tracing the history of this emergence that Foucault considers how different eras have problematized 'sexuality', making it an object for thought and intervention. This is important, Foucault suggests, because it is in studying "sexuality" as a problematization that one finds that people's identities have become increasingly tied to their practices around sex. To understand why, one must examine the bodies of (scientific) knowledge about 'sexuality' and the political structures, laws and regulations that surround sexual practices.

"One starts ... with practices", then, because these are what "render complex relational phenomena problematic" and, in the process, produce them as 'objects' for thought (Bacchi, 2012, p. 4). In other words, if 'sexuality' is an object for thought, then people situate themselves within its framework of principles and values through their practices. If one is to scrutinise the limits of this domain, then one must deconstruct these objects of power to show how it is that relations of power give rise to such practices. In *The History of Sexuality, Vol. 1*, for example, Foucault deconstructs 'sexuality' to show that people's sexual practices assume the principles of morality (heterosexuality as an ethical code) and science (heterosexuality as a biological imperative). The effect is that these taken-for-granted assumptions render subjects both intelligible (as sexual subjects) but also circumscribe the forms of sexual subjectivity that may be taken. It is in deconstructing objects of power that Foucault's study of problematizations makes us pointedly aware of this dual-function and its relational nature. This is the 'reality' of subjugation: that relations of power simultaneously function as a condition for the possibility of ethics and politics and, yet, also circumscribe its forms of discourse (Bacchi, 2012; also see Taylor, 1989).

This leads us to how Foucault deploys the concept of problematization in a secondary manner: to refer to those historical processes that produce objects for *critical reflection*. It is this process that establishes "a certain objectivity, the development of a politics and a government of the self, and the elaboration of an ethics and a practice in regard to oneself" (Foucault, 2000b, pp. 116–117) that produces the objects to be problematized. Foucault demarcates this as the "history of problematics" or *problematizations* – the politics that shapes how people live. It is up to us to come to grips with those relations of power *that do the actual shaping* and to begin to understand how these relations work. Here, Foucault provides us with additional insight:

> What distinguishes thought is that it is something quite different from the set of representations that underlies a certain behaviour; it is also quite different from the domain of attitudes that can determine this behavior. ... Thought is freedom in relation to what one does, the motion by which one detaches from it, establishes it as an object, and reflects on it as a problem. (Foucault, 2000b, p. 117)

Foucault is suggesting here that 'thought' is one of the means through which people exercise their agential power. It is the mechanism through which people reflect, critically, upon the fields of experience that shape their lives. To study problematizations, then, is to examine how people dismantle these objects. It is to inquire into the politics of people's self-constitution and to make sense of how these objects emerge for thought (Foucault, 2000b, p. 118). This is what is so compelling about Foucault's second interpretation of problematization: *objects of power* are deconstructed and replaced with relations of power as people move, in thought, to gain a critical sense of the limits and exclusions of the systems within which they act. In other words, it is through the exercise of agency, of detachment and problematization, that one finds how people transform taken-for-granted assumptions into something else.

Of course, such a move of reflexive thought, is always preceded by new forms of experience, which constitute what those different solutions will be. "It is a question, then", argues Foucault (2000b), "of thinking about the relations of these different experiences to politics" and how it is that these experiences make possible the transformation of "obstacles of a practice" into problems for which one can offer practical solutions (p. 114). "But", Foucault (2000b) warns, "it is also necessary to determine what 'posing a problem' to politics really means" (p. 114). One cannot simply state that politics is the constituent of experience. Rather, the task is to elaborate on "*whose* consensus, *whose* values, [and] *whose* traditions constitute the framework for a thought and define the conditions in which it can be validated" (Foucault, 2000, p. 114; emphasis added). It is to make a judgement about how people have placed themselves, suitably, within a framework of principles and values that are recognised, accepted and questioned. Thus, Foucault's concept of problematizations also brings to the fore the spatial-temporal dimension of identity formation. For it is in studying problematizations that one explores the "interconnections, the relations, the movement that results in specific effects in specific 'places'" (Bacchi, 2012, p. 6).

Foucault's concept of problematizations serves two important functions, then. First, it gives us a sense of how a norm comes to *be*; as something which has been problematized, historically, leading it to become an object of thought and of power. This is as much a political process as a sociological one. For what *is* normal cannot be separated from the politics and governance of the self, now that we recognise the ubiquitous nature of power. This leads us to the second function of problematizations: to recognise the reflexive and affective nature of human agency. It is to say that people will always step back and reflect upon their experiences of others who evaluate their social practices. This supplementary meaning of the concept is crucial for us because we consider it to be the pivot on which the norm's 'Janus-faced' function rests. The norm neither excludes nor rejects, rather, it takes on a relational nature when it is problematized and, as such, can be linked to new forms of positive experience. It is the aim of the remaining two sections to establish *how* this process might occur, drawing on the conception of relational reflexivity offered by Archer (2012): the process of problematization requires relational subjects to be

Subjects or Subjected?

reflexive about their social relationships, in the context of their wider concerns, which gives norms their power as something more than prohibition or bureaucratic sanction.

Critical realism and normativity

One recent and influential attempt to theorise normativity from a critical realist[3] standpoint has been the account of 'norm circles' offered by Elder-Vass (2010, 2012). On this view, the operation of normativity is seen to be attributable to the causal powers of specific groups, 'norm circles' coalesced around a particular norm, which have the emergent capacity to influence their members by virtue of how they interact within them. This power rests in the collective intention that members of the circle have to *endorse* and *enforce* a social practice congruent with this norm. As Elder-Vass writes,

> They may support the norm by advocating the practice, by praising or rewarding those who enact it, by criticizing or punishing those who fail to enact it, or even just by ostentatiously enacting it themselves. The consequences of such endorsement and enforcement is that the members of the circle know they face a systematic incentive to enact the practice. (Elder-Vass, 2010, p. 124)

This knowledge works to generate a *tendency* to increase conformity to a given norm. The concept of 'norm circle' works to explain the role of normativity in engendering social action. Rather than attributing causal power in a nebulous fashion to 'social normativity', this account instead focusses upon the relational characteristics of specific groups, foregrounding the embodied actions through which we begin to develop a feel for the normative characteristics of our environment; coming to a fallible understanding of the benefits and sanctions which tend to be attached to particular courses of action. It draws our attention to the role that recurrent exposure by individuals to action that endorses and enforces norms plays in shaping our dispositions to act.

Given the normative heterogeneity of late modernity, every individual is enmeshed within an array of potentially conflicting norm circles, with the implication that they must "sometimes negotiate a path that balances normative commitments that are in tension with each other" (Elder-Vass, 2010, p. 143). However, it is in accounting for these moments of reflexivity that the limitation of Elder-Vass's account becomes apparent. The underlying mechanism through which individuals come to apprehend a normative order is seen to be neurophysiological, with emerging dispositions encoded in our neurological structure in a social process with a physiological substratum:

> It is the effects on our neural networks, and therefore on our beliefs, of our experiences that "condition" us to possess certain mental states. Such conditioning need not be conscious – if we experience a particular pattern of events repeatedly then our brain will learn it without any necessary conscious intervention as, for example, in the phenomenon of subliminal learning (Freeman, 2000, p. 191). (Elder-Vass, 2007, p. 337)

There is nothing intrinsically problematic about the notion that neuroplasticity should be incorporated into social analysis. However it leaves Elder-Vass unable to offer traction upon the important questions illuminated by his conceptual framework: how do individuals choose which sanctions should be confronted and which should be avoided when forced to decide between the demands of competing norms? The virtue of the account is the tendency towards the specificity it engenders when discussing the operation of normativity, leading us to focus upon specific relationships and interactions but without *reducing* the operation of normativity to them. But Elder-Vass struggles to account for the *emergence* of norm circles and through addressing this problem we begin to reach the point

Subjects or Subjected?

where Foucauldian concerns converge with critical realist ones without ever having 'met in the middle'.

Explaining the emergence of norm circles entails accounting for how individuals come to *endorse* norms. Opening up this question in terms of individual subjectivity does not entail a repudiation of Elder-Vass's dispositional account. He is surely correct that we gain an understanding of our normative environment through repeated apprehension of norm behaviour. The problem lies in his invocation of neurophysiology as a 'blackbox' to make sense of a process that is largely evaluative. It's clear *that* things matter to people but it's not clear *why* they matter (Sayer, 2011), for the language with which he describes the affective dimension of normativity sterilises the *force* that human experience(s) have on the construction of the self. The subject is not taken at their word, as a person who subjectively reflects upon his or herself in relation to their objective circumstances (see Archer, 2003), but rather is reduced to a minimum set of the neural networks that condition behaviour.

Once we begin to flesh out the notion of *endorsement*, we are left with a more complex picture in which the enforcement of norms *we ourselves endorse* comes to seem a very different matter from the enforcement of norms *we do not endorse*. With regards to the former, normative action resonates with us, as the action of other(s) leads us to recognise ourselves as having fallen short of some standard we accept. With regards to the latter, normative action is experienced as a basically arbitrary exercise of power, one to which we might pragmatically acquiesce but that has no accompanying experience of feeling bound by the standard in question. The relationship between norms and values is a profoundly complex question (Joas, 2000), which is ultimately beyond the scope of this chapter, yet the underlying distinction is an important one for our argument. In accounting for the former but not the latter, Elder-Vass leaves himself unable to offer adequate explanations for how norm circles come into being. What we are asserting here is what Joas (2000) describes as the irreducible character of the cultural in which questions of value (and evaluation) come to be seen as central to sociological explanation (p. 6).

Considered in these terms, we begin to prise apart the notions of endorsement and enforcement that are conflated with Elder-Vass's account of normativity. Returning to this chapter's fundamentally micro-social frame of reference, we can accept the thrust of the norm circles approach while resisting the emptying out of moral experience entailed by it. The value of his approach lies in its capacity to conceptualise the operation of normativity in terms of the causal powers of groups of individuals and the relations between them. Elder-Vass usefully distinguishes between *proximal*, *imagined* and *actual* norm circles for a particular person and a particular norm. The *proximal* norm circle is the set of actual individuals who have contributed to the formation of the disposition to act in accordance with the norm. The *imagined* norm circle is the group outside of the local context that is believed, implicitly or explicitly, to endorse and enforce the norm in question. The *actual* norm circle is a matter of the objective extension of this group, i.e. all those individuals who are *actually* disposed to act in accordance with the norm (Elder-Vass, 2007, pp. 127–128). Once we begin to recognise the role of evaluation in the emergence of norm circles, with individuals coming to invest themselves (albeit often inchoately) in the endorsement and enforcement of particular norms, we are left with an increasingly multifaceted picture; one which recognises a recurrent evaluative moment in the operation of normativity but nonetheless contextualises this in terms of the ubiquity with which power is exercised relationally towards normative ends.

To see the implications of this, let us consider the notion that certain institutions are 'compulsory', which has been so influential within the study of sexuality and gender and which

Subjects or Subjected?

will be taken up in the case study of asexuality. Lesbian feminists and gay liberationists formulated the concept of compulsory heterosexuality in the 1960s and early 1970s in deliberate opposition to the moral individualism common amongst earlier homophile activists and liberal feminists (Seidman, 2009, p. 18). Perhaps the most influential theoretical formulation was Rich's (1980) account of compulsory heterosexuality and lesbian existence, which has constituted a potent source of inspiration for those seeking to understand the operation of normative power in many other areas of sexual life (see, for example, Fahs (2009) on a growing tendency for heterosexual-identified women engaging in homoerotic behaviour with other women). Rich offers a vivid account of "numberless women psychologically trapped, trying to fit mind, spirit, and sexuality into a prescribed script because they cannot look beyond the parameters of the acceptable" (Rich, 1980, p. 657) through the operation of compulsory heterosexuality, with its discursive erasure of woman-identified experiences.

Agreeing with Rich, we focus upon how this institution:

> has been organized and maintained through the female wage scale, the enforcement of middle-class women's 'leisure,' the glamorization of so-called sexual liberation, the withholding of education from women, the imagery of 'high art' and popular culture, the mystification of the 'personal' sphere, and much else. (Rich, 1980, p. 659)

However, we believe that the most fruitful route to such an investigation is to 'open up' the concept of the institution itself. In doing so, we overcome the inability of 'compulsory heterosexuality' to render agency and transformative change comprehensible (Seidman, 2009, pp. 22–23) while also avoiding the abandonment of social structure in the critique offered by queer theory (Seidman, 2009, p. 225). The norm circles approach encourages us to look towards the operation of normative power in everyday life (family, friends, peers, etc.) through often mundane interactions which serve, tacitly or explicitly, to enforce particular norms of behaviour and comportment. Furthermore, the force or lack thereof possessed by such ubiquitous interventions can be seen to depend both on wider social processes beyond everyday life (the *imagined* norm circle) and how the individual has been shaped by their prior history of normative interaction.

We recognise the omnipresence of normative power (with all social situations entailing the endorsement and enforcement of some norm, in fact being partly constituted in this way) but nonetheless recognise the variable force with which that power operates. As we shall argue in the following section, this variability should be understood *biographically*: it is not a matter of unencumbered self freely evaluating the circumstance in which she finds herself but rather a path-dependent process of *making one's way through the world* (Archer, 2007). On this view, our attention is turned towards the processes through which individuals are able to call into question the proximal norm circles through which power operates repressively and the sources provided by alternative norm circles through which power operates productively; in the case of asexuality, the substitution of a local reference group which stigmatises a lack of sexual attraction for a dispersed reference group which normalises it. What we are trying to stress is that "trying to fit mind, spirit, and sexuality into a prescribed script" is a process which is both repressive and agentive. Unpicking the interplay between the two can be achieved by looking at the biographical trajectories of particular individuals *over time* but doing so in a way which recognises the ubiquity of normative power at *any particular point in time*.

A case study: asexuality and allosexuality
In recent years, asexuality has emerged as a social identity achieving ever wider recognition, at least in the Anglo-American world. Commonly defined as "someone who does not experience sexual attraction", it has been suggested that between 0.5% and

1% of the UK population may be asexual (Bogaert, 2012, p. 45). However, these figures relate to the underlying experience of *lacking sexual attraction* as opposed to self-identification as asexual. In order to understand how the former leads to the latter, it is necessary that we look towards the qualitative experience of *being* and *becoming asexual*, something which has been the focus of increasing numbers of qualitative researchers (Chasin, 2011, 2013; Dawson, McDonnell, & Scott, 2016; Scherrer, 2008, 2010a, 2010b; Scott & Dawson, 2015). In spite of the diversity of experience which soon becomes apparent when one begins to investigate the asexual community, particularly as reflected in contrasting orientations to sex and romance, there is a striking point of commonality: the experience of having self-pathologised and of being pathologised by others in relation to the experience of an underlying lack of sexual attraction (Carrigan, 2011, 2015; Pryzbolo, 2011, 2013). In coming to recognise themselves as somehow different from their peers, often when confronted with the emergence of a demonstrative adolescent sexuality which had no resonance in their own experience, the inevitable question is confronted of *what* this difference is: 'why aren't I like everyone else?' Attempts to discuss it with friends and family will tend to elicit a range of responses which when recounted in the context of qualitative research become eerily familiar:

- Maybe you're just a late bloomer?
- Maybe you haven't met the right person yet?
- Is something wrong with your hormones?
- Were you abused as a child?
- Have you been to the doctor?

While the precise formulations vary, recurrent themes are clearly identifiable (Carrigan, 2011, 2012). What such responses share is an underlying assumption of the *universality* and *uniformity* of sexual attraction, i.e. everyone experiences it and it is fundamentally the same thing in each case. The belief that everyone experiences sexual attraction inculcates a propensity to *explain away* apparently deviant cases; some other causal factor is identified (hormones, psychology, abuse, late development, etc.) which is assumed to have disrupted an otherwise inexorable process. This is something which Carrigan (2012), Chasin (2013) and Pryzbolo (2011, 2013) suggest has potentially radical implications for sexual culture, as the increasing visibility of asexuality provokes changes in its non-asexual *other*. But how might we conceptualise such a process in terms of the lived realities of personal life (Smart, 2007)? Can we specify how this 'sexual assumption' might lead to macro-social change through micro-social interaction? Through doing so, we intend to shed light on the puzzle of identity in neoliberal times.

While a simple repudiation of this assumption could prove an adequate foundation for an (a)sexual cultural politics, it is analytically unsatisfactory for us to remain on this level. What *is* this assumption? What *is* the relation in which one acts upon this assumption? The notion of the 'sexual assumption' is nothing more than a conceptual construct, formulated to draw out the empirically identifiable convergences in the reactions received by those who identify themselves as asexual. In other words, the construct is an attempt to make sense of a cultural formation with its own history of emergence that encourages some forms of intimate sociality and discourages others. However, what we wish to consider here is the *encounter* itself, as a meeting between embodied persons within hierarchically organised social space. As Ahmed (2002) usefully reminds us, "to be touched a certain way, or to be moved a certain way by an encounter with an other, may involve a reading, not only of the encounter, *but of the other that is encountered as having certain characteristics*" (p. 20). Intra-action and interaction are cognitively and affectively interwoven through the encounter, as the allosexual confronts the other whose difference is not immediately apparent. This is a term commonly used within the asexual community to refer to those who *do* experience sexual attraction. It is deployed from this point onwards for two reasons. Firstly, it avoids the use of phrases like 'sexual people' or 'non-asexual' that might be pragmatically tenable but are semantically obtuse given the dominance of the sexual assumption. Secondly, it avoids the universalism inherent in contrasting the particularism of asexuals to (sexual) people as such, i.e. the two descriptors are accorded equal status rather than one being the negation of the other. While the term has provoked debate within the asexual community about its desirability, we feel it is socially tenable (analogous to the use of *cis-gender* with regard to *trans identities*) and analytically useful (even as a place-holder for a more substantial sense of identity-as-sexual which may emerge with time).

Though many asexuals reject the language of 'coming out' (Carrigan, 2012) the dynamics of information control nonetheless resemble what Goffman states: "to display or not to display; to tell or not to tell; to let on or not to let on; to lie or not to lie; and in each case, to whom, how, when, and where" (Goffman, 1963, p. 57). Assumptions of the universality and uniformity of sexual attraction are encountered in everyday interaction, posing questions of how to make clear that these are not true of oneself. But *what is it like* to be an allosexual, one who has never even been brought to reflect upon these assumptions *as* assumptions, to be confronted with someone now asserting that *actually* they do not experience sexual attraction? Why is it so bewildering and why does this incomprehension provoke attempts to *explain away* asexuality? Carrigan (2012) and Dawson, McDonnell, and Scott (2016) offer more empirical detail about how these dynamics play out in difference spheres of personal life. But their focus is upon the asexual whereas, as Scott and Dawson (2015) argue, relationality is key to understanding these dynamics. This is most pronounced in intimate relationships: "Partners, who research indicates are unlikely to identify as asexual themselves (Carrigan, 2012), will have to adapt to the identity presented to them, and consider how it will affect the way they relate to one another" (Scott & Dawson, 2015, p. 10). But the point applies more broadly to the entire assembly of social relations which constitute the personal lives of asexual people (Smart, 2007).

While a thorough examination of asexual experience, its continuities and discontinuities, remains beyond the scope of this chapter, our intention is to illustrate how the biographical process of *coming to identify as asexual* needs to be understood in terms of a particular pathway through serial encounters within social space. The 'sexual assumption', as with compulsory heterosexuality (or any putative variant thereof), remains on this picture as something enacted through interpersonal interaction, often operating within existing webs of relationships (Taylor, 1989) between the person being compelled and the friends, family or peers who are enacting norms in a way which is restrictive and pathologising. Rather than imputing oppressive power to a disembodied institution, our focus looks towards a *relation* that is recurrent (such that P1 acts towards P2 in a way that renders a characteristic of P2 problematic) and then seeks to explain that recurrency. In this sense, it is not so much a rejection of the putative institution, as much as a change in emphasis; we would see the institution as constituted and reconstituted relationally but with the caveat that we can only understand its history of emergence if we examine typical instances of its composite interactions. In doing so, our attention is drawn towards the beliefs and normative dispositions of *both* parties, as well as the biographical consequences of the encounter for each.

To put it another way: an understanding of asexuality goes hand-in-hand with an understanding of *allosexuals confronting asexuality* and how asexuals, so to speak, confront these confrontations. So we 'open up' the institution, considering the types of interaction which shape and are shaped by it, as well as the range of effects such interactions have for individuals recurrently exposed to them, e.g. the allosexual who suddenly realises that 'maybe some people just *are* this way' after encountering someone claiming to be asexual for the nth time. Or, more importantly for our argument, the biographical implications for the asexual who recurrently finds themselves pathologised when they attempt to convey their experience of lacking sexual attraction. In many cases, these continual encounters with the sexual assumption lead them to consult expert systems: going to the doctor, consulting a counsellor, seeing a sex therapist (etc.) in the hope of making sense of this sense of difference (Carrigan, 2015). However, those who come to identify as asexual tend to find such interventions unhelpful at best and actively harmful at worst, often serving to reinforce the experienced force of the sexual assumption and intensifying the distress and confusion that provoked the consultation in the first place. In contrast, the experience of encountering asexuality in the media or discovering asexual resources online through searching, 'do not experience sexual attraction' or some equivalent search term can prove transformative (Carrigan, 2011). In such cases, the meaning ascribed to one's own lack of sexual attraction undergoes a dramatic reversal, with an individualising and pathologising understanding of it coming to be replaced by a communalising and normalising evaluation. Far from being a *deviation from the norm*, as was previously entailed in relation to a local reference group which affirmed the sexual assumption, someone undergoing this transition instead recognises themselves as an *embodiment of another norm*, newly identifying themselves in terms of a dispersed reference group encountered through the online asexual community. The prevalence of the sexual assumption does not subside as a result of this biographical process but the *value* the individual places on it does change. People still react in stigmatising ways but the normative content of these interactions no longer resonates intra-actively; the sexual assumption has been rejected and its enactment in everyday life constitutes, at worst, an obstacle of frustration and distress to be negotiated. The sexual assumption has been problematized and the form taken by this is one that, we have argued, can be best understood biographically. This can prove richly generative of new descriptions, concepts and identities (Chasin, 2011; Scherrer, 2010a). But this discursive elaboration needs to be understood in terms of the relational reflexivity exercised by asexual individuals as they make their way through recurrent social situations, characterised by the normative dynamics identified here.

Finally, let us return to the theoretical issue of neoliberal subjectivity and how our case study intersects with it. We have suggested that Foucault's problematization requires a greater consideration of biography and narrative conceptions of the self in order to understand the reflexive relations between practices and subjects' capacities to deliberate reasonably. This would be a much 'thicker' concept of subjectivity than is typical of post-structuralist accounts, which assume that governmentalities work through an endeavour to synergise rationalities and subjectivities. Thus, on the terrain of advanced liberalism and neoliberal-subjectivity, we find accounts of the individual that operate on "extremely thin concepts of malleable subjectivity" (Barnett et al., 2008, p. 644), where the governance of practices often transform people's subjectivities in a very strong sense towards instrumental rationality. This is most apparent in discussions of the 'entrepreneurial self' (Scharff, 2014), where is it argued that the political and economic rationalities of contemporary society now govern to create subjects who internalise the values of autonomy and competition but at the cost of excluding those regarded as insufficiently ambitious.

Subjects or Subjected?

We would contend this characterisation of identity formation insofar as it is clear from our discussion of the sexual assumption that individuals can change the emphasis that they place on norms when establishing values. Norms only function as norms because of the capacities of people to reflect on them in the context of their 'ultimate concerns' (see Archer, 2000). It is through this self-reflexive capacity, which is interpretive but also communicative and interactive, that we find Foucault's problematization a useful means of 'opening up' *how* subjectivity is embedded in "rhetorical dynamics of accountability in the company of others" (Barnett et al., 2008, p. 644). In other words, by looking at social reflexivity and the forms of communicative reasoning that people deploy when confronted with the sexual assumption we see the often "discretionary, elaborative, and ad hoc" (McCarthy, 1993, p. 30 cited Barnett et al., 2008, p. 647) manner through which people *come to identify* as asexual. Thus, subjectivity is appropriately embedded within broader practices of self-making and personhood without any need to succumb to the "careless nominalism of the self, characteristic of generic post-structuralism more broadly" (Barnett et al., 2008, p. 644). The relational realist framing of problematization we have offered, through the case study of the asexual and the allosexual, illustrates how we can retrieve identity in neoliberal times in a way that avoids voluntarism and recognises the 'Janus-faced' character of normativity.

Conclusion
We began this chapter with a puzzle and we have cleared some of the conceptual terrain needed to move towards its understanding. In an effort to abandon any dualistic notion of the 'subject' or the 'subjected', we have excavated, from the resources of critical realism and Michel Foucault, a new conceptual approach that makes sense of subjectivity in relational terms. The purpose of this has been to make sense of the proliferation of subjectivities without falling into the trap of either

voluntarism or determinism. Rather, what we have offered in this chapter is a modest account of how identity emerges reflexively, seeing subjection and subjectivity as two moments of a biographical process. In particular, our account has focussed on the routes *into*, *through* and *out* of the recurrent social situations in which normative power operates. In any particular situation an individual is subject to a variety of normalising and disciplinary forces, yet they enjoy a *degree* of freedom in their movements *through* situations. It is to the 'Janus-faced' nature of normativity that we owe our original puzzlement and, yet, through realist-informed biographical research and Foucault's concept of problematization, we now have a better understanding of *how* it is that agents affirm their critical reflexivity. Indeed, it may be said that the process of *becoming* asexual is an iterative unfolding of agential politics and problematization(s), rather than polemics.

Notes

1. See Al-Amoudi (2007) for an insightful discussion of why this assumption is mistaken.
2. This chapter is fundamentally exploratory and makes no claim to offering a comprehensive account of Foucault's voluminous output.
3. Critical realism is a philosophy of social science that was founded through the earlier works of British philosopher Roy Bhaskar and developed in sociology by Margaret Archer, Andrew Collier and Andrew Sayer. Critical realism is a new ontology that gives primacy to the emergent nature of real causal properties and powers through the discovery and description of social causal mechanisms that constitute the motive force for social change. This realist ontology is built on the assumption that critical thinking plays an important role in registering a critique of ideology and power through an understanding of these (often unobservable) mechanisms. See Gorski (2013) for a helpful introduction on 'What is critical realism?'

References

Ahmed, S. (2002). The contingency of pain. *Parallax*, *8*(1), 17–34.
Al-Amoudi, I. (2007). Redrawing Foucault's social ontology. *Organization*, *14*(4), 543–563.
Archer, M. S. (2000). *Being human: The problem of agency*. Cambridge, United Kingdom: Cambridge University Press.
Archer, M. S. (2003). *Structure, culture and the internal conversation*. Cambridge, United Kingdom: Cambridge University Press.
Archer, M. S. (2007). *Making our way through the world: Human reflexivity and social mobility*. Cambridge, United Kingdom: Cambridge University Press.
Archer, M. S. (2012). *The reflexive imperative in late modernity*. Cambridge, United Kingdom: Cambridge University Press.
Bacchi, C. (2012). Why study problematizations? Making politics visible. *Open Journal of Political Science*, *2*(1), 1–8.
Barnett, C., Clarke, N., Cloke, P., & Malpass, A. (2008). The elusive subjects of neoliberalism. *Cultural Studies*, *22*(5), 624–653.
Bogaert, A. F. (2012). *Understanding asexuality*. Lanham, MD: Rowman & Littlefield Publishers.
Carrigan, M. (2011). There's more to life than sex? Difference and commonality within the asexual community. *Sexualities*, *14*(4), 462–478.
Carrigan, M. (2012). How do you know you don't like it if you haven't tried it? Asexual agency and the sexual assumption. In T. G. Morrison, M. A. Morrison, M. Carrigan, & D. T. McDermott (Eds.), *Sexual minority research in the new millennium* (pp. 3–19). Hauppauge, NY: Nova Science.
Carrigan M. (2015). Asexuality. In C. Richards & M. J. Barker (Eds.), *The Palgrave Handbook of the Psychology of Sexuality and Gender* (pp. 7–23). Basingstoke, United Kingdom: Palgrave Macmillan.
Chasin, C. J. (2011). Theoretical issues in the study of asexuality, *Archives of Sexual Behavior*, *40*(4), 713–723.
Chasin, C. J. (2013). Reconsidering asexuality and its radical potential. *Feminist Studies*, *39*(2), 405–426.
Cresswell, M. & Brock, T. (2017). Social movements, historical absence, and the problematization of self-harm in the UK, 1980–2000. *Journal of Critical Realism*, *16*(1), 7–25.

Dawson, M., McDonnell, L., & Scott, S. (2016). Negotiating the boundaries of intimacy: The personal lives of asexual people. *The Sociological Review, 64*(2), 349–365.

Elder-Vass, D. (2007). Reconciling Archer and Bourdieu in an emergentist theory of action. *Sociological Theory, 25*(4), 325–346.

Elder-Vass, D. (2010). *The causal power of social structures: Emergence, structure and agency.* Cambridge, United Kingdom: Cambridge University Press.

Elder-Vass, D. (2012). *The reality of social construction.* Cambridge, United Kingdom: Cambridge University Press.

Fahs, B. (2009). Compulsory bisexuality?: The challenges of modern sexual fluidity. *Journal of Bisexuality, 9*(3–4), 431–449.

Foucault, M. (1998). *The history of sexualilty, Vol. 1: The will to knowledge.* London, United Kingdom: Penguin.

Foucault, M. (2000a). Technologies of the self. In P. Rabinow (Ed.), *Michel Foucault: Ethics: Subjectivity and truth (Essential works of Foucault, 1954–1984, Volume 1)* (pp. 223–251). London, United Kingdom: Penguin.

Foucault, M. (2000b). Polemics, politics and problematizations. In P. Rabinow (Ed.). *Michel Foucault: Ethics: Subjectivity and truth (Essential works of Foucault, 1954–1984, Volume 1)* (pp. 111–119). London, United Kingdom: Penguin.

Foucault, M. (2002). The subject and power. In P. Rabinow (Ed.), *Michel Foucault: Power: (Essential works of Foucault, 1954–1984, Volume 3)* (pp. 326–348). London, United Kingdom: Penguin.

Foucault, M. (2004). *Abnormal: Lectures at the Collège de France, 1974–1975.* New York, NY: Picador.

Foucault, M. (2008). *Psychiatric power: Lectures at the Collège de France, 1973–1974.* Basingstoke, United Kingdom: Palgrave Macmillan.

Gill, R. (2008). Culture and subjectivity in neoliberal and postfeminist times. *Subjectivity, 25*(1), 432–445.

Goffman, E. (1963). *Stigma: Notes on the management of spoiled identity.* London, United Kingdom: Penguin.

Gorski, P. (2013). What is critical realism? And why should you care? *Contemporary Sociology: A Journal of Reviews, 42*(5), 658–670.

Joas, H. (2000). *The genesis of values.* Chicago, IL: University of Chicago Press.

Subjects or Subjected?

Kelly, M. (2013). Foucault, subjectivity and technologies of the self. In C. Falzon, T. O'Leary, & J. Sawicki (Eds.), *A companion to Foucault*. London, United Kingdom: Wiley-Blackwell.

Miller, P. & Rose, N. (2008). *Governing the present*. Cambridge, United Kingdom: Polity.

Mouzelis, N. (1995). *Sociological theory: What went wrong? Diagnosis and remedies*. London, United Kingdom: Routledge.

Pryzbolo, E. (2011). Crisis and safety: The asexual in sexusociety. *Sexualities*, 14(4), 444–461.

Pryzbolo, E. (2013). Afterword: Some thoughts on asexuality as an interdisciplinary method. *Psychology and Sexuality*, 4(2), 193–194.

Rich, A. (1980). Compulsory heterosexuality and lesbian existence. *Signs*, 5(4), 631–660.

Rose, N. (1990). *Governing the soul: The shaping of the private self*. London, United Kingdom; New York, NY: Routledge.

Sayer, A. (2011). *Why things matter to people: Social science, values and ethical life*. Cambridge, United Kingdom: Cambridge University Press.

Scharff, C. (2014, 1 April). Gender and neoliberalism: Exploring the exclusions and contours of neoliberal subjectivities. Retrieved from http://theoryculturesociety.org/christina-scharff-on-gender-and-neoliberalism/

Scherrer, K. (2008). Coming to an asexual identity: Negotiating identity, negotiating desire, *Sexualities*, 11(5), 621–641.

Scherrer, K. (2010a). Asexual relationships: What does asexuality have to do with polyamory? In M. Barker & D. Langdridge (Eds.), *Understanding non-monogamies* (pp. 154–159). London, United Kingdom: Routledge.

Scherrer, K. (2010b). What asexuality contributes to the same-sex marriage debate. *Journal of Gay and Lesbian Social Services*, 22(1–2), 56–73.

Scott, S. & Dawson, M. (2015). Rethinking asexuality: A symbolic interactionist account. *Sexualities*, 18(1–2), 3–19.

Seidman, S. (2009). Critique of compulsory heterosexuality. *Sexuality Research & Social Policy*, 6(1), 18–28.

Smart C. (2007). *Personal life: New directions in sociological thinking*. Cambridge, United Kingdom: Polity Press.

Taylor, C. (1989). *Sources of the self: The making of the modern identity.* Cambridge, MA: Harvard University Press.

Tyler, I. (2010). Designed to fail: A biopolitics of British citizenship. *Citizenship Studies, 14*(1), 64–74.

Tyler, I. (2013). *Revolting subjects: Social abjection and resistance in neoliberal Britain.* London: Zed Books.

Weeks, J. (1977). *Coming out: Homosexual politics in Britain from the nineteenth century to the present.* London, United Kingdom: Quartet Books.

CHAPTER SIX

EJACULATORY TIMING AND MASCULINE IDENTITIES:
THE POLITICS OF AB/NORMALISING
SEXUAL PERFORMANCE

Hannah Frith

> The inability to control ejaculation sufficiently for both partners to enjoy sexual interaction [...] occurrence of ejaculation before or very shortly after the beginning of intercourse (if a time limit is required: before or within 15 seconds of the beginning of intercourse). (World Health Organization, International Classification of Diseases – 10, 1992)
>
> Size may not matter but length of sexual performance is important to both men and women so delay the inevitable orgasm with double strength Stud D-Lay Cream for longer-lasting, fulfilling sex that ticks everyone's box again and again. (Bondara, Advertising for Stud D-Lay Cream™)

Sexual intimacies – including orgasm and ejaculation – are subject to temporal regulation. The timing of orgasm is not simply a matter of physiology; cultural assumptions and ideologies frame how this embodied experience is worked up, felt and made sense of. Researchers distinguishing between 'clock time' and the 'natural' timings of the body argue that modernity is characterised by attempts to regulate bodies by bringing them into line with normative temporal expectations of behaviour. For example, the times and locales for defecation and urination have come under tighter regulation in the modern West to meet an increasing demand – explicitly articulated in workplace rules and regulations – that people relieve themselves *not* whenever or wherever they feel like it but at an appropriate time and place (Inglis & Holmes, 2000). Similarly, the 'natural' rhythms of mothers' bodies are regulated, mechanised, fragmented and alienated as both mothers and midwives are expected to monitor their own and the baby's behaviour in relation to the time and efficiency of the working week (Simonds, 2002). As Turner (2003) points out, "the polite management of human deposits – excrement, urine, spit and sperm – is fundamental to the civilising process" (p. 3). Using the opening quotes as a springboard, I argue that ejaculation is subject to such a 'civilising' process and focus on how temporality – ejaculating at the 'right time' – is regulated through the interweaving of neoliberal discourses about the rational management of (heterosexual) sex and discourses of masculine sexual 'performance'. A range of commercial and professional interests converge in the civilising of men's ejaculation. I demonstrate that neoliberal ideals of masculinity are institutionalised and legitimated in definitions of premature ejaculation (PE) circulating in international classifications of physical and mental health. These in turn provide normative benchmarks for assessing functional and dysfunctional sexual performance, for generating and creating consensus about the prevalence of sexual problems, and for legitimating interventions into the intimate sphere of sexuality. These neoliberal norms (and anxieties) about sexual performance are cascaded down to mass audiences through popular culture, including the mass marketing of sex-related products (such as creams, lotions, devices) and the selling of expert advice in lifestyle magazines and self-help books. Ultimately, these norms shape meaning-making between couples trying to make sense of their sexual interactions and permeate men's interpretation of their own embodiment and sexual subjectivity. I argue that ejaculation, which is 'out of time', is firmly positioned as a failure of the neoliberal masculine subject, and that professional and commercial interests collude in offering mechanisms for men's rehabilitation towards the perfect intercourse performance.

Neoliberalism and the 'perfect intercourse performance'

The entry of neoliberalism into the intimate sphere has seen both a re-conceptualisation of sex, and the construction of a new sexual actor. Rather than an irrepressible force of nature, neoliberalism has increasingly reframed sexuality as subject to rational management as something to be continually worked on, improved, made efficient, developed, invested in, and capitalised upon (Jackson & Scott, 1997; Tyler, 2004; Gill, 2009; Frith, 2015a). Sexual pleasure is refashioned as a rational goal to be pursued through the accumulation of knowledge and skill and as governed by expert knowledge (Marshall, 2002). Alongside this, the neoliberal actor is recast as rational, calculating, self-regulating and engaged in sexual encounters based on contractual exchange. Sexual practices and lifestyles are positioned as the outcome of deliberate and purposeful individual choices which are made in the pursuit of sexual self-actualisation. Neoliberal sexual subjects are characterised as entrepreneurial actors acquiring sexual knowledge, skill, bodily capital and expertise as a form of cultural capital with which to compete in the socio-sexual hierarchy. This 'intimate entrepreneurship' forms part of the project of the self and fuses with gendered discourses of sexuality to produce obligations for women to become 'sexual adventurers' who are continually 'up for it' (Gill, 2009), and men to become 'sexual champions' (Stibbe, 2004) who deliver a 'perfect intercourse performance' (McCarthy & Metz, 2008).

This 'perfect intercourse performance' is central to hegemonic masculinity – or the "culturally idealised form of masculine behaviour" (Connell, 1987, p. 83). Within this ideal, men are depicted as being naturally driven by sex, as constantly seeking and ever ready for sex, as actively initiating and 'doing' sex to women, and as in competition with other men. A focus on hardness, strength, endurance, control and activity is intimately tied to the function of the penis and the physical performance of sex, where sex is narrowly defined as inserting an erect penis into a bodily orifice ending with climax and ejaculation. Critical work has focussed on exposing the ways in which medical and sexological discourses reproduce heteronormative masculinity by presenting a penis which is erect for the purposes of vaginal penetration as the model of healthy and functional male sexuality (Tiefer, 1994). Specifically, this work examines the construction of 'erectile dysfunction' as a biomedical problem requiring a pharmacological quick fix, and the mass market expansion of these drugs through promises of 'enhanced' sexual performance for all men by 'guaranteeing' harder, reliable and longer-lasting erections (Marshall, 2002; Grace, Potts, Gavey, & Vares, 2006; Potts, Grace, Gavey, & Vares, 2004). Building on these analyses, my focus here is on the ideological work done by ejaculation and its temporal regulation.

I have argued elsewhere that if being 'good at' sex is a neoliberal imperative, the pursuit of an increasingly spectacular orgasmic experience – having longer, more frequent and more intense orgasms – is positioned at the tangible end product (and reward) of sexual labour (Frith, 2015a, 2015b). For men, orgasm and ejaculation are treated as synonymous and interchangeable despite evidence that they are governed by different physiological mechanisms and are experienced as distinct phenomena (see Mah & Binik, 2001 for an overview). Shifting gender relations and the positioning of sex as central to marital stability have meant that 'good sex' has become culturally defined as reciprocal and mutually pleasing – typically idealised as simultaneous orgasm during intercourse or (at the very least) the mutual exchange of orgasms (Braun, Gavey, & McPhillips, 2003). In this context, ejaculation holds considerable social meaning. As Johnson (2010) points out, "The ability to ejaculate, the quantity of the semen produced, and the forcefulness of their ejaculation all become the hallmark of a hegemonic masculine ideal, to which males aspire" (p. 239). Male ejaculation signals the culmination or end of sexual activity in a way which women's orgasm does not (Muehlenhard & Shippee, 2010). I will argue that this ejaculatory performance must be delivered after a deliberate period of delay in order to meet the obligations and responsibilities accorded to the masculine neoliberal subject.

The two opening quotes, the definition of premature ejaculation as a recognised sexual dysfunction offered by the World Health Organization and the advertising of commercial products purporting to delay ejaculation, both illustrate three key aspects of heteronormative male sexuality which I explore in this chapter. First, premature ejaculation is constructed as a problem of timing which is subject to surveillance and measurement – 'within or before 15 seconds of intercourse'. Second, men are given responsibility for their partner's pleasure – it is important to control ejaculation so that *both partners* enjoy sex, so that it 'ticks *everyone's* box again and again'. Third, premature ejaculation is constructed as a problem of control, of mind over matter. Together these position 'lasting longer' or 'delaying' ejaculation as a marker of neoliberal masculinity, and conversely, premature ejaculation as a failure of masculinity.

Cumming 'too soon'
Heterosexual intercourse is simultaneously positioned as 'real sex', the most natural and desirable expression of heterosexuality, and as inherently problematic, tricky or difficult. This difficulty is ascribed to essential differences between the sexuality of men and women – exemplified by their different orgasmic responses. Men's orgasms are typically represented as rapid, urgent, inevitable, immediate, and uncomplicated, while the female orgasm is depicted as elusive, complicated, difficult and slower to achieve (Nicolson & Burr, 2003; Lavie-Ajayi & Joffe, 2009). Scientific sex surveys, for example, consistently report an 'orgasm gap' in which men orgasm more frequently during sexual intercourse than women (Richters, de Visser,

Rissel, & Smith, 2006), and laboratory studies claim to have discovered a 'timing gap' in which woman take longer to orgasm during intercourse (Masters & Johnson, 1966). Despite being consistently challenged as being a methodological artefact produced by a heterosexist focus on orgasm during intercourse (e.g. Conley, Moors, Matsick, Ziegler, & Valentine, 2011), this scientific discourse provides legitimacy to what are routinely popularised in the mass media as essential differences between men and women.

While all men are impelled to 'last longer', the demarcation of premature ejaculation as a sexual dysfunction, positions some performances as especially troublesome and in need of expert intervention to restore 'functional' sexuality. It is timely to explore discourses about premature ejaculation since they coalesce around competing professional and commercial interests that position PE as either a physiological dysfunction *or* a psychological disorder. A similar trajectory was seen in the medicalisation of 'impotence' to 'erectile dysfunction' (ED), which positioned ED as a physiological, not an emotional or psychological problem, and smoothed the way for quick fix pharmacological solutions (Marshall, 2002). Classificatory systems such as the World Health Organization's International Classification of Diseases (ICD) and the American Psychological Association's Diagnostic and Statistical Manual of Mental Disorders (DSM) represent two powerful documents in which the standards for physical and mental health are constructed, and which in turn legitimate and limit access to treatment. Prompted by the success of Viagra™ and the commercial and clinical need to determine clear benchmarks against which the success or failure of interventions can be assessed, the importance of establishing definitively 'how soon is too soon', when it comes to ejaculation, has intensified. Up until this point, definitions remained remarkably vague about the question of timing. The DSM refers only to ejaculation 'before the person wishes it', while the ICD guideline of 'within 1-2 minutes' is criticised for lacking a sound evidence base (Waldinger & Schweitzer, 2006). This intense focus on timing represents a pivotal medicalising moment since it rationalises the body by identifying a set of universal body norms against which individuals can be measured and compared. Waldinger (a key proponent of this approach) suggests that 'intravaginal ejaculatory latency time' (IELT), defined as the time from vaginal penetration to the start of ejaculation (neatly sidelining gay men), ideally measured with a stopwatch, provides a suitably objective measure of PE (Waldinger, Hengveld, & Zwinderman, 1994). Using this method, an 'objective' cut-off time of one minute has been suggested (Waldinger, Hengveld, Zwinderman, & Olivier, 1998).

Problematically, this objective measure fails to map neatly on to men's own perception of whether they experience PE or not, or their own levels of distress about rapid ejaculation (Waldinger et al., 1998). Some men experience themselves as having PE despite 'lasting' for up to 25 minutes (Patrick et al., 2005 – see also Hartmann, Schedlowski, & Kruger, 2005). In practice, clinicians rely more on their own impressions and client distress than a stopwatch measure of timing (Perelman, 2006), and consider timing to be less meaningful than perception of control or satisfaction with intercourse in determining PE (Althof, 2006). Whilst clinicians and pharmaceutical companies may be keen to fix the timing of ejaculation so as to delineate the normal from the abnormal, and to be able to measure the effects of pharmaceuticals, stopwatch measures separate the physical response from the socio-emotional context in which this becomes meaningful. Men's perceptions of ejaculating 'too soon' may bear little resemblance to the amount of time it actually takes them to ejaculate, and stopwatch measures tell us little about the meaning of this timing for men themselves. However, clock time does offer a mechanism through which ejaculatory performance can be more closely monitored, and generates norms and standards against which men can be assessed or measure themselves.

For men who are not specifically labelled with premature ejaculation, popular culture recasts the failure of heterosex to deliver reciprocal pleasure as a problem of 'timing' which can be overcome by 'speeding up' women and 'slowing down' men:

> In some ways simultaneous orgasm is the ideal solution to the 'problem' of human sexuality: the fact that men and women are running on unsynchronized watches. The fact that men tend to be easily and quickly aroused; women tend to be slowly and intricately aroused: the whole sweet task of loving is to slow him down and speed her up so you meet somewhere in the middle. (Bechtel & Stains, 1996, p. 273)

The inherent complexity of the female orgasm and the natural discrepancy between the timing of men and women's sexual responses, shape the imperative for men to delay their ejaculatory response. The generation of anxiety about sexual performance, coupled with neoliberal imperatives for constant self-improvement, create a market for products and advice through which failures of masculinity can be recuperated. Men are impelled to 'work at' developing their sexual stamina through consumption and bodily practices. Creams which promise to "enhance your lovemaking prowess" by helping men to "perform for longer", condoms laced with anaesthetic gels are perfect for those who want to "last longer" (Durex Performa™ condoms, n.d.), self-help books promise to help men to *Command Your Ejaculation* (Reynolds, 2013), and lifestyle magazines offer tips on how to train PC[1] muscles, vary the depth of thrusts, or use the 'squeeze' technique to help delay their ejaculation (Stevens & *Men's Fitness* Editors, n.d.). 'Lasting longer' becomes a competitive advantage in the sexual marketplace – an aspect of sexual capital which can be worked at, not only for men who are labelled as premature ejaculators, but for any (rational) man who wants to improve their sexual performance.

Satisfying her
> No three words deflate a man's ego faster than 'Is that it?' The Sexual Dysfunction Alliance reports premature ejaculation comes top of your list of bedroom anxieties. It's little wonder. Lasting less than three minutes reduces her chances of orgasm by over 80%, according to a study in the *Journal of Sexual Medicine*. (*Men's Health*, 2014)

Neoliberal sexual actors are typically depicted as self-interested individuals who must take responsibility for themselves; their moral autonomy is measured by their ability to 'self care', provide for their own needs and service their own ambitions (Adam, 2005). Yet, scientific definitions of PE and popular articulations of the imperative to 'last longer' often position female orgasm (rather than clock time) as marking how long is long enough. While 'unsuccessful' sexual interactions with a partner are often an implicit criterion for sexual dysfunctions, PE is *explicitly* constructed as a problem defined by the (lack of) sexual satisfaction of a *partner*. The ICD describes PE as the "inability to control ejaculation sufficiently for *both partners* to enjoy sexual interaction" (WHO, 1992, emphasis added). Not only does this affirm intercourse and an erect (but non-ejaculating) penis as integral to women's pleasure, it also positions men as *responsible for* women's orgasm and sexual satisfaction. When asked how long they felt a man ought to be able to delay or control his ejaculation for, the majority of men (both those who did and did not experience PE) indicated that this was "until the partner has experienced her orgasm" (Hartmann et al., 2005, p. 98). Although there is very little exploration of the relational dynamics of PE, in response to a series of questions posed in an internet survey, 70% of men reported seeking treatment because they wanted to better sexually satisfy their partner (compared to 61.2% who wanted to increase their own pleasure) (Porst et al., 2007). Moreover, more than 20% also sought help because their partner became concerned, upset or angry when they climaxed quickly, and nearly 15% because their partner asked them to (Porst et al., 2007). In qualitative interviews, men experiencing PE report concerns about establishing new relationships or distress about not satisfying existing partners: "It does bother me sometimes that I can't make my spouse achieve an orgasm" (Symonds, Roblin, Hart, & Althof, 2003, p. 366). PE impacts on their sexual confidence ("When you can't satisfy your woman, you somehow feel like there's a large part of you missing or failed", Revicki et al., 2008, p. 38), and their sense of masculinity – "you're only half the man you should be" (Symonds et al., 2003, p. 366). This moral imperative for men to satisfy their partner runs counter to the typical construction of the neoliberal actor as self-interested yet is firmly embedded in masculinity.

One way of making sense of this is to explore how the ethic of reciprocity which governs committed heterosexual relationships fuses unevenly with gendered discourses to open up different entitlements and obligations around orgasm for both men and women (Braun et al., 2003). The ethic of reciprocity offers an uneven moral reasoning based on contractual interaction which places obligations on men to 'give' orgasms to female partners *before* 'taking' their own. Within this discourse, the mutual (though not necessarily simultaneous) exchange of orgasm is constructed as 'right' and desirable while non-reciprocal pleasure is portrayed 'wrong' or problematic (Braun et al., 2003). The construction of a timing gap, the positioning of male sexuality as active and agentic, and the representation of male ejaculation as signalling the end or culmination of sexual activity, all coalesce to place obligations on men to delay their orgasm until after they have 'given' an orgasm to their female partner. This simultaneously speaks to the ethic of reciprocity necessitated by shifting gender roles and the feminist critique of heterosexuality, whilst reasserting male dominance. Being 'good at' sex requires men to gather technical 'know how' or learn 'tips and tricks' with which they can consistently and efficiently deliver the more elusive and complex female orgasm to their partner. Men's lifestyle magazines depict women's unpredictable and elusive sexual responsiveness and their "constant demands for 'better' orgasms" as a source of worry for men who are blamed if this satisfaction is not forthcoming (Rogers 2005, p. 185). Men's ability to give orgasms is portrayed as a form of "masculinity-on-trial" (Rogers, 2005, p. 185), and female orgasm signals the successful resolution of this obligation. Some have argued that this is a *pseudo*-reciprocal contract since the positioning of men as actively seeking sex, and women as permitting or denying access to her body, means that in return for the promise of an orgasm-during-intercourse, the man must "'try to please the woman" by "trying to 'give' the woman an orgasm" (Gilfoyle, Wilson, & Brown, 1992, pp. 217–218). Certainly, this strategic approach of 'giving' orgasms in order to secure access to more frequent or 'better' sex is a recurrent message in men's lifestyle magazines (Farvid & Braun, 2014). Yet, both men (Gilfoyle et al., 1992) and women (Roberts, Kippax, Waldby, & Crawford, 1995) position men as being generous, kind, skilled or caring lovers if they wait for their partners to orgasm before 'taking' their own, or conversely of being selfish and inconsiderate if they do not. The work that men put into 'giving' an orgasm is taken as a sign of their love and commitment. Conversely, premature ejaculation represents a failure to fulfil the demands of the ethic of reciprocity – the man has taken his own ejaculation 'too early' and has failed in his moral duty to delay his own orgasm in order to deliver hers first.

Controlling the (leaky) body
The obligation to both maintain an erection and to 'hold back' the inevitable ejaculation requires a 'mindful mastery' over the

body to monitor and control the timing of ejaculation. Bodily control over ejaculation is a key dimension distinguishing sexual function from dysfunction – as reflected in debates about the definition of PE circulating in scientific discourse, classificatory systems, lay accounts of PE and popular discourse. The website of the Victoria State Government of Australia, for example, describes PE as "a lack of control over ejaculation so that it often happens sooner than the man or his partner would want" (Victoria State Government, n.d.). It asserts that while some men "ejaculate as soon as foreplay starts" others "*lose control* when they try to insert their penis" (emphasis added). The 'inability to control ejaculation' remains central in the ICD-10 definition of PE with which this chapter opened, although the inclusion of a "recurrent and persistent absence of reasonable voluntary control of ejaculation" has been dropped from the latest versions of the DSM (see Waldinger & Schweitzer, 2006 for an overview of changing definitions of PE).

Some argue that ultimately PE *is* subjective with feelings of control being central to men's experience of PE and essential to measures of treatment success (Althof, 2006). Commenting on what successful treatment for PE would offer, one participant said that "the ultimate success would be unlimited control" (Revicki et al., 2008, p. 36), and men with PE describe being "totally preoccupied with thoughts about controlling their orgasm" rather than on feelings of arousal (Hartmann et al., 2005, p. 93). Both psychosexual treatments and commercial products draw on a discourse of control to describe their benefits. Talking about the possibility of combination treatment, Perelman (2006, p. 1010) claims that pharmaceutical treatments may produce a "critical teachable moment" in which, by delaying the moment of ejaculation, men can learn to recognise and respond to the physical sensations allowing these "newly empowered men to feel 'in control'". Similarly, the popular start/stop technique in which men delay ejaculation by squeezing the tip of their penis is routinely described in popular magazines and websites as offering men the chance to learn how to "control ejaculation through education and by practicing the simple techniques" (Medline Plus, n.d.).

This emphasis on mindful mastery over the body neatly dovetails neoliberal concerns with a managerial approach to the body, and the rationality of hegemonic masculinity. Holding back the ejaculatory response is a demonstration *par excellence* of mind over matter. Premature ejaculation has often been constructed as a problem with the mind – a 'performance anxiety'. For example, Relate (a UK based charity offering psychosexual therapy and counselling to couples) advises that for most men who experience premature ejaculation it is "likely to be to do with anxiety" and that "Feeling anxious that you may ejaculate quickly is more likely to make you ejaculate quickly" (Relate, n.d.). Emotional control and the denial of vulnerability are cornerstones of hegemonic masculinity, banishing anxiety by controlling ejaculation affirms the rationality of hegemonic masculinity and neoliberalism. The forceful and purposeful ejaculation of semen from the penis at the culmination of sustained sexual activity marks a 'successful' sexual performance – perhaps most clearly articulated in the ubiquitous iconic 'cum shot' of pornography. Conversely, leaky bodies – bodies which secrete fluids involuntarily – cause embarrassment and shame since they indicate a senility or loss of mind in which we are unable to control our bodily functions (Turner, 2003). The mistiming of ejaculation transforms the penis from an active organ which dynamically ejects semen, to a dysfunctional leaky body from which semen shamefully passes at inappropriate or unwanted moments. Neoliberal discourses position the sexual body as an instrument to be managed and deployed in the pursuit of sexual pleasure by the purposeful actor/manager. A leaky body from which semen flows involuntarily represents a failure of masculinity and a failure of neoliberal rationality.

Recent attempts to recast PE as a medical dysfunction rather than a psychological disorder – including the removal of 'voluntary control' from the DSM – may pave the way for a greater uptake of sexo-pharmaceuticals which offer a technological fix. This solution is removed from the feminised sphere of emotional and relational difficulties, and instead reaffirms the body as a functioning machine which can be made to run more efficiently in the rational pursuit of better sex.

Concluding comments

The experience of orgasm is typically understood as a private, individual, physiological response, yet I have demonstrated that ejaculation is subject to a temporal civilising process in which men are expected to delay ejaculation until an appropriate time. A perfect intercourse performance is constructed in medical and popular literature alike as necessitating an ejaculation which is 'delayed' (rather than 'too soon'), timed *after* ensuring the orgasmic satisfaction of a (female) partner, and is mindfully controlled before being purposely released from the body. The neoliberal reframing of sex as work which is subject to rational management filters down from the institutionalised global (such as the World Health Organization) into even the most intimate spaces. While researchers, scientists and medics work to measure, categorise and define premature ejaculation with increasing precision in order to identify the physiological mechanisms of its problematic existence and pharmaceutical quick fixes, men (and sometimes their partners) are encouraged to 'work at' their sexual performance by drawing on expertise to guide embodied practice. Neoliberal imperatives to 'be good at' sex and to constantly improve one's performance and pleasure fuse with hegemonic masculinity to shame men who fail to regulate their physiological responses appropriately. Neoliberalism positions sexual problems as individual failures, malfunctions which result from personal shortcomings (irresponsibility, immaturity, poor judgement, lack of control, etc.), which should be corrected through intimate entrepreneurship – a commitment to self-improvement through the consumption of products, knowledge and expertise, and the development of skills, techniques and bodily capital.

These neoliberal responsibilities to deliver the perfect intercourse performance meld neatly with the requirements of hegemonic masculinity in propelling narrowly gendered versions of heterosexuality. The discursive construction of PE neatly fuses the requirement for subjectivities which are rational, self-determining and autonomous, and masculinities which privilege the dominance of the mind over the body, and male responsibility for female pleasure delivered through penile-vaginal intercourse. The necessity for intercourse to be constructed as reciprocal and as delivering mutual pleasure in order to fortify heterosexuality's place at the apex of the sexual hierarchy, has generated rights and responsibilities which are heavily gendered. Being able to 'give' an orgasm is taken as evidence of men's skill and sexual expertise, while being able to delay his own orgasm until after his partner is satisfied is taken as evidence of self-control and appropriate exercise of bodily capital. The imperative to be a 'real man' realised through an appropriate ejaculatory performance, operates simultaneously at the interpenetrating scales of the body (when ejaculation happens and is experienced as timely or out of time), the interpersonal (when couples decide there is/isn't a 'problem'), and the institutional (the 'fixing' of definitions of PE and associated treatment regimes). Normative standards about the control and timing of ejaculation is one of the ways in which men are held accountable for their sexual performance.

There is an enormous amount of labour (both individual and institutional) invested in the scaled mobilisation of sexual anxiety and the promise of sexual rehabilitation. Neoliberal drives towards sexual self-improvement, coupled with the masculine imperative to initiate and direct sexual interactions, makes the male body an ideal site for ideological work. Following the huge commercial success of Viagra™ for 'treating' erectile dysfunction, it is perhaps no accident that interest in premature ejaculation has increased. Anxiety about sexual performance serves the commercial interests of those who seek to develop, distribute and profit from sexo-pharmaceuticals and other commercial products who require the production of men to whom these reparative solutions be marketed. It also serves the professional (and financial) interests of those whose jobs and credibility rest on their 'expertise' in diagnosing and treating sexual dysfunction and/or offering advice about managing sexual performance. Discourses and practices around ejaculatory timing harness and fix sexual intimacies and put them to work in the reproduction of capitalist, patriarchal, heteronormative social orders as these have been reconfigured by neoliberalism.

Note
1. The PC muscles are the pubococcygeus or pelvic floor muscles.

References
Adam, B. M. (2005). Constructing the neoliberal sexual actor: Responsibility and care of the self in the discourse of barebackers. *Culture, Health and Sexuality, 7*(4), 333–346.
Althof, S. E. (2006). Prevalence, characteristics and implications of premature ejaculation/rapid ejaculation. *The Journal of Urology, 175*, 842–848.
American Psychiatric Association (1980). *Diagnostic and statistical manual of mental disorders*. Washington, DC: American Psychiatric Association.
Bechtel, S. & Stains, L. R. (1996). *Sex: A man's guide*. New York, NY: Rodale Press Inc.
Bondara (n.d.). Advertising for D-Lay Cream™. Retrieved from http://www.bondara.co.uk/delay-cream-100ml [Accessed 18 September 2012].

Bondara (n.d.). Advertising for Stud D-Lay Cream™. Retrieved from http://www.bondara.co.uk/stud-d-lay-cream [Accessed 18 September 2012].

Braun, V., Gavey, N., & McPhillips, K. (2003). The 'fair deal'? Unpacking accounts of reciprocity in heterosex. *Sexualities, 6*(2), 237-261.

Conley, T. D., Moors, A. C., Matsick, J. L., Zeigler, A., & Valentine, B. A. (2011). Women, men, and the bedroom. Methodological and conceptual insights that narrow, reframe, and eliminate gender differences in sexuality. *Current Directions in Psychological Science, 20*(5), 296-300.

Connell, R. W. (1987). *Gender and power.* Sydney, Australia: Allen and Unwin.

Durex Performa™ condoms (n.d.). Retrieved from http://www.durex.co.za/products/condoms/durex-performa [Accessed 28 February 2017].

Farvid, P. & Braun, V. (2014). The 'sassy woman' and the 'performing man': Heterosexual casual sex advice and the (re) constitution of gendered subjectivities. *Feminist Media Studies, 14*(1), 118-134.

Frith, H. (2015a). *Orgasmic bodies: The construction of orgasm in contemporary Western culture.* Basingstoke, United Kingdom: Palgrave.

Frith, H. (2015b). Sexercising to orgasm: Embodied pedagogy and sexual labour in women's magazines. *Sexualities, 18*(3), 310-328.

Gilfoyle, J., Wilson, J., & Brown, B. (1992). Sex, organs and audiotape: A discourse analytic approach to talking about heterosexual sex and relationships. *Feminism & Psychology, 2*(2), 209-230.

Gill, R. (2009). Mediated intimacy and postfeminism: A discourse analytic examination of sex and relationships advice in a women's magazine. *Discourse & Communication, 3*(40), 345-369.

Grace, V., Potts, A., Gavey, N., & Vares, T. (2006). The discursive condition of Viagra. *Sexualities, 9*(3), 295-314.

Hartmann, U., Schedlowski, M., & Kruger, T. H. (2005). Cognitive and partner-related factors in rapid ejaculation: Differences between dysfunctional and functional men. *World Journal of Urology, 23,* 93-101.

Inglis, D. & Holmes, M. (2000). Toiletry time: Defecation, temporal strategies and dilemmas of modernity. *Time and Society, 9*(2/3), 223–245.

Jackson, S. & Scott, S. (1997). Gut reactions to matters of the heart: Reflections on rationality, irrationality and sexuality. *The Sociological Review, 45*(4), 551–575.

Johnson, M. (2010). 'Just getting off': The inseparability of ejaculation and hegemonic masculinity. *Journal of Men's Studies, 18*(3), 238–248.

Lavie-Ajayi, M. & Joffe, H. (2009). Social representations of female orgasm. *Journal of Health Psychology, 14*(1), 98–107.

Marshall, B. L. (2002). 'Hard science': Gendered constructions of sexual dysfunction in the 'Viagra Age'. *Sexualities, 5*(2), 131–158.

Masters, W. H. & Johnson, V. E. (1966). *Human sexual response.* Toronto, Canada; New York, NY: Bantam Books.

Mah, K. & Binik, Y. M. (2001). The nature of human orgasm: A critical review of major trends. *Clinical Psychology Review, 21*(6), 823–856.

McCarthy, B. W. & Metz, M. E. (2008). The 'good-enough sex' model: A case illustration. *Sexual and Relationship Therapy, 23*(3), 227–234.

Medline Plus (n.d.). Premature ejaculation. Retrieved from http://www.nlm.nih.gov/medlineplus/ency/article/001524.htm [Accessed 3 March 2014].

Men's Health (2014, 28 January), Are you good in bed? Retrieved from http://www.menshealth.co.uk/sex/better/are-you-good-in-bed-428773?click=main_sr [Accessed 3 March 2014].

Muehlenhard, C. L. & Shippee, S. K. (2010). Men's and women's reports of pretending orgasm. *Journal of Sex Research, 47*(6), 552–567.

Nicolson, P. & Burr, J. (2003). What is 'normal' about women's (hetero)sexual desire and orgasm? A report of an in-depth interview study. *Social Science and Medicine, 57*, 1735–1745.

Patrick, D. L., Althof, S. E., Pryor, J. L., Rosen, R., Rowland, D. L., Ho, K. F., McNulty, P., Rothman, M., & Jamieson, C. (2005). Premature ejaculation: An observational study of men and their partners. *Journal of Sexual Medicine, 2*(3), 358–367.

Perelman, M. A. (2006). A new combination treatment for premature ejaculation: A sex therapist's perspective. *Journal of Sexual Medicine, 3*, 1004–1012.

Porst, H., Montorsi, F., Rosen, R. C., Gaynor, L., Grupe, S., & Alexander, J. (2007). The Premature Ejaculation Prevalence and Attitudes (PEPA) Survey: Prevalence, comorbidities, and professional help-seeking. *European Urology, 51*, 816–824.

Potts, A., Grace, V., Gavey, N., & Vares, T. (2004). 'Viagra stories': Challenging 'erectile dysfunction'. *Social Science and Medicine, 59*, 489–499.

Relate (n.d.). Sex common problems. Retrieved from http://www.relate.org.uk/relationship-help/help-sex/sex-common-problems/i-have-problems-premature-ejaculation [Accessed 24 February 2014].

Revicki, D., Howard, K., Hanlon, J., Mannix, S., Greene, A., & Rothman, M. (2008). Characterizing the burden of premature ejaculation from a patient and partner perspective: A multi-country qualitative analysis. *Health and Quality of Life Outcomes, 6*, 33–43.

Reynolds, C. W. (2013). *Command your ejaculation: 12 best kept ways to boost your ejaculatory threshold and become An ENDLESS MAN in bed*. Kindle edition.

Richters, J., de Visser, R., Rissel, C., & Smith, A. (2006). Sexual practices at last heterosexual encounter and occurrence of orgasm in a national survey. *Journal of Sex Research, 43*, 217–226.

Roberts, C., Kippax, S., Waldby, C., & Crawford, J. (1995). Faking it: The story of 'ohh!'. *Women's Studies International Forum, 18*(5/6), 523–532.

Rogers, A. (2005). Chaos to control: Men's magazines and the mastering of intimacy. *Men and Masculinities, 8*(2), 175–194.

Simonds, W. (2002). Watching the clock: Keeping time during pregnancy, birth, and postpartum experiences. *Social Science & Medicine, 55*(4), 559–570.

Stevens, E. & *Men's Fitness* Editors (n.d.). 9 ways to last longer in bed! *Men's Fitness*. Retrieved from http://www.mensfitness.com/women/sex-tips/last-longer-in-bed-sex-experts-tell-you-how?page=4 [Accessed 3 March 2014].

Stibbe, A. (2004). Health and the social construction of masculinity in *Men's Health Magazine*. *Men and Masculinities, 7*(1), 31–51.

Symonds, T., Roblin, D., Hart, K., & Althof, S. (2003). How does premature ejaculation impact a man's life? *Journal of Sex and Marital Therapy, 29*(5), 361–370.

Tiefer, L. (1994). The medicalization of impotence: Normalizing phallocentrism. *Gender & Society, 8*(3), 363–377.

Turner, B. S. (2003). Social fluids: Metaphors and meanings of society. *Body & Society, 9*(1), 1–10.

Tyler, M. (2004). Managing between the sheets: Lifestyle magazines and the management of sexuality in everyday life. *Sexualities, 7*(1), 81–106.

Victoria State Government (2012). Premature ejaculation. Retrieved from https://www.betterhealth.vic.gov.au/health/healthyliving/premature-ejaculation. [Accessed 24 February 2014].

Waldinger, M. D., Hengeveld, M. W., & Zwinderman, A. H. (1994). Paroxetine treatment of premature ejaculation: A double-blind, randomized, placebo-controlled study. *American Journal of Psychiatry, 151*, 1377–1379.

Waldinger, M. D., Hengeveld, M. W., Zwinderman, A. H., & Olivier, B. (1998). An empirical operationalization study of DSM-IV diagnostic criteria for premature ejaculation. *International Journal of Psychiatry and Clinical Practice, 2*, 287–293.

Waldinger, M. & Schweitzer, D. H. (2006). Changing paradigms from a historical DSM-II and DSM-IV view toward an evidence-based definition of premature ejaculation. Part 1–validity of DSM-IV-TR. *Journal of Sexual Medicine, 3*, 682–692.

World Health Organization (1992). *The ICD-10 classification of mental and behavioural disorders: Clinical descriptions and diagnostic criteria for research.* Geneva, Switzerland: World Health Organization.

CHAPTER SEVEN

NEOLIBERAL IDEOLOGY AND SHIFTING
'SALARYMEN IDENTITY' UNDER CORPORATE
RESTRUCTURING IN JAPAN

Nana Okura Gagné

In societies around the world, the 1980s seemed to herald a global shift towards a new logic of political, economic, and social governance grounded in the growing interconnectivity of global capital and an unshakable belief in the advantages of marketisation (Harvey, 2005). Since then, this growing hegemonic logic of neoliberalism has become orthodoxy among many national governments, multinational corporations, international financial institutions and transnational NGOs across the globe. Crucial to the global permeation of neoliberal logic has been the consent of local governments and citizens in accepting – or even embracing – neoliberal policies as the only choice for competing in the global economy. The push by states, corporations and transnational institutions to find new markets and avenues for capital throughout the world has gone hand-in-hand with the "construction of consent" for neoliberal policies among citizens (Harvey, 2005, p. 39) and "market deepening" that bind citizens to global capital through increasingly interconnected public services, NGO aid regimes, and private enterprise (Carroll, 2012a, p. 356; 2012b, pp. 379–380).

In this way, the past several decades have been the story of state policies shifting from Keynesian-style regulated welfare economies, to "roll-back" notions of market deregulation, and to "roll-out" strategies of public-private partnerships and targeted regulation to keep global capital expanding (Carroll, 2012a, p. 354; see also Harvey, 2005). As with many other regions,

Japan was also affected. Japan's penetration by global neoliberal policies also began with privatisation of certain public services in the 1980s and 1990s under the Liberal Democratic Party Prime Ministers Yasuhiro Nakasone and Ryutaro Hashimoto. By the late 1990s and early 2000s, Japan was fully engaged in new debates over the needs for developing new models of flexible labour and capital accumulation, financial deregulation and entrepreneurism that have been the hallmark of neoliberalism around the world.

Despite these similarities, however, Japan offers a unique case of the intersection of neoliberalism and local responses. Unlike many other states that have undergone a radical transformation in political-economic systems under the expansion of capitalism, the concepts of marketisation and economic efficiency have long been embedded in Japan (e.g., Howell, 1995; Matsuo, 2009). Moreover, what is seen as the 'neoliberal' path of outsourcing social services to the private sector also has a long history in Japan, especially in the post-war Japanese state's project of relegating welfare responsibility to corporations (Borovoy, 2012; Gordon, 1993). As such, the rise of neoliberal rhetoric in post-bubble Japan was met with neither complete bewilderment nor unbridled enthusiasm.

After the bursting of Japan's bubble economy in the early 1990s, there was a general consensus that Japanese companies had to change in order to survive in the global market.[1] Neoliberal advocates in particular felt that inflexible labour laws and ballooning corporate welfare costs for the ageing workforce were holding Japanese companies back. Thus, the problems since the 1990s were an opportunity to fully embrace neoliberal policies that were already the orthodoxy across much of the Western world (Tanaka, 2002; Yoda, 2006; Steven Vogel, 2006). According to most observers, while the post-war domestic economic system seemed to have achieved enviable levels of productivity and affluence according to its own terms, by the

Neoliberal Ideology in Japan

1990s economically liberal places such as the US became the 'universal' symbols of winners of global capitalism. In contrast to the Japanese corporate world, American corporations seemed able to take risks and foster dynamic competition, transparency, accountability and entrepreneurial spirit (Steven Vogel, 2006).

At the same time, even as politicians and corporations in Japan have moved to embrace further deregulation, cost-cutting, and labour reforms, the by-products of such deregulation and reforms – layoffs, a rising irregular labour force, and growing talk of a 'new stratified society' within Japan – have been cited by critics as proof that Western neoliberal policies are not the answer to Japan's socio-economic difficulties. These mixed reactions typify the ways that neoliberal logic has come to be seen as both the cure and the cause for what ails contemporary Japan.

During my fieldwork with a range of salarymen who worked in large and medium sized companies in various sectors from 2006 to 2016, I witnessed how the alienating effects of neoliberal reforms often took very personal forms. Each salaryman I interacted with was a 'neoliberal subject' affected by some sort of corporate restructuring, including job-transfers, institutional marginalisation and sudden layoffs. And yet the ways that they experienced these changes differed greatly, as did the ways that they responded to their conditions and reflected on them. In the midst of these far-reaching and deep-cutting changes around the world, how have neoliberal reforms affected individuals and their life histories? Has neoliberal restructuring produced new kinds of subjectivities among those who are affected? In order to understand some of the effects of neoliberal reforms on individuals, it is necessary to contextualise Japanese economic history alongside the individual life histories of those who have been directly involved with and affected by corporate reforms. The intertwined dynamics of restructuring and reflection by both management and employees highlights a key site for the anthropological study of neoliberalism as both a hegemonic discourse as well as a form of governance with concrete effects.

As Orta (2014) has argued, "the anthropology of capitalism requires ethnographic attention to capitalism at key sites of its production, as well as analytic recognition of the compulsive force of capitalism as it is produced and reproduced through a multitude of connected practices" (p. 38). To this end, this chapter aims to understand the complex and ambiguous responses regarding neoliberal economic reforms among Japanese workers, known as 'salarymen'.[2] I aim to shed light on the ways that the subjectivities of individual workers who worked under Japan's post-war economy have been forged in and reshaped by Japan's economic rise and fall in the last several decades. Specifically, by focussing on the macro structural changes in Japan and two life histories, this chapter shows how a combination of neoliberal reforms, interpersonal workplace tensions and family obligations reveal the complex emotional and social dynamics that striate the seemingly technocratic and rational logic of neoliberal policies in Japan. Further, it reflects on the ways that structural reforms have destabilised the social identity of salarymen, revealing the economic and emotional vulnerability of these men.

Globalisation and neoliberalism at work: increasing economic competition, unemployment and rising suicide rates in Japan

During Japan's post-war 'economic miracle' from 1954 until the early 1970s, the Japanese economy expanded rapidly, transforming both the national economy and the lifestyles of everyday people from war-weary poverty to unprecedented prosperity (Gordon, 2013, p. 243). Over time, as Japanese salarymen came to symbolise the economic and cultural prosperity of modern Japan, salarymen's social identity became shaped through the stability of long-term employment and corporate welfare. Specifically, in return for their hard work, salarymen were rewarded with corporate family housing, access to healthcare and leisure, and economic stability for life-planning. As Japanese corporations required long and demanding working hours from employees, it simultaneously gendered the social institutions of Japanese society – men as a central breadwinner and women as professional housewives (E. Vogel, 1963; Suzanne H. Vogel, 1978).

In this way, Japanese salarymen and their families came to represent the emergent lifestyle of the 'new middle class' as a symbol of desirable modern life. These aspirations were not limited to those who worked at large corporate organisations; they became embraced by those across all walks of life (Kelly, 1986; Plath, 1964; E. Vogel, 1963). Altogether, as people's lives became increasingly centred on corporations for their livelihood and welfare from the 1960s onwards, Japanese salarymen became the icon of the Japanese economy, and by extension, Japan writ large. Accordingly, Japan became characterised by the ideology of "economic nationalism", which bundled economic growth and private consumerism for national prosperity along with prosperity for citizens' middle-class lifestyles (Dower, 1993, p. 31; Garon, 2013, p. 112).

In the past two decades, however, increasing economic liberalisation and globalisation have put pressure on such corporate welfare and employee-centred corporate practices that previously protected Japanese salarymen and their families against economic downturns. Alongside a significant shift of the labour force from manufacturing to services, many Japanese corporations confronted the backlash from the bursting of the economic bubble and resulting deficits through downsizing and layoffs. The restructuring of the labour force had the support of the state, which saw the recession and the growing global discourse of neoliberal fiscal and labour policies as an opportunity to reorganise post-bubble corporate and social institutions in Japan.

From 2001 to 2006, the Junichiro Koizumi administration's aggressive neoliberal policies promoted deregulation and privatisation within a broader restructuring and the economy began to show signs of recovery. Building from the initial moves towards privatisation of certain industries by Nakasone and Hashimoto in the 1980s and 1990s, Koizumi took a more drastic approach to privatisation and deregulation than his predecessors, following the well-worn path of neoliberal reforms in the US and the UK. He made moves to transfer a range of 'inefficient' public services such as the postal service and postal savings bank, regional railways, and power utilities to private sector businesses (with only partial success) in order to foster market-based 'efficiency' and 'productivity' while reducing government deficits. He also pushed for more 'flexible and responsive' labour laws (Lechevalier, 2014; Tiberghien, 2014).

As the economic recession deepened, unemployment rose from roughly 2.1% in the early 1990s to a peak of 5.5% in mid-2002. By 2003, the economy began to show signs of improvement and unemployment seemed to turn around at last, falling to 4.1% in 2006 (Ministry of Internal Affairs and Communications (MIAC), 2013). Yet, while Koizumi was celebrated for his changes, his policies did not necessarily solve Japan's economic woes. The reality on the ground behind the changing employment numbers was a restructuring of the labour market. Many companies simply reduced the number of regular employees and increased the number of temporary workers without extending full employment benefits (MIAC, 2013). Furthermore, the 2007–2009 global financial crisis rocked the Japanese economy again, affecting corporations more broadly than before due to increased international capital flows. The crisis triggered layoffs and bankruptcies across the increasingly interconnected world of global capitalism, and unemployment

Neoliberal Ideology in Japan

rose again to 5.5% in mid-2009, leaving both regular employees and the growing number of irregular employees who were hired during the Koizumi administration vulnerable to layoffs and downsizing (MIAC, 2013).

There was a deeper human toll behind these employment statistics as well. As the fallout from the post-bubble recession deepened, in 1998 incidences of suicide hit the highest levels (32,863) since the late 1950s. Since then, the number remained high throughout the 2000s (more than 30,000 suicides per year), peaking at 34,427 in 2003. According to official statistics, nearly half of these suicides (16,307) were committed by individuals classified as unemployed, and thus many were likely to be affected by labour deregulations. Finally, in 2012 the number of suicides dipped below 30,000 (to 27,853) for the first time in 14 years (National Police Association, 2013).

Economic restructuring: shifting corporate structures and governance in Japan

The bursting of the economic bubble in 1990 revealed both international and domestic pressures on the post-war model of Japan's corporate-centred society. In addition to the changing demands of increasingly competitive global product markets and the subsequent hollowing-out of Japanese industry, corporations faced a declining need for maintaining the same levels of labour power within their corporations as in the past (Moriya, 2005). Under the Koizumi administration, "Without structural reformation, no economic recovery" became the slogan (Tanaka, 2002) and many corporations began seeking solutions for rationalising their business practices (Miyata, 1999; Moriya, 2005; Tanaka, 2002). In order to strengthen Japan's global competitiveness, the Japanese management system was reanalysed against the competitive corporations in the US. As a result, many corporate leaders began questioning the Japanese employment practices that had been so successful in maintaining labour power without laying workers off (i.e. in maintaining long-term employment), and the Japanese management system itself became a target of critique.

The Japanese management system was actually a bundle of practices including long-term employment, a seniority-based wage system, slow evaluation and promotion, non-specialised (generalist) career paths, implicit control mechanisms and collective decision-making and responsibility. Together, this system facilitated rigid internal labour markets and limited labour mobility while also fostering company-based unions, internal competition, and a corporate-centred social contract through which individuals' social identities were tied to their place of employment. As the Japanese economy imploded in the early 1990s, however, this system was called into question not only by neoliberal advocates but also by individual corporations. Industry lobbyists and policymakers took advantage of the growing discourse of neoliberalism to reduce barriers for corporations, enabling them to implement policies that would protect the close relationship between companies, politicians and bureaucrats that marked Japan's so-called 'iron triangle'.

Rather than simply a direct implementation of global market-centred ideology, then, the logic of neoliberalism was co-opted by Japanese corporations through various new forms of corporate governance to mobilise workers. These included replacing full-time employees with temporary employees, hiring freezes, promoting early retirement, and implementing the new merit system to reengineer Japanese corporate practices (Sato & Imai, 2011). In other words, the ideal solution to win over global competition seemed to be to replace 'Japanese-style management practices' with what has typically been characterised as 'American-style management practices': short-term and flexible employment, rapid evaluation and promotion, specialised career paths, explicit control mechanisms, and individual decision-making and responsibility. All of this came as a top-down strategy for reconfiguring the workplace, which had unexpected and unintended effects on the social relations among workers and the social identities of salarymen in Japan more broadly.

From exclusion to destruction: two case studies of salaryman subjectivity

In Japan, the main targets of criticism that were used to rally support for the acceleration of neoliberal reform were in fact the older experienced class of salarymen, the same men who had piloted Japanese companies to domestic and global success until the late 1980s (Sato, 1994). Thus, while the growing numbers of young temporary workers or *haken* have frequently been raised as the primary victims of neoliberal reforms (Fu, 2013), the majority of salaried employees who remained employed are also both subjects and agents directly involved in these reforms (Conrad & Heindorf, 2006; McCann, Hassard, & Morris, 2006; Meyer-Ohle, 2009). Specifically, in the face of the 1990s recession the supporters of neoliberalism blamed senior salarymen for resisting the implementation of the new merit system (Tanaka, 2002). They lambasted senior salarymen for being privileged by the 'old' system and for reproducing outdated and inefficient practices through such traditional systems as so-called 'lifetime employment' and seniority-based promotion.

Such criticisms were often misplaced, however, as my fieldwork revealed a much more complex reality. In contrast to the image that 'lifetime employment' was an uncontroverted reality in Japan, in the early post-war years many workers changed their jobs often due to the volatility of the market, and it was not until the late 1950s that employment stabilised (Gordon, 2002). Moreover, since the end of the 1960s, there was a fundamental shift in employers' attitudes towards life-stage adjusted wage systems by expanding the 'merit' component within the same wage system, and by pursuing various 'intra-(group) firm employment adjustment' and 'labour lending' In the past, these methods enabled employers to adjust their labour force by transferring workers to other companies, usually to their own subsidiaries (Inagami, 2004).

Senior salarymen of this generation told me that while there was no explicit contract of 'lifetime employment' upon their entry into the company (see also Brinton, 1993, p. 50; Itoh, 1994, p. 235), they "had no incentive to leave the company" as "they had struggled to be hired in the first place" and "they had to work to support their household". Thus, without any probation period or explicit limit of tenure (such as a fixed-term contract), employees worked hard from the beginning for this tacit 'long-term' employment based on mutual efforts and trust. In other words, as much as long-term employment had been bitterly fought for through the efforts of labour unions in the post-war period and it was commonly marked as 'distinctively Japanese' by foreign observers, for many of the post-war generation employees long-term employment was not even brought into their consciousness. Indeed, as the following illustrations demonstrate, it was accepted *tacitly* (*anmoku no ryōkai*) with the condition of mutual efforts and trust by both management and employees.

Through such arrangements, salarymen's subjectivities as employees had been subsumed within the broader ideologies of home and work that solidified over the past half-century. This came with a distinct gendering of social life as well. As the development of Japan's 'corporate-centred society' was fundamentally a 'gender-exclusive society' (see Osawa & Callon, 1992) post-war gender ideology relegated men to the role of corporate-centred breadwinner while at the same time the ideology of economic nationalism tied salarymen's identities as workers at specific corporations to their contribution to the nation's post-war recovery.

By the early 2000s, however, neoliberal reforms opened the door for such tacit arrangements and resilient ideologies to be radically altered under the banner of 'restructuring'. Theoretically, this neoliberal logic implies that changing workplace governmentality into a system emphasising "individual autonomy" will transform workers' subjectivity into "homo-economicus", a kind of subjectivity rooted in the self-regulated autonomy of individuals (Read, 2009, pp. 30–31). As Read (2009) notes, "The operative terms of this governmentality are no longer rights and laws but interest, investment and competition", and the victims (and beneficiaries) produced by this unbridled competition are legitimated by the discourse of self-responsibility which justifies winners and losers through the logic of efficiency, flexibility and results. As a result of this self-directed discourse of competition and flexibility, neoliberal governmentality is seen as co-opting and corroding rival discourses by subsuming all of human activity within its hegemonising worldview, premised on the idea that individuals have the freedom and obligation to carve out their own identity within the competitive marketplace of ideas. In other words, neoliberalism is assumed to preclude resistance to its ideology and policies by charging all individuals to find success within the system, thereby cultivating a 'neoliberal subjectivity'.

Despite the global expansion of neoliberal ideologies, however, this seemingly 'rational' logic of competition, flexibility, and self-regulated autonomous workers can also serve as a smokescreen for local manipulations and more politically or personally motivated restructuring. In Japanese workplaces, rather than transforming workers' consciousness into a 'neoliberal subjectivity' motivated by independent and autonomous notions of success, 'restructuring' played on and pried open the differences between workers and management without empowering workers. At the same time, it unleashed the sticky, personality-driven conflicts that had long been held in check in the pre-neoliberal workplace. The following are case studies of my informants who experienced corporate restructuring directly, which had various effects on their individual and family lives, and which revealed complex subjectivities tangled between their workplaces, their families and their futures.

Ken Fukawa[3]

Ken Fukawa, a former salaryman in his late 50s, was one of the early victims of restructuring in Japan. Fukawa-san was 45 years old when he was laid off unexpectedly in 2002. Fukawa-san had lived through the economic boom years and had ridden the waves of economic success as a salaryman at a prestigious fisheries company. Long-term employment, a stable and predictable seniority-based salary scale, and a strong connection with his company had been a given. What is more, what marked Fukawa-san was that he had been a very productive employee, and spent several years in Spain as a business expatriate. However, Japanese neoliberalism became painfully real when he was fired from his company. From his perspective, what lay behind his restructuring was not the economic logic of neoliberalism per se, but rather the way that his bosses used neoliberalism as retaliation against him as an outspoken and therefore unwanted and problematic employee. As a result, the impact of neoliberal policies at his workplace spurred Fukawa-san on to reflect upon the strengths of the previous system, while also revealing the fragility of salaryman subjectivity.

Fukawa-san was born in 1958 in Kumamoto to a small family. He grew up near the water and became interested in the sea and fisheries. After attending Tokyo University of Marine Science and Technology, he applied for a job in the fisheries division of one of Japan's largest fishery corporations. Fukawa-san got the job with the vague idea that he would work for the company until he retired – a feeling that many of my informants shared.

During his first 21 years with the company he rose through the ranks in various departments, from middle-management in the trawler business and development departments to chief of the sales division – including five years of expatriate work in

Spain. As a team leader he earned ¥500–700 million a year for the company, but he spent only eight hours a day at home, including sleep. In 1998, he was temporarily sent to a small subsidiary as third manager of the sales department in Tokyo to help reduce their deficit. Though he worked hard to reduce costs the subsidiary did not improve and they had to close it in 2002. After its closure, Fukawa-san was sent back to the parent company as a counsellor in the personnel department, but at the same time he was told that he would be laid off in six months.

Neoliberal employment policies are frequently advertised as imparting positive flexibility in terms of opportunities for experienced middle-aged men like Fukawa-san to be attractive candidates for headhunting or re-employment (e.g., see Lane, 2011; Van Oort, 2015). However, Fukawa-san told me how helpless he felt. In Japan, he explained, it is more difficult for a senior salaryman to get re-employed, as he would simply be a burden (*meiwaku*) to a new employer; as a senior in age and experience, his status and skill would require a high position, but as an older 'outsider' among younger employees who had more experience with the particular company, he reasoned that his presence would upset the internal dynamics of the company.

Fukawa-san's layoff was ostensibly part of broader restructuring in the company. However, he also knew that his particular situation was much more 'personal'. Fukawa-san was the only one laid off in the division – everyone else was simply transferred to different divisions. He talked about his feelings about the layoff as "agonizing" particularly because it could not be justified by the collapse of the bubble economy; it had everything to do with the personal tension with his boss, who used corporate restructuring as a retaliatory rationale to get rid of him as an apparent burden due to his age and experience. Fukawa-san described this boss as the CEO's "pet" who never really thought about the management and continuity of the corporation. When they faced the deficit problem in the subsidiary, Fukawa-san felt that moving their office from the expensive World Trade Center building would be the first thing to do, but his boss did not even consider his opinion. As a consequence, they could not sustain the subsidiary and it went bankrupt, and Fukawa-san was fired. Under a pure merit system Fukawa-san could have been prized as a top employee, but neoliberal tools of restructuring and the 'flexibilization' of employment meant that Fukawa-san became a viable target of retaliation as a senior employee who was increasingly seen as a burden to the company. Indeed, Fukawa-san claimed, "that is why I *do* believe in the importance of lifetime employment *and* the merit system coexisting together, to protect people from this kind of discrimination".[4]

He received the premium period of six months of job-loss insurance (¥18,000 per day) and ¥10 million in severance pay. After a year of looking for a job without success, he felt helpless at not being able to support his family properly in the future and with 15 years left on a 30-year home loan. Although his wife works, both his and his wife's attitudes that a man should be the breadwinner are hard to change. Fukawa-san explained that his wife would still demand his monthly salary for basic living expenses regardless of his unemployment situation. He described that moment as presenting him with only two options: either committing suicide so that his family could collect his life insurance, or starting his own business. In 2003, Fukawa-san decided to launch a small tuna fishing business. He eked out a living for his family, but by 2007 his sales stagnated and it became very difficult to sustain his lifestyle. In 2008 he began doing part-time jobs at night including as a security guard, bartender, and deliveryman for fish markets.

Fukawa-san reflected that during his salaryman period he was never conscious of the long-term employment system. His exclusion from it made him gradually realise how important it is to have such a system to protect employees, not only from economic downturn, but also from restructuring that is driven by incompatibility with bosses and other delicate human relations in the company. He reflected, "now I think that the lifetime employment system means basically working for one person so that you can plan your life, which is very important not only for my own peace of mind, but also for the peace of mind of my family".[5]

As someone who had witnessed first-hand the transformation of contemporary business practices, rather than embracing a 'neoliberal subjectivity' as a flexible and autonomous agent (see Lane, 2011; Urciuoli, 2008), Fukawa-san's desire for stability increased. As a result, he came to see the deployment of corporate restructuring on the ground as a threat to personal security. Now, even in his late 50s he was constantly negotiating the constraints of his family expectations and obligations, coming to terms with his 'unfair' treatment by the company that he had worked for single-mindedly for nearly 21 years.

Ichiro Otsuka

While Fukawa-san became subject to the capricious flexibility of neoliberal restructuring in the form of a sudden layoff, the 50-year-old salaryman Ichiro Otsuka experienced neoliberalism as the inflexibility of being stuck between marginalisation at work and economic woes at home.

Otsuka-san came across as humble and sympathetic when we met in 2011, but he explained that he used to be "an arrogant man" with the "three Hs" (highs) lauded by Japanese society: high income (coming from a rich family), height (being six feet tall), and high intelligence (having high academic scores). Indeed, he had just received an award for 30 years of service from his company in 2010, and by all estimates he should have been at the top of the corporate ladder in his company. Instead, he explained that he had gone through "a turbulent life", and he reluctantly described himself as a "crushed person". Like

Fukawa-san, he had been on track for a stable and successful life at a major corporation. Unlike Fukawa-san, Otsuka-san had a plan to become successful so that he could leave his company in the future in order to take over his father's business. However, neoliberal reforms at his company forced him to reflect on the social and personal meanings of employment, and to reconcile his future options with his family's needs.

Otsuka-san was born as the eldest son to a wealthy family in Fukushima in 1963. He was a good student in school and he planned to study architecture and civil engineering to take over his father's business. However, the course of his life took an unexpected turn when he took an early entrance exam at a prestigious technical high school in Tokyo with the intent of using it as a way of preparing himself for upcoming high school entrance exams. To his and his family's surprise, he unexpectedly passed the exam, and suddenly everything changed.

The high school was a special technical high school where students studied the electrical business without paying tuition but with the obligation to work for one of the major electric companies upon graduation. Thus it would effectively determine his future career. His school urged him to accept the prestigious offer, and Otsuka-san eventually assented thinking that he would become successful enough that he could eventually leave the company to take over his family's business upon his father's retirement.[6]

Otsuka-san entered the affiliated Tokyo Electric University after high school, and he was assigned to work in the Tokyo office of his company during his junior year in 1982. At the time he also began a relationship with a divorced woman who was five years older than him, although his family kept encouraging him to get settled and married with a more "proper" partner. Against the wishes of his relatives, Otsuka-san and his girlfriend decided to conceive a baby to persuade them to accept their marriage.

Neoliberal Ideology in Japan

The strategy of forcing his family's acceptance worked, and Otsuka-san married in 1983. He and his wife soon had a daughter and son, and he was later transferred to Ibaragi prefecture in 1986. From the start of his career in the company Otsuka-san worked hard and showed progress. With the seniority and merit systems, he was comfortably climbing up the corporate ladder. Everyone knew he would be a big man in the company in the future, and soon Otsuka-san was even able to do business with his father's company, building towards his vision to take over the company in the future. However, his father's business fell into debt and eventually went bankrupt in 2001.

After his father's bankruptcy, Otsuka-san took on some of his father's debts as the eldest son. He suddenly found himself the owner of ¥20 million of debt. Moreover, he had just bought a house and he had been counting on the company's support through promotions and bonuses to pay for his growing family. As he had always been taken care of by his boss in the company, he turned to him for advice. Astounded by such an amount of debt, the boss consulted with his own boss, and eventually the news reached the head of the department. As it is usually the top manager who must take responsibility for his subordinate's deeds in Japanese companies (see Matsuo, 2009), Otsuka-san's debts were interpreted as a sign of untrustworthiness and a potential threat to his company in the middle of its corporate restructuring. As a result, Otsuka-san was taken out of the management track. Although he continued to work hard, he never again received any promotions.

Otsuka-san recalled that what was most regrettable was his naïve trust of his boss and company, which turned out to be non-reciprocal. He had worked for them since he was 14 years old and always showed progress and achievement, but when he needed their support the most he felt that the company betrayed him. Since then he had never received challenging tasks but kept working on mundane tasks just to fill out his remaining working years.[7]

While such marginalisation led Otsuka-san to feel like a "crushed human", he and other informants I spoke with who were in similar situations also noted that despite such feelings of helplessness and mental anguish, they still felt fortunate to receive a pay cheque. It took Otsuka-san a long time to accept this reality, and there were many moments when he seriously considered quitting the company. But given his mortgage and his children's future college expenses, he decided to keep working to support his family.

Otsuka-san was not merely a passive victim, however. When we first met in 2007, his original plan of taking over his father's business was over, but he had made a new "secret plan" to start pursuing what he really wanted: to start his own restaurant business in Tokyo in 2010. He described his agenda as "revenge" against what happened to his and his father's careers, and he used his free time to study cooking and plan for opening his own business. This dream, too, ended in 2009, however. With the fallout of the global financial crisis destabilising the Japanese economy, Otsuka-san's wife and son begged him to stay on at the company where he had stable employment instead of pursuing his risky, entrepreneurial dream. According to Otsuka-san, this was largely driven by the fact that his son was on the job market and having a father without a stable job might disadvantage his son's job possibilities. In the end, he chose to respond to his family's expectations of him and opted for the long-term security of his continued employment. Nonetheless, on 11 March 2011 the Great East Japan Earthquake struck, sending shockwaves through the power industry. As a result, Otsuka-san's retirement package was significantly reduced, and he regretted not taking early retirement when he had the chance for better conditions.

Nonetheless, when I met Otsuka-san again in February 2017, he looked happier than before. Reflecting back, he told me how lucky he was to be able to be employed after all of the things that happened to him and his company. Ironically, this was the first time I heard that he felt so happy not to have quit before.

Ultimately, for Otsuka-san it was his father's unexpected bankruptcy that was used by his company as a reason to demote him from the promotion track. In his case, neoliberal reforms struck twice: new management systems legitimated the differential treatment that led to his marginalisation, and flexible labour regulations enabled his company to dismantle his previously stable retirement package. At the same time, this treatment also allowed him to look back on the experience as a part of human maturity, even as his past and future career choices were nonetheless bounded by his family's expectations and gendered pressures to maintain a stable life for his family. From this perspective, both Otsuka-san and his company chose reliability and stability over potential risks as a way to protect themselves within the uncertain economy.

Conclusion

The two narratives presented here articulate how each salaryman was a neoliberal subject affected by some sort of corporate restructuring, whether it was sudden layoffs or institutional marginalisation. What is significant in these two cases is that despite the claims by neoliberal advocates that neoliberal policies would liberate individuals from parochial, 'feudalistic' logic through the freedom of rational, economic market logic and flexibility, the actual forms of restructuring have largely resulted in *freeing companies* from social responsibility for their workers and in the increased flexibility of capital. This left many individuals locked into a tight labour market with a narrow and shaky path to work and family stability. For experienced salarymen, the unsettling impact of neoliberal policies came almost unexpectedly, yet through highly personal circumstances that cannot be explained simply by an economic formula of cause and effect.

In this way, the impact of the continuing deployment of neoliberal ideologies and policies in Japan offers an insightful contrast with neoliberalism in other parts of the world since the 1980s. In many societies, especially developing nations emerging from colonialism or socialism, the greatest challenges confronting neoliberalism as a policy bundle and ideology are institutional, legal and political (Carroll, 2012a; Goldman, 2001; Harvey, 2005). In Japan, in contrast, neoliberal policies and ideology have been welcomed by corporations, enabled by legal institutions, and pursued by decades of entrenched politicians and technocrats who have been insulated from many of the pressures of politics found in other societies (see Tiberghien, 2014). Despite the new forms of flexibility that neoliberalism enabled for corporations, however, it certainly did not provide 'positive' flexibility, namely flexibility to enable stability, for individual salarymen. Underneath the vastly transformed corporate environment that has embraced neoliberal reforms for global competitiveness in post-bubble Japan lies a much more conflicted local ecology of the workers themselves who are faced with the majority share of risk without the personal or social safety nets needed to catch them should they fall. Moreover, as the icon of 'the salaryman' as a stably employed worker for the Japanese nation becomes a vestigial social identity, salarymen themselves (and their families) also face a lack of social understanding of their newly precarious and unstable social position.

This is not to say that individual employees have demonstrated an *ideological* resistance to neoliberal policies. Both Fukawa-san and Otsuka-san would generally agree with their companies' economic logic as well as the goals of individual economic success, and indeed Otsuka-san had been on the brink of taking advantage of just such an entrepreneurial pursuit. At the same time, they also continued to value dominant social attitudes regarding the company as a *socio*-economic institution that is responsible for providing welfare for employees. Even in their unexpected economic turmoil, it is clear that they continue to accept the resilient gender ideology and familial expectations to provide security to their families, while they are faced with the reality that it is increasingly difficult to fulfil such corporate, familial and social expectations in contemporary Japanese society. Put differently, while they still *identify themselves with* the social identity of the salaryman who dedicates his life to the company in order to support his family, they are finding it increasingly difficult to *identify themselves as* such a salaryman as their subjectivity has shifted in the new economy from central pillars holding up the home to shaky pillars struggling to shelter their home from the capricious flows of global capitalism.

Ultimately, despite the discourse of neoliberalism as a global hegemonic regime, each salaryman was affected by and creatively responded to the large-scale restructuring of the Japanese economy, becoming 'neoliberal subjects' while actively eschewing, or else not being able to develop, a 'neoliberal subjectivity'. Certainly, the drastic socio-economic changes in contemporary Japan have impacted salarymen's sense of self and their attitudes toward work. However, rather than internalising the neoliberal market logic that encourages individuals to embrace risk and internal competition as an autonomous worker (i.e. Giddens, 1991; Lane, 2011; Urciuoli, 2008), Japanese employees like Fukawa-san and Otsuka-san developed a critical and reflexive awareness of the fragility of work stability and the importance of avoiding risks as a way to protect their jobs and their families' livelihood.

It was only in retrospect after being subjected to new forms of neoliberal evaluation, being laid-off, or becoming structurally marginalised that many salarymen were able to re-evaluate the previous systems such as long-term employment, and by extension reconsider what it meant to be a worker in the Japanese economy. As the previous corporate-centred safety nets began to unravel beneath them, many salarymen like my informants gained a new awareness of how the previous system had enabled their corporate life as well as their stable family life. Rather than giving birth to a new kind of neoliberal identity, then, the restructuring of the Japanese economy instead highlighted the increasing gap between the realities of the Japanese economy on the one hand, and on the other, the resilient expectations, aspirations and subjectivity of post-war salarymen as family breadwinners and as indispensable members of the national economy. Furthermore, as neoliberalism took concrete forms in their workplaces, many salarymen saw the human costs of 'restructuring' come into focus, while their own futures became increasingly unclear.

Notes
1. Indeed since the birth of the Japanese management system, there have been ongoing changes to adjust labour within many Japanese companies since the 1960s.
2. 'Salarymen' technically means salaried full-time white-collar and blue-collar male workers. In Japan, the wages and working conditions of male blue- and white-collar workers in same-size companies are almost identical (Gordon, 2013, p. 254).
3. All names of companies and informants are pseudonyms.
4. Interview with Fukawa-san. Tokyo, May 2007.
5. Interview with Fukawa-san. Tokyo, December 2010.
6. The relationships between junior high schools, high schools and companies are built on long-term relations of school-assisted placement. Thus, if a student rejects an offer from a prestigious school or company, it can damage the long-term relationships between the institutions (see Kariya, 1998). In Otsuka-san's case, the school urged him to accept the offer, despite his and his family's misgivings about it deciding his career track.

7. In fact, encouraging an employee to quit or take early retirement of their own will is one of the company's intentions of sidelining employees in such ways. This enables companies to rid themselves of undesired employees without going through the difficult legal and personal process of officially firing him/her. It was developed over the long years of Japan's rigid labour market and continues in the new era of more flexible layoff rules. While it has become much easier for companies to lay off employees under newly flexible labour laws, such as in Fukawa-san's case, terminating an employee still costs the company considerable money in terms of severance pay and unemployment assistance. In contrast, if employees quit or take early retirement of their own volition it is not reflected in the company's layoff statistics and, more importantly, it costs the company comparatively little. This strategy reflects the resilient cultural strictures that continue to restrain many companies from firing employees as easily as in the US, for example. Indeed, this strategy has been refined even more in recent years, with some companies even setting up specific departments, colloquially called 'banishment rooms' (*oidashibeya*), designed precisely to make employees quit (e.g. Suzuki, 2012).

References

Borovoy, A. (2012). Japan as mirror: Neoliberalism's promise and costs. In C. J. Greenhouse (Ed.), *Ethnographies of neoliberalism* (pp. 60–74). Philadelphia, PA: University of Pennsylvania Press.

Brinton, M. (1993). *Women and the economic miracle: Gender and work in postwar Japan.* Berkeley, CA: University of California Press.

Carroll, T. (2012a). Introduction: Neo-liberal development policy in Asia beyond the post-Washington consensus. *Journal of Contemporary Asia, 42*(3), 350–358.

Carroll, T. (2012b). Working on, through and around the state: The deep marketisation of development in the Asia-Pacific. *Journal of Contemporary Asia, 42*(3), 378–404.

Conrad, H. & Heindorf, V. (2006). Recent changes in compensation practices in large Japanese companies: Wages, bonuses, and corporate pensions. In P. Matanle & W. Lunsing (Eds.),

Perspectives on work, employment and society in Japan (pp. 79–97). Basingstoke, United Kingdom: Palgrave Macmillan.

Dower, J. (1993). Peace and democracy in two systems: External policy and internal conflict. In A. Gordon (Ed.), *Postwar Japan as history* (pp. 3–33). Berkeley, CA: University of California Press.

Fu, H. (2013). Fragmented work in post-bubble Japan: Negotiating identity, gender, age, and class in triangular employment relationships. *Anthropology of Work Review, 34*(1), 27–38.

Garon, S. (2013). Saving for 'My own good and the good of the nation': Economic nationalism in Modern Japan. In S. Wilson (Ed.), *Nation and nationalism in Japan* (pp. 97–114). London, United Kingdom: Routledge.

Giddens, A. (1991). *Modernity and self-identity: Self and society in the late modern age.* Stanford, CA: Stanford University Press.

Goldman, M. (2001). The birth of a discipline producing authoritative green knowledge, World Bank-style. *Ethnography, 2*(2), 191–217.

Gordon, A. (1993). *Postwar Japan as history.* Berkeley, CA: University of California Press.

Gordon, A. (2002). The short happy life of the Japanese middle class. In O. Zunz, L. Schoppa, & N. Hiwatari (Eds.), *Social contracts under stress: The middle classes of America, Europe, and Japan at the turn of the century* (pp. 108–129). New York, NY: Russell Sage Foundation.

Gordon, A. (2013). *A modern history of Japan: From Tokugawa times to the present* (3rd ed.). Oxford, United Kingdom: Oxford University Press.

Harvey, D. (1991). Flexibility: Threat or opportunity? *Socialist Review, 21*(1), 65–78.

Harvey, D. (2005). *A brief history of neoliberalism.* Oxford, United Kingdom: Oxford University Press.

Howell, D. (1995). *Capitalism from within.* Berkeley, CA: University of California Press.

Inagami, T. (2004). Changes in the employment system and future labor policies. *Japan Labor Review, 1*(1), 39–51.

Itoh, H. (1994). Japanese human resource management from incentive theory. In M. Aoki & R. Dore (Eds.), *Japanese firms: The sources of competitive strengths* (pp. 233–264). Oxford, United Kingdom: Oxford University Press.

Kariya, T. (1998). From high school and college to work in Japan: Meritocracy through institutional and semi-institutional linkage. In Y. Shavit & W. Müller (Eds.), *From school to work: A comparative study of educational qualifications and occupational destinations* (pp. 311-335). Oxford, United Kingdom: Clarendon Press.

Kelly, W. (1986). Rationalization and nostalgia – cultural dynamics of new middle-class Japan. *American Ethnologist, 13*(4), 603-618.

Lane, C. (2009). Man enough to let my wife support me: How changing models of career and gender are reshaping the experience of unemployment. *American Ethnologist, 36*(4), 681-692.

Lane, C. (2011). *A company of one: Insecurity, independence, and the new world of white-collar unemployment.* Ithaca, NY: Cornell University Press.

Lechavelier, S. (2014). Capitalism and neo-liberalism – Lessons from Japan. In S. Lechavelier (Ed.), *The great transformation of Japanese capitalism* (pp. 157-162). Abingdon, United Kingdom: Routledge.

Matsuo, T. (2009). *Shounindo no susume.* Tokyo, Japan: Fujiwara Shoten.

McCann, L., Hassard, J., & Morris, J. (2006). Hard times for salarymen: Corporate restructuring and middle managers' working lives. In P. Matanle & W. Lunsing (Eds.), *Perspectives on work, employment and society in Japan* (pp. 98-116). Basingstoke: Palgrave Macmillan.

Meyer-Ohle, H. (2009). *Japanese workplaces in transition: Employee perceptions.* London, United Kingdom: Palgrave Macmillan.

Ministry of Internal Affairs and Communications (2013). *Labor force survey.* Retrieved from http://www.stat.go.jp/data/roudou/report/2011/pdf/summary2.pdf

Miyata, Y. (1999). *Nihonteki soshiki, jinji, koyou seido no henka, ittaikagenri kara no dakkyaku o mezashite.* Tokyo, Japan: Fujita Mirai Kenkyujo.

Moriya, T. (2005). *Nihon kigyo e no seika shugi donyu: kigyonai kyodotai no henyo.* Tokyo: Japan: Moriyamashoten.

National Police Association (2013). Suicide statistics. Retrieved from https://www.npa.go.jp/safetylife/seianki/jisatsu/H22/H22_ji satunogaiyou.pdf

Orta, A. (2014). Response to Karen Ho on cultures of capitalism, contexts of capitalism. *American Ethnologist, 4*(1), 38-39.

Osawa, M. & Callon, S. (1992). Corporate-centered society and women's labor in Japan today. *U.S.-Japan Women's Journal, English Supplement No. 3*, 3–35.

Plath, D. (1964). *The after hours: Modern Japan and the search for enjoyment.* Berkeley, CA: University of California Press.

Read, J. (2009). A genealogy of homo-economicus: Neoliberalism and the production of subjectivity. *Foucault Studies, 6,* 25–36.

Sato, H. (1994). Employment adjustment of middle-aged workers and keeping workers employed. *Japan Labor Bulletin, 33*(2), 8–15.

Imai, J. & Sato, Y. (2011). Regular and non-regular employment as an additional duality in Japanese Labor Market: Institutional perspectives on career mobility. In Y. Sato & J. Imai (Eds.), *Japan's new inequality: Intersection of employment reforms and welfare arrangements* (pp. 1–31). Melbourne, Australia: Trans Pacific Press.

Suzuki, T. (2012). *Kaiko no saizensen: PIP no Shuurai [The frontline of layoffs: The Incursion of Performance Improvement Plans].* Tokyo, Japan: Junposha.

Tanaka, H. (2002). *Nihongata Salaryman wa fukkatsusuru.* Tokyo, Japan: NHK Books.

Tiberghien, Y. (2014). Thirty years of neo-liberal reforms in Japan. In S. Lechavelier (Ed.), *The great transformation of Japanese capitalism* (pp. 26–55). Abingdon, United Kingdom: Routledge.

Urciuoli, B. (2008). Skills and selves in the new workplace. *American Ethnologist, 35*(2), 211–228.

Van Oort, M. (2015). Making the neoliberal precariat: Two faces of job searching in Minneapolis. *Ethnography, 16*(1), 74–94.

Vogel, E. (1963). *Japan's new middle class.* Berkeley, CA: University of California Press.

Vogel, Suzanne H. (1978). Professional housewife: The career of urban middle class Japanese women. *Japan Interpreter, 12*(1), 16–43.

Vogel, Steven. (2006). *Japan remodeled: How government and industry are reforming Japanese capitalism.* Ithaca, NY: Cornell University Press.

Yoda, T. (2006). A road map to millennial Japan. In H. Harootunian & T. Yoda (Eds.), *Japan after Japan: Social and cultural life from the recessionary 1990s to the present* (pp. 16–53). Durham, NC: Duke University Press.

CHAPTER EIGHT

URBAN TRANSFORMATIONS, WORK AND THE IDEA
OF SOCIAL SOLITUDE AMONG TWO GENERATIONS
OF MEN IN SURABAYA, EAST JAVA

Matteo Carlo Alcano

Introduction
The implementation of political decentralisation in Indonesia from 2001 has had a negative effect on informal sector workers, with many small enterprises being pushed into the formal economy and street vendors evicted from public space (Wilson, 2010, p. 117). The present chapter is centered on the life experiences of two generations of men who live and work in the informal sector in the low-income neighbourhood of *kampung* Malang, Surabaya, East Java.[1] More specifically, it describes the relationship between the recent transformations of the urban landscape, the practice of work and an idea of social solitude. While Surabaya has been re-imagined and constructed as a city of transit and passage (see Peters, 2013) and a key point for the transit of people and goods towards Eastern Indonesia, its inhabitants have experienced dispossession, reduced mobility and unemployment and have been left facing the consequences of economic and social change. The chapter looks at how social actors embody, reproduce, inflect and react to such change.

Ultimately, the chapter discusses subjectivity and personal growth. The language of subjectivity has been employed to offer a dynamic perspective of processes of selfhood (see Blackwood, 2010). As Sherry Ortner (2005) pointed out in her seminal essay about the theoretical and ethnographic implications of the notion of subjectivity through the analysis of work, subjectivity comprises the cultural and social formations that shape, organise and provoke the ensemble of modes of perception, affect, thought, desire, fear and so forth that animate acting subjects.

This chapter is divided into three sections. The first introduces the city of Surabaya and the neighbourhood of *kampung* Malang, located south along Surabaya's main river; it describes the politics of urban re-qualification that have been carried out by the municipality since at least 2008, with a focus on the nature of policy relating to governance of the urban informal sector. From this point of view, it looks at the implementation of neoliberal policies and the privatisation of markets. The second analyses the impact of these new regulations on the lives of the older generation of inhabitants of *kampung* Malang, a group of men aged 40 to 65. It explores their ideas and thoughts about community, work and uncertainty and a concern about the future of their sons, grandsons and nephews. It shows how neoliberalism produces imaginaries through which people understand the possibilities and the limits of the urban experience (Brenner & Theodore, 2010) and reflect upon the changes they experience. The third section shifts the focus on to the current generation of adolescents of *kampung* Malang and on to youth street gangs, and the ways that young men seek to approach adult life and create a better present and future for themselves in a climate of material and social insecurity. It analyses how in the urban context of Surabaya, neoliberalism, with its discourses and ideology, generates strategies, struggle and a reworking of the conceptions about everyday life. The ways young men from a specific area of an Indonesian city engage with, resist or inflect urban and social change show how market-based regulatory arrangements necessarily interact with non-market and 'socialized' forms of coordination and aggregation.

Surabaya and *kampung* Malang: order and erosion
Surabaya is Indonesia's second largest city, the capital of the province of East Java and the home of the country's navy. It is located in the mouth of the Mas River, and along the edge of the

Madura Strait. It is a gigantic port strewn with cranes, construction sites, corporate buildings, wide roads and shopping malls. For local residents Surabaya is closely linked to the birth of the Indonesian nation, as it is in Surabaya that the battle for independence began and peaked in 1945. To them, it is the city of heroes, and statues commemorating independence are scattered all over the city.

Between 1998 and 2008 Surabaya witnessed a decade of profound urban transformations, as the municipal government strove to achieve order and legibility to complement the needs of the emergent middle class. The overall goal was to facilitate the circulation of persons, vehicles and goods and to qualify Surabaya as a city of passage and consumption. Among the most prominent transformations was the restructuring of road transportation through the unclogging of existing roads (*jalan, jalan raya*[2]) and their conversion into spiralling one-way circuits (see Peters, 2010). This process involved the clearance of the informal economy from the streets, and the progressive elimination of any sign of disorder from the public space through what Harvey would call the politics of 'dispossession' – the attempt to accumulate by dispossessing people of their economic rights and various forms of ownership and economic power (see Harvey, 2003). As a consequence, the poor were relegated to the confined alleys of the neighbourhoods of the inner city. By mid 2008, according to local newspaper reports (as quoted for instance in Peters 2009, 2010), Surabaya's civil policing arm achieved a thorough clearance of makeshift food stalls (*warung*), mobile vendors, marketplaces and pedicab (*becak*) drivers from the city streets in order to abate congestion and increase the flow of traffic. Order also manifested itself through rapid proliferation of plazas. While the conversion of roads served the purpose of eradicating any pause in the constant flow of traffic and avoiding congestion, the latter functioned to negate and visually deflect poverty (Peters, 2009, 2010).

Edges of Identity

The growth of plazas and hotels has been particularly rapid over the past decade and a half in the central urban sub district of Tegelsari, and is most apparent in the old Ngagel industrial estate situated across the river from *kampung* Malang.

Kampung Malang spans an area of no more than one square kilometre. It is actually a cluster of about 100 neighbourhoods, each comprising about 100 officially registered residents, making an approximate total of 10,000 inhabitants. As mentioned, *kampung* Malang sits across from the once heavily industrialised industrial estate that now forms part of a congested central service district. An enormous one-way road, a bridge, the Mas river, and then abandoned factories, as well as new hotels, malls and apartment complexes merge around an intersection that borders the *kampung*.

In Surabaya, *kampung* Malang is widely regarded as a slum neighbourhood, a *lorong*. The term *lorong* literally means narrow corridor. However, it is also loosely used by some to refer to the slum areas in many big cities in Indonesia (see, for instance, Nasir, 2006; Nasir & Rosenthal, 2009). In the *lorong*, clusters of alleyways commonly known as *gang* link the slum area to more affluent parts of the city. As Nasir and Rosenthal (2009) point out, with some geographical and sociocultural differences, similar areas can be found in many developing or even developed countries, and the *lorong* can be compared to the 'favelas' of Rio de Janeiro, the poor neighbourhoods in Colombia and Guatemala, or the 'ghettos' usually inhabited by the Latinos, the so-called 'barrios', and by African-Americans in the United States. What these areas have in common is that they are known in slum literature as "clusters of disadvantage" (Chambers, 1983, p. 112), that is areas that present severe socio-economic deprivations that interact to create various kinds of vulnerabilities.

To the naked eye, the landscape of the area surrounding *kampung* Malang is characterised by an excessive number of buildings under construction, empty lots and half-finished buildings – so many in fact that many *kampung* residents describe the city as "not yet ready" (*belum siap*) and as a site of perennial construction work. The city is unfinished, not yet developed, and the construction sites are a constant reminder of that. Overall, the efficient, industrial feel of Surabaya and its appearance of order is quite deceptive. In his vivid accounts about the streets of Surabaya, Stephen Christopher Brown described the city as a "strikingly protean place" (2009, p. 34), extremely variable in shape and form, a site of swift changes, where urban transformations occur in a short period of time and uncertainty is palpable:

> I have watched mildewed plaster literally peel off an interior wall of its own accord during another soggy day in the wet season; construction bricks are often so soft they crumble to the touch. In one of the gleaming marble and metal temples Javanese people use for banking, the entire polished stone counter crashed to the floor one day when I leaned down to speak through the hole in the glass. (Brown, 2009, p. 34)

Surabaya is a city where plans are constantly deferred to the future and where various sites are identified by both government officials and local residents as "not yet developed" (*belum dibangun*). This contributes to create a sense of uncertainty, both spatial and temporal:

> Over the decade or so since I first visited the city buildings, skyscrapers and malls have gone up, been torn down or burned down, been replaced by newer and seemingly more fragile ones. Roads are changed and the everyday routes are subject to constant revision. Warung pop up like mushrooms, transforming the landscape for a six or eight-hour spell before their orange and blue plastic tarpaulin walls are struck again and melt away into the air. Some districts reinvent themselves three times a day, selling for instance flowers in the morning, beer and chicken in the afternoon, brightly colored aquarium

fish in plastic baggies by night. The most enduring landmarks these days are perhaps a few construction projects halted long ago amid disputes over debt and ownership; their rusted iron frames diminish almost imperceptibly each night, as gleaners sell scrap metal by the kilogram, but the indeterminacy of ownership is, paradoxically, the one constant that can be relied upon. (Brown, 2009, pp. 34-35)

The Mas river: work and aggregation

A great portion of *kampung* Malang occupies the area along the riverbank: this is a former residential area that grew around a weaving factory and used to house factory workers at least until the early 1990s when the factory was closed down and demolished. The older men of *kampung* Malang attach a profound meaning to the river and to the land that surrounds it. They enjoy sitting by the water and recounting their sons' and grandsons' anecdotes about the Mas River that borders the Eastern entrance of their home village. Some of these stories are tales of events past, while some others are reflections about the present and the future. The river has been, and still is, a part of their everyday life and what surrounds it tells a lot about macro and micro economic and social changes and how they have been internalised.

First and foremost, the river is the "Blood River" (*Sungai darah*), a terminology that refers to those periods in the city's history – such as during the struggle for independence, the overthrow of the Communist Party and the licensed assassination of criminals by the police – when the river swept the discarded corpses of the victims of politically motivated violence downstream towards the sea (see Peters, 2010). The riverbanks are associated with death and with the passage of large masses of dead bodies, the carcasses of local heroes whose epic deeds animated much of the local and national history. More recently, according to the older men I talked to in *kampung* Malang, the river washes away the solitary corpses of young adolescents, those who have ventured out in the city streets in search for employment but have become involved with street gangs, petty crime and substance abuse; they have vanished and never returned home: victims of personal retaliation or vendettas, often consumed by drug and alcohol addiction, their dead bodies are sporadically found by the river banks, their faces barely recognisable. While some of these stories are exaggerated and have become part of a local mythology, they are nevertheless symptomatic of a diffused sentiment of anxiety and worry.

To many, the river is nowadays *sepi* – that is, 'void of any human activity'. As I have shown, the acceleration of road transport in Surabaya did not take place through the construction of new roads but through the unclogging of existing roads. Such a process affected the main alleys of *kampung* Malang as well as its riverbank area. In accordance with the municipal agenda the main alley of the *kampung* was indeed set to become a thoroughfare linking two main roads at separate ends of the *kampung*. Sustained police operations attempted to clear the main alleyway of all economic activities and to dislodge the illegal barracks that were built by the river, with dramatic consequences for the lives of the *kampung*'s inhabitants.

The male population of *kampung* Malang relies heavily, if not exclusively, on work in the informal sector. The informal sector in Indonesia covers a wide range of economic and income generating activities that fall outside of formal government regulation and taxation including casual jobs, small-scale entrepreneurial activity and home industry. It also includes the black market and the illegal market. It is mostly territorially based, operating in open spaces, from residences and backyards (Wilson, 2010, pp. 113–115). With the high dependence of formal sector employment upon global markets, the informal sector has expanded particularly during times of global economic downturn such as the Asia Financial Crisis of 1997. As such it has provided a safety net against abject poverty in the absence of extensive functioning social welfare services in Indonesia (Wilson, 2010, p. 114).

The informal sector in Surabaya thrives on networks of socialisation and mutual help that are best understood through the local notion of *berkumpul*. *Berkumpul* (sometimes also *bergaul*, literally the practice of socialisation, aggregation, coming together) is mostly a male institution. Through networks of socialisation and thanks to the possibility of getting together at a certain time and in a particular place, *kampung* men share information about job opportunities, exchange goods and spend time together. While men mingle at an intersection, or most often at a street food stall (*warung*), they hear information about work available for the day: some find a small job opportunity painting a house, a peddler of second-hand clothing finds some customers, a scrap picker meets someone willing to buy his scrap metal, a petty criminal finds a buyer for some illegal substance he had purchased and a broker finds a buyer for a watch he wants to sell. Through the exchange of information, men gain access to work and generate an income. There are numerous activities that are subsumed under the category of *berkumpul*: these range from meeting and talking at a street food stall of the *kampung* main alley, to exchanging goods at the market, to gambling and pigeon racing, to organising rotating credit associations. Reciprocally, the practice of work stimulates the desire to meet and to continue to stick together (*bersama-sama*) and share the flow of information. *Berkumpul* is a form of communication among *kampung* men, an opportunity to interact, a practical need and a way to make a living. It is also associated among my informants with the transition to adult life, and with the ability for a person to provide for himself, his family and extended kinship network and to meet the expectations of the community that are known as *kerja bakti*, the "duty work" and include specific tasks around the *kampung*.

Urban Transformations, Work and Social Solitude

With the attempted re-qualification of the *kampung* main alley by the municipal authorities, many among my informants saw the coming of the end of *berkumpul*. This is where the impact of neoliberal ideologies is most visible. In fact, while most *kampung* women handle the household business and the micro economic activities that revolve around the house, the great majority of men are currently unemployed. These men are left with 'nothing to do', with no activity (*aktivitas*, also *urusan laki-laki*, the 'male activities' or 'male business') as they maintain, and worry about their future and the future of their sons and grandsons. The river is 'void of any human activity' because the frequent police attempts to vacate the area make it difficult for them to come together and find work. By its own definition, work in the informal sector is fluid, flexible and insecure. At some existential level, everybody knows it. However, nowadays the men I have talked to feel *sendiri*, ("lonely"), as they strive to find space to meet and new opportunities to seize, and also lament a new sense of disconnection from the flow of opportunities. In their eyes, such opportunities are to the exclusive advantage and benefit of the new middle class. From their perspective, they wonder how their sons are going to be able to "become men" (*menjadi laki laki*) and find their place within Indonesian society.

Local markets and pigeons: apprenticeship and circulation
This section takes a closer look at the importance of local markets and pigeon racing in the social economy of *berkumpul*, to further demonstrate the repercussions of urban transformations and of the regulatory measures that are central to neoliberal processes on the lives of the men who live in *kampung* Malang.

The story of the men of *kampung* Malang is particularly tied to the fortunes and misfortunes of two local markets, Pasar Turi and Keputran, which are quite well known across Indonesia and are most certainly part of the history of East Java. Both markets burned down following arson attacks; while the former was completely destroyed and the area reconverted into a plaza, the latter was displaced and traders were scattered in the urban periphery. Temporary contracts were issued through a new municipal regulation stipulating that licences and agreements should be renewed on a yearly basis; these new temporary contracts exposed traders to the ever-present possibility of non-extension and their replacement with others capable of paying the inflated rents and service costs for space in the new mall (Peters, 2009, p. 913). Among the men of *kampung* Malang, the importance of market activities lay, and still lies today, in the association of work and personal growth. By working at the market stalls, men say they would pick up the tricks of a particular trade, and more generally learn about discipline and dedication towards the practice of work: "Men who work at the market, carry their business around all the time; wake up early, prepare their goods, and really just care about what they do." (Joko, 42 years old).

A youth, especially, would learn the art of a business by working at different market stalls over the course of his adolescence; he would rotate on a timely basis and become a trade apprentice before eventually moving on and trying to own his own business:

> Children must learn all sorts of activities, from as many people as they can. This way they can find out what they want to do, and really gain experience and wisdom. (Joko)

Because each market stand is usually associated with a particular family or a particular household, youths would circulate among different families and households and be treated as part of the family, as well as a business protégé:

> In the village children move around to live and work with a family, and then another family, and they also become part of the family's activity. When you go to the market you see them work at the stand, and then at another stand, and then at another stand again. Sometimes they go live with another family, maybe a relative, maybe not, sometimes they only

Urban Transformations, Work and Social Solitude

stay there during the day and then come home at night. It depends, if there is enough room, or if the kids are grown up and want to do their own thing, maybe hang out with their friends and then come home at night. (Joko)

The special thing about the market is that when a child goes to work he becomes a man, and also travels from one place to another in the village. (Wawan)

These forms of rotation are social institutions that can be partly assimilated to the customary habit of sending children off in an informal fostering arrangement to become a trade apprentice or business protégé, where they learn how to collaborate and operate together under the same roof. The social practice of 'borrowing' children was described by Hildred Geertz (1961) among others and more recently revisited by Brenner (1998). According to these scholars, there are links that are constructed through apprenticeship rather than blood, and children have historically been 'loaned' among relatives, even distant relatives. Quite often these exchanges involved monetary transactions, which would somehow, as these authors maintain, help to secure the recognition of the child's status and rights (see Brown, 2009).

Berkumpul is also associated with recreational activities, such as pigeon racing and gambling. It is worth noting that the playful aspect of such practices is intimately intertwined with its economic and social valence and efficacy. As described in great detail by Peters (2010, 2013), pigeon racing (*merpati belap*) brought more men together than any other *kampung* institution. It took place in the main alley of *kampung* Malang, which formed the end point to a race between two male pigeons. In the geography of order of Surabaya, pigeon racing had to be extirpated because of the land-use pattern it represented.

What is important about the structure and the dynamics of pigeon racing for the present discussion is that they express the need to create bonds of solidarity. Much like in the case of local rotating credit associations disguised through lottery games (see Brown, 2009 for a discussion on *arisan*), pigeon racing defines whom to trust within the community. Money, respect and social prestige are involved and one only plays games of racing with those who are considered trustworthy among fellow community members.

Furthermore and equally important, *kampung* men often use pigeon racing and pigeons as a metaphor of life and its trajectories, a way to speak about the incompatibility of urban rational projects and the lived experience. There is a widespread symbolic association between the return of pigeons to their cages after a race and the return home of children and young men after a long day of work. As many maintain, it is hard to train pigeons nowadays: races are banned and illegal, the locations change at the very last minute and most events are ended abruptly by the police; as a consequence many wonder "how can we teach a pigeon where to go? ... They [the pigeons] get lost, don't know where they are and can't find their way back." Youths seem to share a similar fate, according to my older informants. The markets have closed down, and their sons have had very little chance to learn about work; there is hardly any place to meet and make friends, and many youths are forced to venture out alone in the city to find a job. Beyond the river, the city looks an uncertain prospect to the older men of *kampung* Malang. From the riverbanks they turn their gaze beyond the old industrial area and express a pessimistic view about the future: while the horizon discloses bright city lights, all they see is a "labyrinth" (*labirin*), as they say. The city feels intricate, dangerous, a maze: "How can we teach our sons where to go?" Joko said during a conversation. "They don't know anything [....] they get lost, [there are] so many risks there [in the city], and what if they don't come back?"

Youth gangs of *kampung* Malang: small jobs and discipline
There is no doubt that the adolescents who are quickly approaching the world of the informal economy are particularly affected

Urban Transformations, Work and Social Solitude

by the political, economic and social changes that take place in the urban areas of Surabaya, as they begin to struggle to find appropriate sites for aggregation and work. Unemployment and concerns about the future, the absence of recognised social status and a diffused sentiment of being disconnected from the flow of capital, goods, people and ideas that animates life in the city, push a growing proportion of these youngsters to create a network of companions and to develop new forms of support, encouragement, pride and identity (Kristiansen, 2003). These networks represent a margin of creativity and a way to express personal and collective agency. In fact, youths do not feel they are socially isolated. They certainly express a sentiment of dissatisfaction, but do not articulate an explicit discourse about social solitude, as their fathers and uncles do. As they maintain, they have their own way to "move forward" and "develop" (*maju*) in life.

Youth street gangs are perhaps the most manifest form of male aggregation in contemporary *kampung* Malang. About a dozen youth street gangs (*geng*) populate the area. They consist of youths aged 13 to 17. With reference to Indonesia, Wilson (2010) has noted that in a climate of neoliberal regulations the informal sector relies heavily on local gangs to seek protection against eviction and from the intrusion of local authorities. While the nature of youth gangs remains ambiguous (and some are criminalised by the media), in Surabaya and *kampung* Malang they represent a source of security and they are thought to make a contribution to the creation of a safe (*selamat*) environment.

The high level of unemployment provides large amounts of time for youths to interact in the neighbourhood spaces. Many call these activities *nongkrong* (hanging around), or "doing nothing". The actual practice of "doing nothing" includes busy activities such as talking, joking, drinking, singing, recounting details from previous events, playing video games, fiddling with mobile phones, chatting via social networks and exchanging goods (clothes, cigarettes, alcohol), but also passing around and trading information about small job opportunities. In the neighbourhood, youths come together in gangs to "make a living", to "look for money" (*cari uang*). The underlying idea is that a person leaves the home in the morning to try to earn enough to support himself, possibly with the help of others. In a broad sense, in fact, *cari uang* refers not only to the strict acquisition of small money, but also food, cigarettes, drinks and things of everyday usage (as corroborated by Brown, 2009, p. 152).

Youth gangs are territorial. Indeed, each gang controls its own territory in the neighbourhood, what is usually known as the gang's turf (*lahan*): a segment of an alley, a bus stop, a small parking area, the back area of a building (in many cases gangs hang out in the rear of shopping malls, as often the alleyways that depart from the exit of these complexes lead back into the neighbourhood). Within their territory, youth gangs attempt to regulate the flow of wealth, goods and work opportunities. Ideally, all business opportunities should fall under their supervision as gangs extract fees from traders and offer protection from thieves and intruders. In return, they collect information about prospective short-term or long-term work opportunities in the formal and informal market; these include daily jobs as parking attendants, garbage collectors, handymen and food vendors as well as illegal activities such as selling drugs. Gangs also manage to raise money by imposing a payment on those who cross their territory, city dwellers who enter the neighbourhood to look for inexpensive labour or migrants from the surrounding rural areas who travel from one place to another to look for accommodation and a job.

Gang membership relies on the notion of discipline (*disiplin*), which refers to the existence of a code of apprenticeship and behaviour among gang members. The idea of discipline is inculcated into new members as soon as they become part of the group and presupposes that a novitiate must understand the place he occupies within the gang. Not all members are equal, despite a diffused sense of solidarity, and hierarchies and statuses are re-worked on a daily basis. Indeed, they place a strong emphasis on the ability to generate money, income and to gain possession of stolen goods. In particular, gang members who become successful at obtaining a permanent job in the city are highly valued by the rest of the gang as they, in turn, might be in the position to have first-hand information about small jobs and generate further work opportunities. This is the case with youths who find a relatively stable job at one of the stores or food chains at the shopping mall, or who are employed to do occasional repairs and maintenance work at hotels in the city.

On a more intimate level, the idea of discipline presupposes that a novitiate must fulfil a series of duties and obligations and comply with the day-to-day exigencies of the gang, whatever these may be. There is one responsibility in particular that is worth mentioning: it is the duty of the novitiate to 'clean the house'. In *kampung* Malang, youth gangs occupy small barracks, shacks and abandoned homes. These squat settlements are scattered all over the neighbourhood and symbolise the possession of a specific territory; they are considered as the headquarters of the gang and are usually the place where gang members congregate to hang out during the day. Their inhabitants keep these informal and precarious settlements as neat and tidy as possible. The walls are plastered with pictures of relatives and friends who have lived in the same area, as well as with newspaper articles about police raids and local thugs. Bottles, drinks, glasses and snacks are arranged on the small tables which are made out of carton cases and boxes; there is also an old mattress or a couch of some sort to accommodate gang members when they meet. New gang members are usually in charge of keeping the place cosy and comfortable: they wash the dishes, wipe the floor and decorate the room with second-hand materials. While novitiates take care of the gang's home, older gang members usually assemble to play chess or gamble. During these activities new members act as maids (they are ironically referred to as the *pembantu*, the housemaids) and cook and serve meals to other gang members.

New gang members rarely leave their squat unsupervised, as they first have to become familiar with the perimeter of the gang's territory. For this reason, they are chaperoned around the area by the older gang members who show the posts and landmarks that define their territory and point out the areas where the gang operates. New gang members are usually required to memorise and be able to name all these spots.

Discipline is also manifest in the way a gang member carries himself and walks along a neighbourhood alley. In fact, gang members are required to walk in single file and march through the neighbourhood alleyways like miniature soldiers. The idea of walking in single file[3] along the narrow stretched out spaces of the neighbourhood alleyways serves several purposes simultaneously, some practical, some symbolic. First, by positioning themselves in a line, gang members are able to move easily through tight, otherwise impracticable, interstices; second, by treading noisily, they announce their presence and are recognised by the community at large. Also, by walking in line, gang members reiterate the gang's internal hierarchy, as gang leaders usually march in front of the line: in many cases gang members are able to recite the full sequence of names that make up an entire line, and this is all the more impressive as positions, just like statuses, change frequently. To know the names of gang members enhances the self-perception of single gang members and their sense of identity: as many say, "in a line you always know who you are". Moreover, by proceeding in a line, gang members meet the need to avoid backtracking (*mundur*), as they maintain that in a line somebody is always watching somebody else's back.

Curiously, there is an inherent element of ambiguity that seems to characterise the notion of discipline. As implied by numerous gang members, because a gang's configuration might change a lot over a short period of time, it is not always easy to trust a novitiate's commitment to the group. While walking in a line, then, they are torn between the confidence that "somebody always has your back", unconditionally, and the doubt that that same somebody "might stab you in the back".

Across the river: making money and construction sites
Youths do not just look beyond the river, as their fathers and uncles do. They cross the river and explore the city in search of new possibilities and money. While the city looks chaotic to them, this element of disorder does not discourage them from travelling across the bridge.

Gang members flock to the city streets to be close to where they believe the circulation of money to be. This is an important aspect of gang life, one that is perhaps less captivating than those stories of games of territory and honour but that nevertheless provides useful insights in the day-to-day experiences and interactions of youths in this area. In fact, aside from marking their own turf, these young teenagers and adolescents work hard to make a living. Against the regulations of neoliberal urban projects, youths find a way to enter the urban informal sector and make sense of their everyday life experience. A variety of money-generating activities on the streets includes busking, begging, petty trade in magazines and papers or other cheap goods, acting as brokers for people who are looking for more expensive goods, trash-picking, pedalling *becak* (pedicabs), and selling parking vouchers.

One of the jobs that most youths aspire to is to become a driver. Such desire says a lot about the need for youths to be a part of the city, and what better way to integrate into a system based on the idea of unimpeded circulation than by becoming a part of the circulation itself? (Or, as one taxi driver once pointed out with subtle irony, what better way to integrate into a system based on traffic than by becoming the traffic itself?) The tension between the fear of being lost in the maze, as expressed earlier by Joko, contrasts with the desire of the young men to become a part of the city. Becoming a part of the space through its everyday production is reminiscent of Harvey's (2012) notion that the "city is an object of utopian desire, as a distinctive place of belonging within a perpetually shifting spatio-temporal order" (p. xvii). Within this spatial context, taxi drivers are held in high esteem, but it is virtually impossible for adolescents to obtain a licence and collect the money to pay the deposit for the taxi. Bus and micro-bus drivers are less exalted: this is mostly due to the fact that they do not own the vehicle they are driving and work as mere employees. Below them comes the people who work collecting fares from riders (called *konduktor* on city buses and *kernet* on micro-buses). Not all drivers have *kernet*, though most of the time a male passenger will volunteer in the middle of the bus route, by getting aboard and start acting the part, hanging out of the door to call for potential riders and collecting money from passengers before they get off (Brown, 2009, p. 181). This is a small job that many youths try to snatch up on a regular basis. They either know the bus driver and arrange with him to jump on the bus at a certain stop, or they feel entitled to extract fees from bus riders when the bus crosses through an area that constitutes the gang's territory. Often gang members get off after riding for a while and wait for another bus to come by. There is an inherent element of fun in riding the bus all day, and in moving from one place to another.

Concluding remarks: a comparative look at urban change and personal growth
It emerges from research in Surabaya that youths always return home or proudly affirm that it is their intention to do so. While attempting to connect with the new urban landscape of

Urban Transformations, Work and Social Solitude

opportunities that is Surabaya, they also reveal the strong bond that ties them to their neighbourhood village.

The older men of *kampung* Malang envision a present and a future of uncertainty and experience a sense of disquiet. There seems to be little work available by the river, and the networks of friendship and socialisation that sustain the practice of work seem to have weakened. These men can hardly find any physical spot to come together and exchange knowledge, practical skills and information about work. Overall, they experience a sense of disconnection towards the city at large and towards the new middle class: they feel they occupy a marginal position in relation to the flow of goods, people and vehicles that traverse the city with unbroken continuity. They feel they live at the margins of opportunities and cannot fully integrate into the new geography of the urban space. Their view towards life is quite pessimistic and many feel lonely and isolated. As they seem to suffer the consequences of urban and social change, they also worry about the younger generation of *kampung* men: they question the success of their sons' and grandsons' transition towards adult life. The city feels unknown and there is a diffused perception that those who dare to explore the city streets may take a dangerous route and become too vulnerable. Some go as far as saying that men and their sons are drifting apart.

Among the younger generation of men of *kampung* Malang, many youths have embraced urban and social change and have found a niche to experiment with work and social relations. Niches are crucial to explore ways to rethink the subject's position in a context of neoliberal change and to show how social actors adapt to change. I have presented here the case of those youths who seek membership of street gangs and enter the world of the informal economy while developing a sense of solidarity, mutual help and discipline. These young men adapt to social change and find their own path towards adult life while reiterating the importance of local social institutions. In this sense, youth street gangs clearly offer a recreational outlet for those who seek to make friends in the narrow alleys of *kampung* Malang, but more importantly a gang is where a youth learns how to make a living, how to find a job through the help of friends and gang companions and ultimately begins to form ideas about self-sufficiency. In doing so, these young gang members situate their life experience in symbolic continuity with the legacy and the experiences of their fathers and grandfathers, and recognise work and social aggregation as the foundation of a fully fledged masculine identity. These young men do not feel as though they are drifting apart from the world of social values and practices that have historically characterised life in the *kampung*. On the contrary, they draw inspiration from that social milieu while at the same time adjusting to a new landscape of opportunities and creatively attempting to shape their own life. This is indicative of how neoliberalism, as a process, attempts to shape, legitimate, restrict and monitor movement within the urban spaces (Brenner & Theodore, 2010). The consequence of this, however, is a proliferation of geographies that are situated and historicised within a particular legacy. The everyday experience of youths in *kampung* Malang sheds light on the vitality and salience of social values and institutions among local communities in an Indonesian city in a climate of urban economic and social change. Such vitality is also what prompted the following consideration by Ananta, 17 years old and Joko's son:

> My dad always tells me that pigeons only know how to fly when raised and trained by their owners: they have to learn how to return home once they are set free in the open air, they have to know the right trajectory, they have to know where to go: it's not enough for them to be strong and quick. He says that it's hard to train a pigeon these days, that even men can barely recognise the streets of this land. My dad looks sad. I tell him what he always taught me, that pigeons are intelligent, ingenious, that they know their way home even in the

chaos of the rooftops and barracks, and that they are smart enough to move around in groups. I tell him not to worry.

While the integration of *kampung* Malang and Surabaya into regional and global orders and the restructuring of local spaces and streets have had a profound impact on the local practice of male socialisation and on the formation of local subjectivities, ethnography shows how young men have carved out spaces to rethink their present and future by continuing to establish a connection with a specific cultural, social and economic milieu. The relevance of conducting ethnography in a context of neoliberal practices lies precisely in the understanding of the ways that neoliberal ideologies impact on the intimate lives of people and restructure their perceptions of society and social relations. At the same time, such a perspective offers an insight into the ways social actors reflect upon their doubts and fears and continue to inhabit the social niches that they have created for themselves.

Notes

1. When I first visited *kampung* Malang I was not aware of the fact that, under numerous pseudonyms, it had been the subject of scholarly work in the field of sociology and urban development studies. In particular, the seminal study of Robbie Peters provides rich and detailed information about the political, economic and urban changes that have occurred in the area in the past 20 years. Throughout this chapter I make constant reference to this body of work and rely heavily on information provided by the author to substantiate the sociological texture of my research (see Peters, 2009, 2010, 2013). All names used in this article are pseudonyms to protect the identity of my informants. In addition, life history details are altered or purposely left imprecise to maintain anonymity of the individuals.
2. All words in italics are Indonesian terms.
3. A similar idea is evoked by street children and homeless youths interviewed by Brown (2009) to describe movement through thin alleys.

References

Blackwood, E. (2010). *Falling into the lesbi world: Desire and difference in Indonesia*. Honolulu, HI: University of Hawai'i Press.

Brenner, N. & Theodore, N. (2010). Neoliberalism and the urban condition. *City: Analysis of Urban Trends, Culture, Theory, Policy, Action, 9*(1), 101–107.

Brenner, S. (1998). *The domestication of desire: Women, wealth, and modernity in Java*. Ithaca, NJ: Princeton University Press.

Brown, S. C. (2009). *Streets and children in Surabaya*. Ann Arbor, MI: Proquest, UMI Dissertation Publishing.

Chambers, R. (1983). *Rural development: Putting the last first*. London, United Kingdom: Longman.

Freeman, C. (2001). Is local: Global as feminine: masculine? Rethinking the gender of globalization. *Signs, 26*(4), 1007–1037.

Geertz, H. (1961). *The Javanese family. A study of kinship and socialization*. Prospect Heights, IL: Waveland Press.

Harvey, D. (2003). *The new imperialism*. Oxford, United Kingdom: Oxford University Press.

Harvey, D. (2012). *Rebel cities: From the right to the city to the urban revolution*. London, United Kingdom: Verso Books.

Kristiansen, S. (2003). Violent youth groups in Indonesia: The cases of Yogyakarta and Nusa Tenggara Barat. *Sojourn: Journal of Social Issues in Southeast Asia, 18*(1), 110–138.

Nasir, S. (2006). *Stories from the lorong: Drug subculture and the social context of HIV-risk behaviours among intravenous drug users in Makassar, Indonesia*. Unpublished thesis, Master of Women's Health (by research). Key Centre for Women's Health in Society, School of Population Health, University of Melbourne, Melbourne.

Nasir, S. & Rosenthal, D. (2009). The social context of initiation into injecting drugs in the slums of Makassar, Indonesia. *International Journal of Drug Policy, 20*, 237–243.

Ortner, S. B. (2005). Subjectivity and cultural critique. *Anthropological Theory, 5*(1), 31–52.

Peters, R. (2009). The assault on occupancy in Surabaya: Legible and illegible landscapes in a city of passage. *Development and Change, 40*(5), 903–925.

Peters, R. (2010). The wheels of misfortune: The streets and cycles of displacement in Surabaya, Indonesia. *Journal of Contemporary Asia, 40*(4), 568-588.

Peters, R. (2013). *Surabaya, 1945-2010: Neighbourhood, state and economy in Indonesia's city of struggle.* Singapore: NUS Press.

Wilson, I. D. (2010). 'The streets belong to who?': 'Governance' and the urban informal sector in Jakarta, Indonesia. In *The elephant in the room: Politics and the development problem*, Asia Research Centre Policy Monograph (pp. 113-133). Perth, Australia: Murdoch University Asia Research Centre.

CHAPTER NINE

NEOLIBERALISING MOSTAR: GOVERNMENTALITY,
ETHNO-NATIONAL DIVISION AND EVERYDAY
FORMS OF RESISTANCE

Giulia Carabelli and Rowan Lubbock

Introduction: Neoliberal geopolitics in the Balkans
For many people, thinking about the Balkans conjures up scenes of horrific warfare, ethnic violence and broken communities. Of course, these ruminations tend to situate themselves in the early 1990s, when such scenes from the former Yugoslavia were flooding the cognitive space of Western media consumers. The academic world was similarly deluged with horror stories of an incomprehensible sort – *Balkan Babel* (Ramet, 1992); *Balkan Ghosts* (Kaplan, 1993); *Yugoslav Inferno* (Mojzes, 1995); *Slaughterhouse: Bosnia and the Failure of the West* (Rieff, 1996); *Rape Warfare: The Hidden Genocide in Bosnia-Herzegovina and Croatia* (Allen, 1996). The legal scholar Theodore Geshkoff once noted that, "[t]he Balkans are usually reported to the outside world only in time of terror and trouble; the rest of the time they are scornfully ignored" (cited in Todorova, 2009, p. 184). As Maria Todorova notes, Geshkoff's comment is as applicable now as it was then. Indeed, barring the recent citizen protests against government policy on travel (June 2013) and workers' struggles over unemployment (February 2014), Bosnia Herzegovina has barely scraped the surface of the international media since the signing of the Dayton Peace Agreements in 1995.

The seemingly inexplicable rupture in 'the Balkans' had also produced an ideological perforation articulated as the resurgence of old conceptions of the Near East. At the same time, the end of the Cold War had, according to Robert Kaplan, led to the loss of geography, or at least our sense of it:

Neoliberalising Mostar

> For suddenly we were in a world in which the dismantling of a man-made boundary in Germany had led to the assumption that all human divisions were surmountable; that democracy would conquer Africa and the Middle East as easily as it had Eastern Europe; that globalization – soon to become a buzzword – was nothing less than a moral direction of history and a system of international security, rather than what it actually was, merely an economic and cultural stage of development. (Kaplan, 2012, pp. 3–4)

How, then, to account for the Balkans' split from the West during a historical moment in which geopolitical boundaries were becoming obsolete? This contradictory phenomenon could be understood as a type of geographical imaginary – a form of discourse that seeks to render contradictory social dynamics as essentially coherent and intelligible (Jessop & Oosterlynck, 2008). The multiplication of social fissures unleashed by the class project of *neoliberalism* (the *socio-political* core of 'globalisation') helped to produce a multiplicity of what Desai (2006) calls 'cultural nationalisms' which seek to normalise the terrain of social inequality and depredation. In the context of Bosnia Herzegovina, as many have argued (for example, Samary, 1995; Petras & Vieux, 1996; Brown, 1997; Gowan, 1999; Hudson, 2003), the central lever that led to Yugoslavia's implosion was the Washington-backed economic reforms of the 1980s, which promised a new path to unity and peace, yet merely exacerbated a multitude of societal fractures. The attempted resolutions of these geopolitical fractures were increasingly addressed through a form of *neoliberal geopolitics*, the specificity of which lies in the fact that, while the Cold War logic rested on one of exclusion and polarisation, the neoliberal era is premised on a fundamental re-integration of those parts of the world that lie outside the circuits of capital accumulation (Roberts, Secor, & Sparke, 2003).

While this type of statecraft often assumes a military role,[1] neoliberal geopolitics also emerges in subtler and more invisible forms of geopolitical 'reconnection'. The relationship between the European Union (EU) and Bosnia Herzegovina (BiH) during the post-Dayton period is a striking case in point, and helps to shed light on why BiH no longer tends to elicit the attention it once did even while it struggles under conditions of *persistent social crisis*. In order to shed light on these dynamics, the chapter will first review Michel Foucault's work on the subjectivity of neoliberalism in order to understand how its various contradictions are made socially comprehensible. Secondly, we will critically engage with Henri Lefebvre's notion of *heterotopia*, which as Harvey (2012) notes is radically different from Foucault's own ideas on this concept. For while Foucault approaches heterotopia as spaces of irreconcilable 'otherness', Lefebvre views these 'other spaces' as potentially liberatory practices emerging "out of what people do, feel, sense, and come to articulate as they seek meaning in their daily lives" (Harvey, 2012, p. xvii). Thus, while Foucault's notion of neoliberal subjectivity goes some way to capturing the post-war dynamics of Mostar, we find Lefebvre's heterotopic thinking as a key cipher in the reading of grassroots strategies and imaginaries that seek to go beyond the discipline of neoliberalism and the division of ethno-national identity. It is, in fact, within Foucault's somewhat neglected concept of *counter-conduct* that it becomes possible to find common currency between the two thinkers' understanding of everyday resistance(s). It is hoped that from the conceptual frameworks of both Foucault and Lefebvre we will be able to dissect the sinews of power that flow between the various actors (both elite and subaltern) involved in the tormented dance of EU-BiH relations.

Contours of global governmentality

At the moment of the post Cold War order – what George Bush Sr. famously called the 'new world order' – we find not merely a new set of material reconfigurations, but also a particular array of discursive and ideational signifiers. As Bush's Secretary of State, James Baker, explained to an audience at the Aspen Institute in 1991, "[w]e must begin to extend the trans-Atlantic community to Central and Eastern Europe and to the Soviet Union". But Baker was clear as to the nature of this possible 'trans-Atlantic' extension:

> the trans-Atlantic relationship stands for certain Enlightenment ideals *of universal applicability*. These values are based upon the concept of individual political rights and economic liberty rooted in European ideals of the 17th and 18th centuries and first planted in the new American nation. (Baker, 1991 emphasis added)

Baker's comments help to underscore the lines of discourse underwriting the emergent neoliberal geopolitics of the US 'hyper-power', which saw its manifest destiny in the universalist project of transforming disconnected locations into an integrated space of global capital. This discursive formation, which Gowan (2001) referred to as 'neoliberal cosmopolitanism', engenders a certain disciplinary logic in which the standards of statehood and economic reform (whose features are often indistinguishable) are subject to the authority of those states within the capitalist core.

These aspects of neoliberal governance outlined by Gowan were first brought to light with the work of Michel Foucault, who sought to identify the contours of power that gave life to a historically specific regime of discipline. Foucault was interested in how the techniques and repertoires of *governmentality* changed over time, particularly in relation to the societal shift from Fordist to post-Fordist modes of governance. In his lectures delivered at the *Collège de France* between 1978 and 1979, Foucault introduced a genealogy of neoliberalism, the specificity of which was not in calculation and rationality per se (as these are indeed what distinguish classical liberalism as a historically distinctive set of governmental practices) but in the internalisation of bourgeois calculation by each individual, who transforms into a private 'entrepreneur' within every aspect of their lives (Foucault, 2008). Here the mechanism of competition obtains directly between individuals, and is established by way of re-conceptualising the notion of individual work itself in terms of seeing human beings as machine-like entities imbued with a set of functional skills that can be (self) exploited in various contexts (Foucault, 2008, p. 224). This relates fundamentally to Foucault's general understanding of power and discipline in the modern era (*biopower*) as one that transcends negative forms of prohibition into modes of power that *enable and give specific agency to individuals*. Endowing individuals with this (neoliberal) agency at once frees and constrains their possible modes of living by forming the strategic field of action beyond which a given agent will find only penalties or 'costs'. In a sense, the neoliberal regime becomes the ultimate expression of 'self government' (Read, 2009).

The formation of *neoliberal subjectivity* therefore becomes a central component for understanding not just the performativity (and therefore effectivity) of neoliberal(ised) societies, but also the contradictions, contingencies and struggles that go into the *process of subject formation* itself. Approaching the problem from this angle helps to mediate between the seemingly pervasive field of power relations bound up with neoliberal governmentality, and the potentials contained within counter-strategies. Foucault's approach to social theory seems to largely fall within the former of these two angles (though more on this below). Indeed, many authors remain highly critical of Foucault's virtual relegation of subjective autonomy from his theory of social practices (see Smart, 1982; Freundlieb, 1994; Newman, 2005, pp. 42ff.), or the short shrift he gives to the possibility of emancipatory practices (see Simons, 1995, pp. 59–67) – although given the breadth of his work, such criticisms may sometimes seem more salient than they really are (see Bevir, 1999). Indeed, only now is Foucault's key notion of 'counter-conduct' beginning to come to light into scholarly circles (cf. Odysseos, Death, & Malmvig, 2016). This term was only briefly addressed in one of Foucault's lectures on 'Security, Territory, Population', on the topic of pastoral power and its historical crystallisation at the dawn of "Western and Eastern" Christianity (Foucault, 2007, p. 196). For Foucault, such forms of counter-conduct are distinct from strictly 'political' or 'economic' struggles, as (respectively) "revolts against power exercised by a form of sovereignty", or those struggles that challenge modes of "exploitation" (Foucault, 2007). Rather, the revolt against what he termed 'the conduct of conduct', is at an immediate level more nebulous, in referring merely to the "struggle against the processes implemented for conducting others" (Foucault, 2007, p. 201). However, as Davidson (2011) points out, Foucault never brought this term to bear on his discussions on neoliberalism in *The Birth of Biopolitics*, which thus leaves a relative gap between the suggestive contours of counter-conduct and his quite substantial explication on the power relations constitutive of neoliberal subjectification (p. 37). It should be noted that Foucault did not render the idea of counter-conduct as merely a fleeting moment of resistance; for although there is a certain immediacy implied by revolts against dominant practices, "In actual fact they are always, or almost always, linked to other conflicts and problems" that transect political and economic terrains of struggle (Foucault, 2007, p. 196). Nevertheless, it is difficult to parse any *substantial* approach of everyday forms of resistance in Foucault. In contrast, the work of Henri Lefebvre, in particular his concept of 'heterotopia', helps to fill in some of the gaps left by a Foucauldian analysis of social movements and grassroots agency. Though Foucault also dabbled with the concept of heterotopia (Foucault, 1986), his usage was (as many scholars have noted) somewhat unsystematic in its elaboration (Harvey, 2000, pp. 537–538; Hook, 2007, p. 182; Saldanha, 2008). Lefebvre's usage, on the other hand, offers a way out of the all-encompassing network of neoliberal disciplines by revealing the often-invisible yet highly creative and spontaneous instances of bottom-up organisation and resistance.

Thus, as we will see, Mostar's urban dynamics can be understood as encompassing a tense interplay between ethno-national 'isotopies' – "places of identity, identical places" – and subversive 'heterotopies' – "the other place, the place of the other" (Lefebvre, 2003, p. 128). In this sense, the production of neoliberal subjectivities in Bosnia Herzegovina generally (and Mostar in particular) reveals the variegated ways in which the performance of neoliberal subject-hood (the abstract self-entrepreneur) becomes complicated through ethno-national identity and authority on the one hand, and the more radical spaces of resistance to such disciplinary devices on the other, each of which reveals the often significant gap between the totalising discourse of *neoliberalism* and the concrete realities constitutive of complex processes of *neoliberalisation* (cf. Peck & Theodore, 2012).

The above considerations further prompt us to inquire into multiple *scales* through which neoliberal discourse and discipline unfolds. Whether in the more global terms of Gowan's neoliberal cosmopolitanism, or in respect to the many localised instances of neoliberal restructuring (Swyngedouw, Moulaert, & Rodriguez, 2002; LeBaron, 2010), it is clear that the formation of neoliberal subjectivity will be sensitive to the spatial and scalar specificities of discourses, forms of authority and discipline, and political practices. In other words, global or international vectors of neoliberal governance/authority will significantly shape more localised processes, and vice versa. Such a multi-scalar approach to neoliberalism again speaks directly to the specific case of Bosnia Herzegovina with respect to how the 'international community' (or rather, the US/EU complex) both negotiated and imposed a particular set of ideological imaginaries and political practices on to Bosnia's post-war settlement, while local actors simultaneously shaped and moulded such directives around their own specific interests and practices.

Spaces of neoliberalism: between Utopia and heterotopia
In order to understand the divergence in ideas, discourses and practices between various agents involved in BiH-EU relations, it is important to recall the basic discursive formations that permeated such relations. In strikingly Foucauldian terms, then US Deputy Secretary of State Strobe Talbott proclaimed in 1996 that, "In an increasingly interdependent world, Americans have a growing interest in how other countries govern, or misgovern, themselves" (cited in Chandler, 1999, p. 27). The type of governance Talbott had in mind was, with respect to Bosnia, shared between both US and European elites, which in the end approximated much more closely to American neoliberalism. This typology of neoliberalism converged around issues of *negative freedom*, far more so than its European counterparts concerned with *positive freedom* (Bohle, 2006).[2] The EU's negative integration approach to its Eastern neighbours therefore assumed a distinctly Americanised geopolitical hue. Again, the discursive core of this geopolitical relationship rests upon a type of *utopianism*: whether in the form of James Baker's invocation of universalist Enlightenment ideals, or in Jeffery Sachs's vision of 'shock therapy' for the entire Eastern European region (Gowan, 1999, Chapter 9), these discourses present a field of knowledge/power that approximates Foucault's notion of *utopia*, which "present[s] society itself in a perfected form, or else society turned upside down, but in any case these utopias are fundamentally unreal spaces" (Foucault, 1986, p. 24). To draw out the lines of contradiction and contestation between international elites in the EU, and local elites and subaltern actors in BiH, the remaining sections will focus on the Bosnian city of Mostar as a way of drawing out the convergent and divergent practices of neoliberalism.

Neoliberalising Mostar: high representations and low politics
The aluminium firm, Aluminij Mostar, was one of BiH's most profitable enterprises.[3] During the war, the firm became a major site of military (and ethno-nationalist) conflict. It was a target of JNA (Yugoslav People's Army) attacks, and subsequently, a target of Croat nationalist aspirations looking to transform the company into a material support for ethnic homogenisation. Thus, while the pre-war composition of the workforce was around 44% Croat, 33% Bosniak and 23% Serb, by 2003 these proportions had changed to 93%, 3%, and 4%, respectively (Amnesty International, 2006, p. 46). Such exclusions occurred either indirectly through 'legal' formalities or directly through physical obstruction; the former via an absentee penalisation policy in which workers unable to reach the factory (through displacement or refugee status) were dismissed, while the latter occurred mostly between 1996 and 1998 when returning non-Croat workers were physically prevented from entering the plant, racially abused by security guards, and confronted by racially derogatory graffiti (Amnesty International, 2006, p. 47). An audit from the Office of the High Representative (OHR) into the privatisation process was heavily criticised due to the passive stance taken by the international community in relation to the Aluminij case, suggesting that, "these 'spontaneous' privatizations have been accepted as a *fait accompli* by the international community" (Donais, 2002, p. 8; see also Pugh, 2002).

Divergent discourses and practices also emerge within the realm of urban imaginaries. In 2003, the OHR reported that uniting Mostar's six municipalities into one was indispensable for the goal of "attract[ing] an ever-larger volume of foreign direct investment and domestic investment" (OHR; cited in Carabelli, 2012, p. 113). Ultimately, the report hinged on a functionalist understanding of 'normal life' in Mostar (institutional unification), which could only be achieved through external interventions. Yet deeper discursive currents reveal an added layer of ideological assumptions on behalf of European elites. While noting that the people of Mostar want a normal city, organised according to normal and widely accepted European standards, the general framing of 'the people' took on a somewhat negative, or 'passive', resonance, in which the very agency of the citizenry was premised upon the external implementation of legal-institutional normality – without the EU, Mostarians could not live (the good life).

These renderings of a (silent) citizenry recalls Agamben's (1996, pp. 30-34) reflections upon the nature of the word 'people' in Western politics and its "amphibolous" nature. In contemporary European languages, 'people' translates simultaneously into a functionally equivalent political subject, and the category of those belonging to lower social classes.[4] Thus, *the People* represent a coherent and formally homogenous 'body politic' (citizens with equal rights and responsibilities); at the same time, *the people* become an amorphous multitude of subaltern classes characterised by their dependency, weakness and exclusion. This double-meaning of 'people' is constructed along the same categories that define, according to Agamben, contemporary (bio)politics: *zoe* (people/bare life) and *bios* (People/political subjectivity). Thus, the term 'people' contains a fundamental fracture – subjects that cannot properly belong to a whole of which they are already a part (see Carabelli, 2012, pp. 118-119).

When analysing the politics and practices of neoliberalism, one must be careful not to imbue a decidedly conscious and predetermined set of strategies upon actors, even those within the neoliberal 'heartland'. As Dardot and Laval (2013, p. 149) note, the analysis must rest squarely upon "a certain 'logic of practices'", within the unfolding of which various agents begin to crystallise and make sense of the wider implications of a political conjuncture. Only from this angle can we make sense of the interaction between elites at the EU and urban level (Mostar).

The road to (neo)liberal governance had to meander through the contours of ethnic division, which compelled both local and international elites to improvise as their conditions of action dictated. The force of unintended consequences cannot, therefore, be underemphasised. If ethno-national war can be seen through the prism of BiH's uneven development in a world system dominated by neoliberal geopolitics, then the post-conflict politics of both international and local elites must be seen as an array of scattered practices that congeal around a common denominator of disciplining the Bosnian citizenry to the logic of economic 'rationality'. Whether that rationality flows predominantly through a framework of ethnic belonging or the 'entrepreneurial spirit' will depend on the socially specific actors involved. Of note is the international community's turn to forms of societal 'resilience'. Disillusioned with the promises of liberal state-building, international elites have now turned to civil society directly as the cipher for post-conflict resolution. Yet such interventions, which may indeed empower certain civil society actors to variously positive effects, generally ignore the larger array of power relations that constitute the field of social antagonism(s) (see Chandler, 2013). A closer look at some of the counter-strategies employed by civil society groups in Mostar helps to reveal these deeper cleavages.

Spaces of heterotopia and everyday forms of resistance
Revealing the (often hidden) contours of resistance against ethno-nationalist divisions in BiH requires a shift of focus to civil society actors that are primarily defined by their relative externality to official political institutions (see Jeffrey, 2013, pp. 107–129). Electoral participation rarely strays from the confines of ethnic identity, while many grassroots organisations obtain their non-nationalist identity formation by actively breaking with such formal channels of political participation, which are often seen as having been historically constructed as a means of excluding non-ethnic or 'Yugoslav' politics (Touquet

& Vermeersch, 2008). Yet these subaltern actors are still trapped in a contradictory position vis-à-vis the dynamics of everyday life. In Mostar, in response to political stagnancy (since 2008, the city has been without an administration because the elected representatives proved unable to decide on the reform of the electoral system, judged as unconstitutional in 2010), the high levels of unemployment, and the bureaucratic burden (legacy and side effect of the power-sharing system), it is common to hear the off-hand remark delivered with a cynical fatalism, "Hey! It's Mostar!" The exclamation signifies the everyday dysfunction of the city which manifests itself along complex ethnic and political dynamics as well as a sardonic and dismissive attitude towards these dynamics that are often overcome through critical and flexible practices enmeshed in everyday life. Thus, citizens are aware of their ethno-national position within the city and they often behave accordingly, partially reproducing such a division; yet everyday movements and actions are not dictated or limited by these divisions. For instance, in 2010, the city offered a few bursaries for university students, which were allocated according to ethnic quotas. In other words, students must have declared their ethnicity to be considered for financial help. Those who struggle to identify with one group because of their parents' different ethnicities or because of their refusal to participate in ethnic-politics, had to decide whether to declare their belonging to an ethnic group (and benefit from financial aid) or to refuse to do so and become unable to submit their applications. Ines, whose parents are Croat and Serb, has been very vocal about taking actions against ethnic politics and never declared her own ethnicity, even when asked during interviews. Yet, she submitted her application as a Serb. In her own words, this did not change her political stand against identity politics in Mostar, but rather it made her even more passionate about the cause as it shows the violence that the system perpetrates on the citizens. Ines needed the financial help to continue her studies and so she decided to become Serb temporarily as a way of navigating the system, although this did not change her political views and activism.[5]

These everyday deviations from the proscribed norm are more than simply random fluctuations against a 'given' social logic. From Henri Lefebvre's perspective, social reality is constituted not merely through social relations and practices, but by *spatial relations and spatial practices*. Thus, in his 'spatial triad' construct, Lefebvre makes note of the tendency of various social classes to predominantly engage in one particular 'moment' of spatial production, even though all three moments are constantly in play.[6] By and large, dominated, or subaltern, actors will tend to engage with 'spaces of representation', which involve variously subversive practices relative to those norms constructed by ruling elites (Lefebvre, 1991, p. 33). As a way of exploring this subaltern space in the context of Mostar, this section will focus on a segment of the activities designed by Abart. This is a platform for art production and urban research active in Mostar since 2009. It was born from the desire to create an alternative narrative for Mostar, not only as the site of ethnic hatred, but rather as the catalyst for grass roots resistance against nationalisms and ethnic divisions. The art collective focusses on the rehabilitation of public space as a means to re-create places for critical dialogue among the citizens. If before the conflict squares and streets were the main sites of socialisation in Mostar, after the war and as a consequence of widespread privatisation practices, they became empty or neglected spaces. Abart works with international and local artists to design participatory projects and site-specific performances that could reflect on the ongoing privatisation of the city that is often hidden by discussions addressing the negative effects of ethnic segregation as the main (and only) problem of Mostar.

'(Re)collecting Mostar' started in October 2010 as a collaborative project developed with students from both universities in Mostar. The initiative wanted to further Abart's investigation into the status and usage of public spaces in Mostar. The project looked at the relationship between public space and public memories to bring back the memories of inter-ethnic social life and account critically for what the city has lost in the post-war scenario. Research into the city archive gave the participants an idea about how the city looked before its destruction and the location of the main social venues. Additional interviews were conducted with older generations of citizens to gather first-hand memories about past urban social life. The material accumulated became the main resource for invited artists and participating students to design a series of art interventions in public spaces. These artworks would share the produced knowledge with a wider public (by reinterpreting it) and also create a joyful moment (and space of encounter) to reflect upon the (problematic) present of Mostar. In doing so, these works created heterotopic spaces in which an alternative to the present of divisions and segregation could be imagined and performed – even if for a few days only.

Boris Orenčuk was one of the students participating in the project. As a contribution, he designed a site-specific installation for a ruined building on the Bulevar (the former buffer zone and internal border). The project, titled *Individualna Radna Akcija 1* (Individual Working Action Number 1), created a utopian space of beauty and *normalcy* within a ruin. The artist spent days cleaning the basement of the building of debris and garbage, then dressed an existing window with red curtains and placed a flower pot in front of it. In fact, the title of his project makes direct reference to what in Yugoslavia was called *radna akcija* – working action – a collective and volunteer effort to build infrastructures or to clean public domains. Young people were usually involved in such activities for the good of society. In the same ways, the artist polished the interior of the decaying building wondering whether we could all (again) work together for the benefit of society – a topic of particular relevance in a contested city. The result was visually uncanny, with the installation creating a visual imbalance between the beauty and colours of the curtain and flowers, and the dirtiness and ugliness of the premises.

Heterotopia as terrain of struggle: between state and civil society
While those working in and around Abart have consistently sought to disrupt dominant political understandings based around ethno-national belonging, there remained a certain limitation to the strategies employed. While these art interventions and other such creative measures (designed to inject a strand of critical thinking into civil society) could be paralleled with Lefebvre's notion of heterotopia – as the construction of other subaltern spaces in the course of struggle – there was an aspect underscored by Lefebvre that is crucially missing from Abart's repertoire of contention. As noted earlier in Harvey (2012, p. xvii), Lefebvre's heterotopia "delineates liminal social spaces of possibility where 'something different' is not only possible, but foundational for the defining of revolutionary trajectories". As an ongoing, evolving and active space of critical dialogue and civic inclusion, Abart represents a veritable heterotopia on the edges of Mostar's rigid mosaic of ethnic identities. However, Abart's strategy for social change tended to fall short with respect to the appropriate sites of struggle and contestation. Its overall view of counter-practices within the interstices of everyday life missed the central problem for any revolutionary force, in the confrontation with concentrated sources of power: *the state*. While Abart's many art interventions help to foster spaces of critical reflection, they do not directly address the political modalities required to achieve concrete change. This issue transcends discussions about Abart's operations by opening up the wider problem of the state/civil society relationship. While the hallmark of capitalist modernity rests on the *formal*

separation of politics and economics (state/civil society) in which the appropriation and execution of *class power* is functionally differentiated from *state power*, this dichotomy is merely an abstraction, an alienating image of reality of capitalist sociality that is in fact shot through with political force (Meiksins Wood, 1981). Whether seen through the coercive measures used to uphold property relations, or through the 'passive' use of legislative measures to regulate society, the state condenses society's wider struggles. And despite their differing conceptions of heterotopia, this critical view of the state-civil society relations was shared by Foucault and Lefebvre, with the former seeing the state apparatus as:

> not a universal nor in itself an autonomous source of power. The state is nothing else but the effect, the profile, the mobile shape of a perpetual stratification … in the sense of incessant transactions which modify … forms and types of control, relationships between local powers, the central authority, and so on. (Foucault, 2008, p. 77)

For Lefebvre, "Social relations, including contradictions that give rise to class struggles, explain the state, not the other way round" (cited in Elden, 2004, p. 217). Thus, while both thinkers saw the state as a relatively demarcated concentration of power relations, it was not somehow externally related to the society over which it governed, but merely represented the congealed site of society's contending groups and power capacities.

Lefebvre's heterotopia directly addresses the necessity of engaging the state as a means of realising a fuller role for *autogestion* (radical democracy). As he argued, "in a broader conception the modalities of *autogestion* may be proposed and imposed at all levels of social practice, including the agencies of coordination" (Lefebvre, [1966] 2009, p. 148). Thus:

> … with the State unable to coexist peacefully alongside radicalised and generalised *autogestion*, the latter must submit the former to 'grassroots' democratic control. The State of

autogestion, which is to say the State at whose core *autogestion* is raised to power, can only be a State that is withering away. (Lefebvre, [1966] 2009, p. 150)

In this way, the everyday practices of activists in Mostar could be understood as grassroots modes of *autogestion* that perceive the state as the site of their struggle. This comes back to the question over the appropriate scale at which struggle must take place with respect to *specific* socio-political goals. The space of Abart, as a *space of encounter*, represents a transnational network in which activists can share experiences that may help to form more coordinated modes of resistance against neoliberal rationality, both within and across state boundaries. At present, however, the relative limitation of Abart's strategic horizon amounts to a somewhat hybrid form of 'counter-conduct' coupled with important interventions into the construction of counter-hegemonic space(s).

Conclusion

As noted at the beginning of this chapter, Bosnia Herzegovina tends only to elicit the attention of the world when there is a full-blown crisis of a magnitude that cannot be easily ignored. It has been almost 20 years since the outbreak of war and the world's attention is now on the divided Balkan country of Bosnia once again. When protests erupted in 2013 over the role of bureaucracy in the issuing of ID cards, the notion of post-ethnic politics was suddenly a possible reality. The most recent citizen protests over the state of the economy are another powerful instance of potentially positive change. Beginning in the North-Eastern town of Tuzla, unemployed workers and a local activist group denounced the state of pensions, unpaid social contributions and the degradation of the quality of life in the town (*The Economist*, 2014a). With the anger directed at the general disarray that privatisation has inflicted on the economy and the fabric of everyday life, it is little wonder that the protests quickly spread throughout the country. Yet beyond the immediate anger of those taking to the streets, there is another development that may spell out a different political future:

> So far protesters have been resolutely anti-nationalist. Now something extraordinary is happening. Led by Tuzla, so-called 'plenums' of fed-up citizens, unemployed workers and intellectuals are springing up to make political demands. On February 11th elected members of Tuzla's cantonal assembly met its plenum to discuss the idea of a government of non-party experts. In the ethnically divided city of Mostar, Croats and Bosniaks are also working together in a plenum.
>
> If the plenums take root, if new leaders emerge and if they focus on realistic demands, something might really change. (*The Economist*, 2014b)

These struggles, which have begun to take on a much more explicit class character, represent a microcosm of the various themes addressed in this chapter. The logic of neoliberal governmentality is only ever just that – a 'logic' that has no embodied essence. The concrete struggles between various elite factions and subaltern actors creates a variegated terrain upon which neoliberal subjectivities will be constantly formed and reformed, yet never reflecting the 'pure' form contained within abstract parameters. Over a decade of ethno-nationalist divisions coupled with repeated attempts by European elites to transform Bosnia into a 'normal' European-type space has merely resulted in a type of capitalist privation that is articulated by divisive identities and social practices. Thus, Bosnia's permanent crisis had tended to become *normalised* to those viewing its political unfolding from afar, while such a normalisation of crisis effectively strips the country of its newsworthiness. The simultaneous work of various grassroots initiatives should not be excluded from this picture, but their strategies of resistance have always fallen short of the wider goal of national reconciliation. Struggling for civic inclusion within a space dominated by socio-political division is always a formidable task. The brief examination of Abart demonstrates the value of such subversive practices, but also the necessity of widening the strategy for urban unification for all citizens. Social movements must always traverse the 'inside/outside' of the state-civil society (false) dichotomy as a means of directly challenging the main apparatuses of power that seek to impose specific rationalities, benefiting only those elites who propagate them, while at the same time maintain their autonomy and freedom of action by actively building their own sites of heterotopic *autogestion*. Such practices resonate with Lefebvre's claim that "there are no ideas without a utopia" (1976, p. 34). The spaces of heterotopia that are opening up across the Bosnian landscape speak to this utopian imagining, in part recalling the old idea of Yugoslav 'community' combined with new ideas of participation and non-bureaucratic popular power. With the current conjuncture of citizen unrest, a vital opening has emerged in which these actors, with their years of organisational experience, can enter into the struggle for a more just, democratic and participatory society. Perhaps now is the moment in which the struggles of everyday life can be transformed and amplified into a truly *socio-political struggle* for Bosnia's future.[7]

Notes
1. For an extensive list of US military interventions during the post-Cold War era, see Hossein-Zadeh, 2006, p. 88.
2. Though even this goal of creating a more participatory and reciprocal political arrangement within the EU has faced innumerable obstacles and setbacks given the inherent contradictions between an elite-led regime of economic liberalisation and the requirements of citizenship (see Bailey, 2006).
3. Though as of June 2013 the company shut down operations completely due to adverse price movements in electricity and aluminium (http://www.aluminij.ba/en/news/624-shut-down-aluminij-dd-mostar-entirely-shuts-down-its-production-facilities).

4. For example, Agamben observes (1996, pp. 30–34) that in Abraham Lincoln's Gettysburg Address (1863), the invocation of a "Government of the people, by the people, and for the people" implicitly contains the ambiguity of the term "people" and what it signifies (see also, Blackburn, 2011, p. 41).
5. For an ethnographic sample of such practices, see Carabelli, 2012, Chapter. 6.
6. Lefebvre's spatial 'triad' consists of the following mutually constitutive elements: *representations of space* (**'conceived'** – abstract and generally elite-led cognitive constructs of how the social world operates); *spaces of representation* (**'lived'** – as the obverse side of elite-led and imposed representations, wherein the dynamics of everyday life emerge within complex constellations of symbols, social practices that are variably 'subversive' modes of life. The sum of which always tends to escape the strictures of elite domination and finite analysis); *spatial practices* (**'perceived'** – in which the combination of elite and everyday practices form into a coherent whole which allows the general structure of the relations of production and reproduction to maintain themselves for a certain historical duration) (see Lefebvre, 1991, p. 33).

References

Agamben, G. (1996). *Mezzi senza fine. Note sulla politica*, Turin, Italy: Bollati e Boringhieri.

Allen, B. (1996). *Rape warfare: The hidden genocide in Bosnia Herzegovina and Croatia*, Minneapolis, MN: University of Minnesota Press.

Amnesty International (2006). *Bosnia and Herzegovina behind closed gates: Ethnic discrimination in employment*. Retrieved from https://www.amnesty.org/download/Documents/76000/eur630012006en. pdf [Accessed 28 February 2017].

Bailey, D. J. (2006). Governance or the crisis of governmentality? Applying critical state theory at the European level. *Journal of European Public Policy*, 13(1), 16–33.

Baker, J. (1991, 18 June). Euro-Atlantic architecture: From West to East, Secretary Baker's address to the Aspen Institute, Berlin, Germany, June. Retrieved from http://www.2plus4.de/USA/ chronik.php3?date_value=18.06.91.&sort=000-000 [Accessed 13 March, 2017].

Bevir, M. (1999). Foucault and critique: Deploying agency against autonomy. *Political Theory, 27*(1), 65–84.

Blackburn, R. (2011). *An unfinished revolution: Karl Marx and Abraham Lincoln*. London, United Kingdom: Verso.

Bohle, D. (2006). Neoliberal hegemony, transnational capital and the terms of the EU's eastward expansion. *Capital & Class, 30*(1), 57–86.

Brenner, N. (2001). The limits to scale? Methodological reflections on scalar structuration. *Progress in Human Geography, 25*(4), 591–614.

Brown, M. B. (1997). The role of economic factors in social crisis: The case of Yugoslavia, *New Political Economy, 2*(2), 299–315.

Carabelli, G. (2012). *Readdressing Mostar: The architecture of everyday life* (Unpublished doctoral thesis). Queen's University Belfast, Belfast, United Kingdom.

Chandler, D. (1999). *Bosnia: Faking democracy after Dayton*. Stirling, VA: Pluto Press.

Chandler, D. (2013). International statebuilding and the ideology of resilience. *Politics, 33*(4), 276–286.

Dardot, P. & Laval, C. (2013). *The new way of the world: On neoliberal society* (Trans. G. Elliot). London, United Kingdom: Verso.

Davidson, A. I. (2011). In praise of counter-conduct. *History of the Human Sciences, 24*(4), 25–41.

Desai, R. (2006). Neoliberalism and cultural nationalism: A *danse macabre*. In D. Plehwe, B. Walpen, & G. Neunhöffer (Eds.), *Neoliberal hegemony: A global critique* (pp. 222–235). London, United Kingdom; New York, NY: Routledge.

Donais, T. (2002). The politics of privatization in post-Dayton Bosnia, *Southeast European Politics, III*(1), pp. 3–19.

Economist, The (2014a, 10 February). Spring in the Bosnian step. Retrieved from http://www.economist.com/blogs/eastern approaches/2014/ 02/bosnias-protests

Economist, The (2014b, 15 February). Protests in Bosnia: On fire. Retrieved from http://www.economist.com/news/europe/21596572-latest-troubles-bosnia-may-wake-up-countrys-inept-leaders-fire,

Elden, S. (2004). *Understanding Henri Lefebvre: Theory and the possible*, London, United Kingdom: Continuum.

Foucault, M. (1986). Of other spaces. *Diacritics, 16*(1), 22–27.

Foucault, M. (2007). *Security, territory, population: Lectures at the Collège de France, 1977–1978*. Basingstoke, United Kingdom: Palgrave Macmillan.

Foucault, M. (2008). *The Birth of biopolitics: Lectures at the Collège de France, 1978–1979*, New York, NY: Palgrave.

Freundlieb, D. (1994). Foucault's Theory of Discourse and Human Agency. In C. Jones & R. Porter (Eds.), *Reassessing Foucault: Power, medicine and the body* (pp. 152–179). London, United Kingdom; New York, NY: Routledge.

Gowan, P. (1999). *The global gamble*, London, United Kingdom: Verso.

Gowan, P. (2001). Neoliberal cosmopolitanism. *New Left Review, 2*(11), 79–93.

Harvey, D. (2000). Cosmopolitanism and the banality of geographical evils. *Public Culture, 12*(2), 529–564.

Harvey, D. (2012). *Rebel cities. From the right to the city to the urban revolution*. London, United Kingdom; New York, NY: Verso.

Hook, D. (2007). *Foucault, psychology and the analytics of power*. New York, NY: Palgrave.

Hossein-Zadeh, I. (2006). *The political economy of U.S. militarism*. New York, NY: Palgrave.

Hudson, K. (2003). *Breaking the south Slav dream: The rise and fall of Yugoslavia*. London, United Kingdom: Pluto Press.

Jeffrey, A. (2013). *The improvised state: Sovereignty, performance and agency in Dayton, Bosnia*. Chichester, United Kingdom: Wiley-Blackwell.

Jessop, B. & Oosterlynck, S. (2008). Cultural political economy: On making the cultural turn without falling into a soft economic sociology. *Geoforum, 39*(3), 1155–1169.

Kaplan, R. D. (1993). *Balkan ghosts: A journey through history*. New York, NY: Vintage Books.

Kaplan, R. D. (2013). *The Revenge of geography: What the map tells us about coming conflicts and the battle against fate*. New York, NY: Random House.

LeBaron, G. (2010). The political economy of the household: Neoliberal restructuring, enclosures, and daily life. *Review of International Political Economy, 17*(5), 889–912.

Lefebvre, H. (1976). Reflections on the politics of space. *Antipode, 8*(2), 30–37.

Lefebvre, H. ([1966] 2009). Theoretical problems of *autogestion*. In N. Brenner & S. Elden (Eds.), *State, space, world: Selected essays* (pp. 138–152. Minneapolis, MN: University of Minnesota Press.

Lefebvre, H. (1991). *The production of space*. Oxford, United Kingdom; Malden, MA: Blackwell.

Lefebvre, H. (2003). *The urban revolution*. Minneapolis, MN: University of Minnesota Press.

Meiksins Wood, E. (1981). The separation of the economic and the political in capitalism. *New Left Review, 1*(127), 66–95.

Mojzes, P. (1995). *Yugoslavian inferno: Ethnoreligious warfare in the Balkans*. London, United Kingdom: Continuum.

Newman, S. (2005). *Power and politics in poststructuralist thought: New theories of the political*. London, United Kingdom; New York, NY: Routledge.

Odysseos, L., Death, C., & Malmvig, H. (2016). Interrogating Michel Foucault's counter-conduct: Theorising the subjects and practices of resistance in global politics. *Global Society, 30*(2), 151–156.

Peck, J. & Theodore, N. (2012). Reanimating neoliberalism: Process geographies of neoliberalisation. *Social Anthropology, 20*(2), 177–186.

Petras, J. & Vieux, S. (1996). Bosnia and the revival of US hegemony. *New Left Review, I*(218), July-August, 3–35.

Pugh, M. (2002). Postwar political economy in Bosnia and Herzegovina: The spoils of peace. *Global Governance, 8*(4), 467–482.

Ramet, S. P. (1992). *Balkan Babel: The disintegration of Yugoslavia from the death of Tito to the fall of Milošević*. Boulder, CO: Westview Press.

Read, J. (2009). A genealogy of homo-economicus: Neoliberalism and the production of subjectivity. *Foucault Studies, 6*, 25–36.

Rieff, D. (1996). *Slaughter house. Bosnia and the failure of the West.* New York, NY: Touchstone.
Roberts, S., Secor, A., & Sparke, M. (2003). Neoliberal geopolitics. *Antipode, 35*(5), 886–897.
Saldanha, A. (2008). Heterotopia and structuralism. *Environment and Planning A, 40*(9), 2080–2096.
Samary, C. (1995). *Yugoslavia dismembered* (Trans. P. Drucker). New York, NY: Monthly Review Press.
Simons, J. (1995). *Foucault & the political.* New York, NY: Routledge.
Smart, B. (1982). Foucault, sociology, and the problem of human agency. *Theory and Society, 11*(2), 121–141.
Swyngedouw, E., Moulaert, F., & Rodriguez, A. (2002). Neoliberal urbanization in Europe: Large-scale urban development projects and the new urban agenda. *Antipode, 34*(3), 542–577.
Todorova, M. (2009). *Imagining the Balkans.* New York, NY: Oxford University Press.
Touquet, H. & Vermeersch, P. (2008). Bosnia and Herzegovina: Thinking beyond institution building. *Nationalism and Ethnic Politics, 14*(2), 266–288.

CHAPTER TEN

URBAN TRANSFORMATIONS IN PHNOM PENH:
CREATIVE COLLECTIVES, THE WHITE BUILDING
AND THE PRODUCTION OF SPACE

Jonathon Louth and Martin Potter

*It's not about blueprints, it's about successions;
it's not architecture, it's music.*
Roberto Unger (2014)

In this chapter we explore the evolving role of art and storytelling programmes in an inner-city building in Phnom Penh, Cambodia, known as the White Building.[1] This work represents a tentative exploration into a community of people and their history – their cultural work and their identity. We chart the history of the Building from the late 1950s, before focussing on art and storytelling programmes from 2008 to the present. The underpinning concept of the programmes under analysis has been around establishing a vision for communal transformation and then acting on that vision through an iterative process of action and reform. Within this setting, art and storytelling practices have become a way of articulating pluralistic modes of struggle in a post-conflict society that is dealing with the onset of a new neoliberal order of accumulation and dispossession. Importantly, these practices look both to the past and to the future. Our interests in these practices lie, in part, through applying a Lefebvrian lens to problematize the contested and dominated nature of the space within which these emergent forms of expression take place. We argue the possibility that the dominant discursive acts of the more powerful can be challenged through the expression of the 'lived' and the elevation of everyday life. Furthermore, we argue that the very perception of the space and the sense of place can be (re)produced through these alternative interactions. Indeed, it is hoped – if the emerging White Building community can hold off government interests and property developers – that current and future programmes play a role in transmitting an inclusive vision of a subaltern community as a form of resistance that comes from, but extends beyond the everyday (see Davies, 2016).

Contested space(s)
Henri Lefebvre's *Production of Space* (1991) has been repopularised and is increasingly applied to the study of neoliberalism and, in particular, to what might be termed the production of neoliberal spaces. Although Lefebvre never directly referred to neoliberalism and his focus was largely upon the 'production' of urban spaces, his ideas have re-emerged as a powerful interpretive analysis of how dominant capitalist practices and ideology are central to the political, social and economic relations that form space. Space, then, is relational – yet common perceptions of space are that it is an abstract notion within which human actions take place. Within this conception, space is simply a "dimension in which matter is located" or it is conceptualised as "a grid in which substantive items are contained" (Agnew, 2011, pp. 316–317; Harvey, 2001, pp. 121–125). The "matter" or the "substantive items" is that which is geometric and locatable within this dimension – or, put more simply: place. (Agnew, 2011). It is a fixed, linear and determinist notion of space (and place) within which interactions take place.

This abstracted notion of space has pedigree; it is, more or less, a Newtonian space. The predictive power that had been unleashed by Newtonianism informed the development of the social sciences. The newly created fields of sociology, political science and economics were particularly enamoured with the scientific and the magisterial influence of Newton (Louth, 2011). As Newtonian physics came to dominate, time and space became empty *abstract* categories; indeed, they became mere containers for events (Harvey, 1990). However, in the work of Lefebvre (and that of David Harvey, whom he influenced), there is a resounding rejection of the 'common-sense' view of Newtonian space:

> ... it is not simply an absolute dimension, an empty container within which socio-ecological processes operate. Instead, space is materially produced by different societies in different ways. (Castree, 2009, p. 32)

The absorption of Newtonian thought (along with Cartesian and Euclidian influences) into academic and popular discourse only furthered the production of 'objective' and 'scientific' space (Louth, 2011). Lefebvre overturned these notions, arguing that space "has always been political and strategic" and that it is "filled with ideologies" (1976, pp. 30–31). Moreover, he recognised that scientific method and procedure infiltrates mental space, which, in turn, comes to represent social space. This, Lefebvre quickly pointed out, becomes the "veil of ideology" (1991, p. 106) – and it is behind this veil that the social nature of space is hidden by ideological domination.

For Lefebvre, "(Social) space is a (social) product" (1991, p. 26). In justifying this assertion he posited a dialectical triad consisting of three dimensions: "spatial practice"; "representations of space"; and "representational space". He distilled this further to the "perceived-conceived-lived" (Lefebvre, 1991, pp. 33, 40).[2] However, it is the dynamic interrelationship between the dimensions – the push and pull of domination and resistance – that gives critical importance to the triad:

1. **Spatial practice** is the *perceived* space. This is where space is produced through formal, economic relations like the hierarchical organisation and the division of labour. It is also where it is socially reproduced through, for example, sexual relations, caring relations, family structures and unpaid domestic work. Production and social reproduction in this sense (Harvey, 1990; Elias & Louth, 2016), acts as a

glue that determines a level of continuity and cohesiveness (Lefebvre, 1991, pp. 33, 38). There is also a connection here with the international political economy of the everyday, where "[h]ow, what, and with whom we spend, save, invest, buy and produce in our ordinary lives shapes markets and the manner in which states intervene". The international political economy is a socially produced space and everyday lives are a part of what constitutes "the global economy in its multiple spatial dimension" (Hobson & Seabrooke 2006, pp. 3-4, 16). What is important here, is that the everyday is part of, and belongs to, the production of space (Merrifield, 1993, p. 523). Agency exists within this space, but it does so within the "repressive 'confines'" (Hobson & Seabrooke, 2006, p. 15) of the dominant social space. However remote, counter-hegemonic possibilities remain a possibility as is explored below.

2. **Representations of space** is the *conceived* space. Here order and ideology are tied to discursive practices; the "conceptualized space" of technocrats, professionals, scientists and the techno-bureaucracy (Lefebvre 1991, 1976; Merrifield, 1993). It is not difficult to bridge to Gramsci's ideas of the role of intellectuals in the production of hegemonic practices (Ekers & Loftus, 2013; Bates, 1975). This is the domain of capital and it plays a dominant role in the production of space (Merrifield, 1993). Here a 'pure' scientific and objective space is produced. In the same manner the town planner or architect appropriates scientific knowledge (Lefebvre, 1976), the absorption of neoliberal practices as 'common-sense' means that not only do the planners and architects of governmental institutions appropriate and absorb a similar language, but that an overarching economic ontology shapes and co-constitutes this space through multiple feedback mechanisms. Political and ideological imperatives drive our understanding of space. Ironically

space is relational, but this dominant space is *conceived* as abstract, linear and Newtonian. In short a Newtonian-inspired Western scientific economic ontology drives technocratic, administrative and pseudo-scientific discursive acts that define the dominant space (Louth, 2012).

3. **Representational spaces** are the *lived* spaces of images and symbols (Lefebvre, 1991). Culture, art, writing, philosophy occur here. Lefebvre did not relegate nor consider this space unimportant. Imagination, creativity and symbolism are distinguishable from, but, at the same time, belong to the physical and social space (Merrifield, 1993). It is a dominated space, yet, irrespective of its domination and its dialectical involvement in the production of space (particularly the space of the everyday), there is the capacity for novelty and emancipatory ideas. Lefebvre (1991) noted that this space of symbols and images "conceals more than it reveals", but still felt strongly "that there are no new ideas without a utopia" (1976, p. 35). This is a thought that indicates that the socially produced 'reality', the expansion and grind of capitalist domination could be overcome or, at the very least, mediated. Indeed, an important spatial consideration prior to any counter-hegemonic process is knowledge and the development of an alternative commonsense (Gill & Law, 1989).

It is with this conception of socially produced space that we will consider the space and place that is the White Building. At one level there is a totality to the breadth of productive and social forces that are at play (Harvey, 2001) and, importantly, we can understand them as scaled and penetrating into "every aspect of everyday life" (Charnock, 2010, p. 1296). We can see this in the White Building via attempts to redevelop the building, to evict the residents and to label them as undesirables. This is capitalist accumulation pure and simple; the ideologically dominant form of space empowers "often by violent means" attempts "to reduce ... obstacles and resistance" (Lefebvre, 1991, p. 49). The current Cambodian experience reveals a process of violent neoliberal accumulation under the guise of clean and order-inducing economic presuppositions. Yet the whole process of producing space is not a neat and linear set of affairs: there is a 'roughness' to the everyday that cannot be wholly subsumed or simply abstracted and reduced into neat economic determinations. Yet this 'roughness', found in the materiality of everyday spatial practices and in the realm of the lived experience, is often ignored or made to fit (violently if need be) with the dominant discourse *on* space. But it is the disjuncture which offers opportunities for emancipatory potential. Public protests are representative of a reclaiming of space. Indeed, the emergence of social movements can be considered to be "manifest expressions of deeper, broader, latent dissatisfactions" (Willner quoted in Springer, 2011, p. 46). Quoting Lefebvre, Wilson points out:

> ... that abstract representations of space cannot succeed in 'papering over all differences' ..., as through the process of their implementation they are confronted by "the materiality of the spatial practices and representational spaces that they have discursively erased, which constitute the grounds for resistance and transformative possibilities. (2011, p. 388)

There is a habit of lionising the possibility of counter-hegemonic potential from speculative theorising as opposed to the empirical analysis of "the spatial dimensions of hegemony, control, and exploitation" (Grovogui & Leonard, 2008, p. 170). Cambodia is a country undergoing rapid economic transformation, with Phnom Penh a new site for neoliberal expansion. Within this, we explore how emergent forms of expression in a small contested social space have generated a creative community and a grass roots resistance to the dominant ideological practices. The White Building is a site of resistance where the everyday and the lived experience has not been successfully 'papered over', that allows us to respond to one of Lefebvre most pertinent questions:

> Given that abstract space is buttressed by non-critical (positive) knowledge, backed up by a frightening capacity for violence, and maintained by a bureaucracy which has laid hold the gains of capitalism in the ascendant and turned them to its own profit, must we conclude that this space will last forever? (Lefebvre, 1991, p. 52)

The White Building: from modernist dreams to the Khmer Rouge devastation

To offer some historical context to the main site of investigation: The White Building is an apartment complex in Phnom Penh, Cambodia. It was built in 1963 as a keystone of the Sihanouk government's urban social housing scheme. In post-independence Cambodia during the late 1950s and 1960s, under the leadership of Norodom Sihanouk, the former King and the then Prime Minister, Phnom Penh underwent a tremendous transformation at an unprecedented pace, with an abundance of newly built public infrastructure, monuments and buildings. Between independence from the French in 1953 and the *coup d'état* by the US-supported Lon Nol regime in 1970, Phnom Penh's population tripled from 370,000 to one million (Keyes, 1995, p. 300). This massive urban migration prompted an urgent need for a housing solution. In an address to Phnom Penh Governor Tep Phan in 1961, Sihanouk declared:

> Finally, our capital must deal with the problem of the urban population ... We must begin the construction of low-cost apartment buildings that can be rented or sold to average and small-income families. This will no doubt take some time and requires progressive planning and investment. (Grant Ross & Collins, 2006, p. 16)

A centrepiece of the response to the "problem of the urban population" was the ambitious Bassac River Front cultural complex that lay on reclaimed land along the Bassac River.

The White Building (originally known as the Municipal Apartments) was a key part of this Bassac River Front cultural complex. Vann Molyvann, the first Cambodian architect to receive a modern education in France, oversaw the entirety of the development of this cultural complex. Vann was immediately appointed Director of Urban Planning and State Architect upon his return to Cambodia in 1956, overseeing numerous urban planning projects (Grant Ross, 2015, p. 168). The inclusion of the White Building in the Bassac River Front cultural complex plan was Vann's first large-scale experiment in applying modern ideas on public housing, and one that was inspired both by Le Corbusier's utopian project La Ville Radieuse (Ly & Muan, 2001) and Ebenezer Howard's concept of the Garden City (Eimer, 2014).[3] This differs from its early European development as a movement that was drawn, to some extent, from anarchist roots (Ward & Hall, 1998). Yet, Castells (1977) is probably closer to the mark describing it as a utopian reactionary movement that expresses a profound demand of the working class, but in a backward-looking ideological envelope. As a movement, its original intent was quickly compromised displaying and, in many ways, reproducing the dominant values held by elements within the British establishment (Foley, 1960). Its original premise was that of locating a "third way between capitalism and socialism", but in actuality it projected a form of urban governmentality (Osborne & Rose, 1999, p. 748). In all, it developed into a conceptualised space of techno-bureaucracy that became hugely influential within modernist town planning ideology, while remaining conveniently "congenial to British values" (Foley, 1960, p. 215). With the "pretensions of expert knowledge" the Garden City utopianism presented a cure for social ills that quickly degenerated into bourgeois self-interest.

In Southeast Asia, from the post Second World War period up until the present day, these ideas have informed a top-down nostalgic fetishisation of community culture (Douglass & Huang, 2007, p. 9).

Consider, then, this influence in the Cambodian context of the 1950s and early 1960s where a modernising desire existed within a newly independent setting that was also entwined with utopian desire and reactionism. This reactionism was in response to the rapid urbanisation and the post-France, post-colonial experience of independence. Despite the universalising pressure of the dominant discursive practices of an expansionary modernist and capitalist outlook, Vann Molyvann's influence exuded distinctly Cambodian characteristics. The backward glances and an imagined utopian modern city merged to form an ideological frame that was evident in the idealisation of Cambodian village life (Chandler, 1984) and in the Sihanouk government's utopian vision of a new golden age of Cambodia harking back to the Khmer Angkorian empire (Falser, 2015, p. 150). Importantly, this historically based idealisation and utopian vision is set within the frame of traditional Cambodian power relations based on the patronage paradigm of power distribution in society (Vickery, 1999; see also Un & Hughes, 2011).

We identify three distinct periods over the life of the building. The first is a period that many Cambodians, artists and historians characterise as a 'Golden Age' in which the God-King shrugged off the cloak of royalty to become the first Prime Minister and to lead the country from the shackles of French colonialism, transforming the capital into the "Pearl of Asia" (Saphan, 2013, p. 64). Sihanouk's substantial and often profligate spending during this period was focussed on building his vision of a modern Cambodia. Inspired by a similar development in Casablanca, the White Building itself was designed by Cambodian architect Lu Ban Hap and Russian architect Vladimir

Bodiansky and inaugurated in 1963 (Sochivy, 2009). Comprising 468 apartments it was the first attempt to offer a multistorey modern urban lifestyle to lower- and middle-class Cambodians (Grant Ross & Collins, 2006) and, as a government led, funded and subsidised initiative, was effectively the first government social housing built in the country. This technocratic drive focussed on significant infrastructure, architectural and monumental works and through the creation of new institutions such as government ministries and universities (See Grant Ross & Collins, 2006; Vickery, 1999). At the same time this *conceived* space of blunt post-independence capitalist transition was seen to be tempered by significant constitutional amendments such as the introduction of Khmer as a national language and the extension of suffrage to women. The lived and the imagined were curated through grand cultural programming such as films, music and dance – all of which Sihanouk and his family were not just patrons of, but participants in (Chandler, 1992).

The second period can be framed as decimation and survival. From 1970 Cambodia fell into civil war, and then the Khmer Rouge regime. After the fall of Khmer Rouge in 1979, as people moved back to the previously abandoned Phnom Penh,[4] the few surviving artists (mostly performing artists) were called to gather and live in the White Building due to its proximity to the National Theatre (Sarath in Potter & Koam, 2012). Many of Cambodia's artists and intellectuals were killed during the Khmer Rouge regime. In 1979, the *Kampuchea Review* wrote "Out of 190 ballet artists, only 40 escaped death under the Pol Pot – Ieng Sary regime" (*Kampuchea Review*, 1979, H1). In 1982, after accepting the position of Minister of Information and Culture, Chheng Phon said: "The genocidal Pol Pot – Ieng Sary – Khieu Samphan regime destroyed our national culture almost completely and killed almost 80 percent of our male and female performers" (*Kampuchea Review*, 1982, cited in Sam-Ang, 1990b; Turnbull, 1999). In an interview with Susan Pack in 1989, Chheng expanded on his earlier statement saying, "there were 385,737 artists and intellectuals (before the Khmer Rouge); during Pol Pot just 300 people survived" (Pack, 1989; Sam-Ang, 1990a). While exact numbers may never be known, what can be seen is that the Khmer Rouge eviscerated Khmer culture and cultural memory with a brutal intent.

Post-Khmer Rouge, and in one of the few acts of cultural renewal by the interim Vietnamese government, from 1979 many of the surviving artists were allowed to live rent free (or at a peppercorn rent) in the White Building and were paid a small stipend to work as artists through the Ministry of Fine Arts and Culture. As Hun Sarath, Chief of Block A in the Building recalls, "the government gathered all the artists to re-build Cambodian culture due to its proximity to the National Theatre" (Sarath in Potter & Koam, 2012). Many of the artists who returned at this time still live in the Building, or have family members who live there and continue to work in arts-related areas. However, despite this support, two decades of crippling economic hardship, natural disasters and ongoing social-political turmoil through the 1980s and 1990s meant that few artists could make a continuous living performing or teaching. At this time just surviving was a triumph.

(Re)producing space: domination and resistance in contemporary Phnom Penh

From the late 1990s two significant threads emerged in the Building's history – one cultural and one commercial. This third period is framed as renewal. In 1998 Arn Chorn-Pond created the Cambodian Master Performers Program. The programme worked with recognised Masters of traditional and royal Cambodian arts (Cambodia Living Arts, 2013). Many of these artists were living in the Building. As a result, the Cambodia Living Arts (CLA) studios were established in 1999 in the White Building and the organisation maintains two studio apartments in the Building to this day. CLA provides an income for many of the Master artists who work as teachers and continues to pay the rent of a number of these artists who were forced to sell their apartments due to financial difficulties in the 1990s and 2000s (Key Mom quoted in Muong, 2015). CLA moved its main offices and studios in the mid-2000s to a different site. However, CLA's work in identifying the importance of this ageing generation of Masters of Cambodian arts laid the foundations for other cultural interventions in the Building.

From around the same time property developers began circling the Building and surrounds, increasingly interested by the prime inner-city real estate and surging Phnom Penh real estate market (Simone, 2008). The majority of the Bassac River Front development had, by this time, been destroyed, demolished or renovated beyond recognition. The National Theatre was burnt during repairs in 1994 and finally demolished in 2008. The charred remains of the theatre were a central feature of Rithy Panh's 2005 film *The Burnt Theatre* representing both symbolic desecration of the 'golden age' of Khmer post-independence culture and metaphor for the struggle to re-build culture from the ashes of Khmer Rouge destruction.

And after almost two decades of no maintenance and ongoing restructuring of the exterior, the White Building was in poor condition – a fading façade with dilapidated infrastructure. Neighbouring squatter communities to the Building such as Dey Krahom and a number of Tonle Bassac communities began to be forcibly evicted from the early 2000s (Cambodian League for the Promotion and Defense of Human Rights 2006, 2008, 2009a; Sisovann & Quinn, 2007; Barton & Cheang, 2006; Community Legal Education Centre, 2006). The most brutal and largest eviction of the Dey Krahom settlement saw about 850 families have their homes bulldozed before they were loaded into trucks and driven an hour north or south of the city and dumped in a field – most of them with no access to running water or electricity, many of them without access to shelter or schooling for their children and none of them with access to local markets. (Cambodian League for the Promotion and Defense of Human Rights, 2009b; LICADHO-Canada, 2008; Shozi, 2014). From inner-city living to the margins of society in a day. The widespread demolition or substantial reconstruction of the Bassac Front development is part of a wider pattern of neoliberal accumulation and spatial reckoning (in the city).

This trend of dispossession and accumulation has continued with the White Building residents living under threat of eviction from their home. Imbricated and very much central to this process is the Hun Sen Government refusal of individual and communal applications which had prevented any substantial renovation or maintenance works. In 2014 there were alleged strategic purchases of White Building apartments by a local developer (Yin, Heng, & Blomberg, 2014) and public statements to demolish the White Building were made by high ranking politicians including Phnom Penh's Governor (Hul & Yin, 2014b), while in 2015 nearby building works caused structural damage to the Building (Sen & Cuddy, 2015). Judging by evictions in surrounding neighbourhoods (Business and Human Rights Resource Centre, 2009), this would result in up to 3,000 people being forcibly re-located to the margins of the city far from their work, markets, schools and their social network (LICADHO-Canada, 2008) and with little compensation or support. However, despite the sustained threat of forced eviction, there has been the emergence of a movement that has challenged the dominant social relations to recognise the White Building as a space of creative resistance, with an intent to collaborate creatively to maximise residents', artists' and the communities' access to resources and opportunity in the city (Simone, 2008). Lefebvre (1984) emphasised the need to excavate everyday life for political possibilities that could point towards alternative visions, and the pragmatic resistance by Building residents appears to be a practical example of this idea. As

Brenner (2001) points out, Lefebvre's dialectical utopianism provides a salient reminder that everyday life under capitalism is permeated with utopian possibilities and strivings – of both reactionary and progressive variants, and with foreboding, benign or emancipatory possibilities.

(Re)producing space: art and storytelling as resistance in contemporary Phnom Penh
From 2008 artists became active in the space again. In 2008 photographer Maria Stott worked with a number of emerging Cambodian photographers including Vandy Rattana to create On Photography Cambodia (OPC) – a series of participatory photography programmes in the Building. OPC was a photographic exploration of Phnom Penh's past, present and future through the juxtaposition of different photographic perspectives – historical photos, family album photos and contemporary images made by community members and professionals – all of which focussed on the White Building. For OPC, the Building simultaneously symbolises "the highpoint of modern Khmer architecture and urban planning, Cambodia's tumultuous past and the urban challenges of today" (Stott, 2009). OPC launched in January 2008, undertook monthly community workshops from October 2008 until the end of 2009 and produced a number of exhibitions from late 2008 and throughout 2009. The project highlighted arts potential for negative capability, redefined by Unger as "the denial of whatever in our contexts delivers us over to a fixed scheme of division and hierarchy and to an enforced choice between routine and rebellion" (2004, pp. 279-280). This understanding of the potential for art and art makers to create resistance (or denial) of perceived fixed divisions and hierarchies is important in the subsequent transformation of the community. Residents of the Building, represented in mainstream media and widely understood as a slum overrun by drugs, gangs and prostitution, could offer alternative visions of the diverse community. OPC also

represented a connective tissue between the end of CLA's localised work in the Building and the emergence of a sequence of new artistic engagements that would ultimately build on the community's artistic history, connect generations of old and new artists, generate new partnerships between the community and external groups and individuals and create new spaces that resist dominant discourses that are perpetuated, both in terms of how the Building and its residents are viewed and the manner in which it has engendered a resistance to the *conceived* dominance of technocratic and neoliberal expansionary practice. As a project it injected fun and enjoyment into the Building, but, as Lefebvre pointed out, it is clear that the "quest for a counter-space" must derive from individual bodies through the appropriation of space – including new spaces for enjoyment (1991, p. 383). Occupation and appropriation of public space is a defining feature of both the right to the city and differential space. The right to collective expression in public is one of the key markers of genuine, democratic public space. OPC pursued a quest for counter-space through re-imagining the Building as a possible site of artistic and creative resistance that could meaningfully and materially impact the everyday lives of residents.

In 2009 and 2010 the two key contemporary, ongoing artistic strands emerged. Inspired by his work with OPC, photographer Vandy Rattana proposed the idea of the creation of a residential community art programme in the Building with the art collective *Stiev Selapak* (Art Rebels), the first Cambodian artist collective. The space would serve as a knowledge sharing space and to support artists to realise new ideas. The vision was for a flexible space, emphasising collaboration and experimentation and named Sa Sa Art Projects – a shortening of *Stiev Selapak* (Nelson, 2012, p. 23). The group also understood the historical context of the space, with Sa Sa co-founder Vuth Lyno observing in Nelson (2012, p. 23) that the Building "is an artists' community". From the outset Sa Sa also embraced fluidity with

Vuth mocking the NGO jargon of sustainability as he discussed the potential impermanence of the community due to the ongoing threat of eviction, as well as Sa Sa's temporal nature and fluid, unregistered structure: "What do we sustain? Ourselves and not the thing that we want to sustain" (Nelson, 2012, p. 24).

From 2010, Sa Sa developed three main programme strands – arts classes and workshops, artist residencies and collaborative projects were held in a re-purposed apartment space in the Building. Numerous events gave some focus to these ongoing activities. Most notably was the White Night, which began in December 2011 as a collaboration between Sa Sa, UK artist The Incidental and some community members. This represented Sa Sa's first substantial collaboration with a foreign artist and saw works exhibited in public and communal spaces (Sa Sa Art Projects, 2016).

The second contemporaneous strand emerged in early 2010 when film-maker (and co-author) Martin Potter and Cambodian film-maker Koam Chanrasmey worked in the Building producing a documentary with the dancer, singer and teacher Hun Sarath. Sarath was a Building resident who was one of the original returning artists of 1979 and was becoming increasingly active in the community. She was, at that time, starting to campaign to become Chief of one of the two blocks of the Building, a campaign that would ultimately prove successful in 2012.[5] In an early interview, Sarath stated that the artists in the Building needed to be active in the community and to be leaders and visionaries (Potter & Koam, 2012). Sarath understood, all too well, the importance of her own lived experience as a means to challenge, alter and ameliorate government and business interest in the building. Indeed, she considered her intervention necessary into order for the Building community to survive. The space, the communities within the Building, could not simply be 'papered' over (see Wilson, 2011; Louth, 2015); the lived, the imagined and the everyday use of the space could not simply be subsumed.

In the numerous, simultaneous programmes running in and around the Building, Potter and Koam (2012) identified potential for partnerships to build a stronger sense of counter-space. However there was little communication between the programmes and, within the general community, communication was highly fragmented. Simone (2008) identifies through interviews with residents of three principal sub-communities in the Building – the sex work section, the artists' section and the police section,[6] with migrants to Phnom Penh from rural areas constituting a highly mobile fourth section. There was no sense of a shared communal identity. The external perspective of the Building as a crime-riddled slum impacted deeply on the residents. The government's refusal to allow restoration works compounded this perspective as the Building slowly decayed. Some residents, driven by perceived fear of gangs in the Building, had installed lockable gates blocking entry to their entire floor. Many residents were ashamed to say they came from the Building. Up to 40% of the Building population had lived in Phnom Penh for less than 12 months and there was a high turnover of residents. Outsiders were often initially treated with varying degrees of distrust (Simone, 2008). This included the Sa Sa Art Projects group who initially found it difficult to engage the broader community. The positioning of Sa Sa as 'rebels' (*Stiev*) indicated to many residents a radical political agenda that was easy to identify. By defining themselves according to an agenda of radical creativity, the outsider, middle-class Cambodian artists struggled to gain the trust of the community and other organisations working in the Building. Their own radicalism resulted in the group being relatively marginalised by the community. Having the Sa Sa gallery space based within an apartment inside the Building and inviting others in was a further condition for marginalisation – a kind of 'fixed space' dilemma. By this we mean that the gallery was open to receive the public but the community were reluctant to enter, while the gallery was the place where artists would do and show work and wait for the public to visit.

The diverse community perspectives about who to trust, how to share power and control and troubled notions of communal identity required both internal and external facilitators working together to create partnerships between groups working independently in the Building, as well as engaging community members in some of the programmes and working across the often siloed community partners, in order to strengthen these partnerships. Working with Hun Sarath, a respected community member, legitimised Potter and Koam to members of the old arts and police section in the Building. The peripatetic nature of the film-making process enabled Potter and Koam to move throughout the Building and to build a network, circumventing the 'fixed dilemma' which had characterised Sa Sa's experience. This meant that as external facilitators, Potter and Koam could easily move across the siloed partners and sub-communities within the Building. After some months of filming Potter and Koam initiated a film programme in August 2012, in partnership with Aziza School which was based in the Building, partly in order to extend the documentary project and partly in response to interest expressed by a group of residents. Participants in the film programme also worked with Sa Sa Art Projects and Aziza School and rapidly developed their creative and organisational skills. As Vuth (2014) observed,

> The group of the video workshop students that we worked with, you could call them the youth leaders in the community, they have a certain spirit of commitment to the community and a spirit of activism, participating in demonstrations or documenting political events. You don't have to tell them; they do their own things.

Edges of Identity

In November, 2012 an exhibition *Snit Snaal*[7] (translation: loving, friendly and intimate with another) was staged to showcase works produced by the participants. Vuth Lyno, in the curator's statement for the programme wrote of the exhibition,

> [It] is intended to be enjoyed by everyday Cambodians, in particular the residents of the White Building themselves. The works are all new, created by twenty young art students and community organisers from the neighbourhood. They look at issues in the White Building community, as well as in their own homes elsewhere in Phnom Penh, and also in the city more broadly. (Potter & Vuth, 2012)

This programme was the most substantial engagement with public and shared spaces in and around the Building. When the Sa Sa gallery hosted an exhibition, other spaces also became exhibition spaces. Video installations were placed in numerous businesses on the ground floor. A local café became a cinema showing films made by the film school participants, as well as films by Cambodian and international film-makers, and one of the Aziza School classrooms became the site for a multi-screen installation work. Most of the films that were featured in the café cinema over the course of a seven-day mini film festival were focussed on people from the Building and life in and around the Building. Film-makers and the participants in the films presented and discussed their stories. As many stories, materials and other resources as possible that were available within the community were used in staging the programme. Video works that were produced were played on TVs and DVDs borrowed from individuals and businesses throughout the Building. The cinema screen was made by Aziza School students; graphic design was done by Building-based designers; promotion of the event within the Building community was by community members, who were also guides for outside guests enabling them to navigate the different sites of the exhibition.

Even community clean-up and maintenance works were organised by community members.

The experience of this event created substantial enthusiasm and interest. The event was a foundation for Sa Sa to initiate an artist in residency programme *Pisaot*.[8] Other non-art outcomes that had formed lead-up events (such as community clean-up programmes and other community organising like shared savings to undertake maintenance works in the Building) became regular activities outside of the art programmes. *Snit Snaal* was the foundation for a subsequent programme in January 2014 called Bonn Phum (The Village Festival). Bonn Phum was a multi-platform and multi-event programme.[9] Again Bonn Phum featured exhibitions in the Sa Sa Gallery, the café cinema festival, video installations in local businesses and Aziza School. The Festival also featured performances on the rooftop of the Building, with almost 1,000 people in attendance to watch original music and choreography created by Building resident Hun Sarath. This performance took classical Khmer court music and dance and re-imagined it for the Building community. Local bands performed at ground level and community archive, reading room and library spaces were opened. An online archive (whitebuilding.org) was also launched at this time. According to a survey by the newly formed White Building Collective, Bonn Phum engaged over 75% of the Building population.[10] It also created the impetus for the creation of the "Humans of Phnom Penh" series initiated by the video group with the support of Damien Rayuela.[11] Vuth (2014) explores the activities of the Bonn Phum programme in depth, and so we will focus on the outcomes and connection to Lefebvre's theories in relation to creative (re)production of the space.

The Bonn Phum festival reiterated and expanded on the *Snit Snaal* model of temporary community action – involving students and White Building residents in actively utilising and transforming existing resources and spaces within the neighbourhood into artistic intervention and engagement, establishing stronger and intimate social relations amongst the community members. This action minimises the dependency of the residents and students on external facilitators such as Sa Sa Art Projects, and enables residents to lead their own future actions. This community leadership and independence was strongly evident when government representatives threatened to demolish the White Building as reported in the *Cambodia Daily* newspaper published on 4 September, 2014 (Hul & Yin, 2014a). That day, the White Building Collective and a few other residents prepared an action plan, organised a community meeting on the rooftop to begin a process of community led consultation and mobilisation. The following week after a sustained campaign in the press the government retracted their statement (Hul & Yin, 2014b). Subsequently Building community leaders met with government and presented a community-led submission to Phnom Penh city council and the Ministry of Planning. This has led to a 'step by step' agreement in July 2015. As Chumm Phanith, White Building Collective member, resident and community organiser, noted in relation to gaining government permissions to do renovation work, "We can do it step by step not all in one time. Because if we ask to do it all, then they don't easy say yes." (P. Chumm, personal communication, 22 November 2015.)

Conclusion: emergence of a radical collective and an art of empathy
The aesthetic of the contemporary arts and media produced at the White Building reflects the multiple facets of the community's responses to contemporary Cambodia. It seeks to experiment and find a new contemporary and communal language and subjectivity by utilising traditional practices and incorporating new technology and modern ideas and collaboration with Cambodian and visiting artists – insiders and outsiders, locals and international guests. Developing spaces that re-imagine the norms of the dominant culture and provide for new

ways to build community, social relations, and the production of new stories and creative acts. This implies the development of forms of art that do not fit neatly within the dominant proto-neoliberal regulatory experience of post-conflict Cambodia (Louth, 2015). The work of making, teaching and sharing – by key groups such as the White Building Collective and Sa Sa Art Projects – responds both to current circumstances as well as larger contemporary issues. It also seeks a practice to address and engage everyday experience and everyday Cambodians with creative and cultural practices outside of the exclusive spaces of galleries and museums. This collapsing of barriers to accessibility and participation produces compelling art and stories and takes on issues of the right to representation, memory and place.

Once art activities occurred at the level of the everyday, relationships and trust emerged (or were re-imagined) within the Building. An ongoing programme of presentations in public and shared spaces that built on an identifiable cultural tradition and practice already present in the Building drew on and encouraged participation of both old Masters and youth residents in the Building. Relationships and trust blossomed between residents as well as between artist facilitators, local organisations and sections of the community. The ongoing, flexible and creative programmes and spaces inside the Building – which become both public and social space – embody resistance. Resistance is spatial in that it has to take place in specific locations under localised conditions by people with alternative opinions, political sensibilities, desires, and the will to make things happen. This doesn't mean that this 'radical space' has to have a radical political agenda that is easy to identify. This was about developing existing spaces throughout the Building where the norms of the dominant culture could be re-imagined, and where there was provision for new ways to build community and social relations through the production of new stories and creative acts. As a result, there has been significant development of individual and collective groups of artists who also now work as teachers, mentors and facilitators to new groups of residents.

The activist and artistic tradition embedded throughout the community across generations has been re-invigorated and when it seemed that the community's demise was a fait accompli – that it was going to simply succumb to the wishes of the government and developers – a path of resistance has emerged. With such a strong creative community in the Building and a history as a site of social inclusion it is unsurprising that artistic expression would form a part of the activism in the space. And this is an activism that is not uncommon, as it appears to pervade many contemporary art movements of Southeast Asia reflecting, as Tan Bun Hui observes, an art of empathy rather than direct activism (Bun Hui in Van den Bosch, 2012). In some sense, we feel that we can offer a qualified answer to Lefebvre's question of whether we must resign ourselves to the dominance of abstract technocratic and bureaucratic space with a tendency towards violent repression (Lefebvre, 1991). Creative resistance – however fleeting – provides an empathetic turn that offers an insight into possible emancipatory moments. Moreover, this 'turn' can translate into material resistance as can be seen by the emergence of a successive series of creative collectives in the White Building.

Notes
1. We use the terms 'White Building and the 'Building' interchangeably.
2. David Harvey (1990, pp. 218–221) interprets Lefebvre's triad as: 1. Material spatial practices (experience); 2. Representations of space (perception); 3. Spaces of representation (imagination).
3. The Garden City (or suburb) is a concept that, while distinctly European, is recognisable in the Southeast Asian early twentieth century colonial context, but in a form that addressed the needs of a colonial expatriate community (Dick & Rimmer, 1998).

4. Phnom Penh was evacuated by the Khmer Rouge within a week of arriving in and taking the capital in April 1975. Many buildings such as government institutions, banks and churches were blown up – however, most homes and businesses were simply locked and left. Fewer than 2,000 people remained in the city during the following three years, eight months with Khmer Rouge cadre only returning to raid businesses and homes for supplies (Kiernan, 1996; Chandler, 1992).
5. For local council administrative purposes the Building is divided into two blocks with a Chief representative elected for each block.
6. According to Simone these are broad, historical categories self-described by residents. However, it must be reinforced that the work of the residents constitutes a more complex cross-section – a fact Simone acknowledges – e.g. of the area defined as the 'police section' Simone (2008, p. 192) notes that most of them "had sold off their apartments and moved elsewhere in the city". The key point is that the community self-siloed its identities.
7. An archive of some of the work produced can be viewed at http://whitebuilding.org/en/collections/snit_snaal
8. Details on Pisaot residencies can be viewed at: http://sasaart.info/pisaot.htm
9. An online archive showcasing some of the work produced and some images from the events can be viewed at: http://whitebuilding.org/en/collections/bonn-phum-the-village-festival
10. The White Building Collective was formed by participants in the video group. The survey was conducted during the week of Bonn Phum and involved content analysis of works produced and the number of active community participants and head count of audience members (combined with head count of community members at events). This formed the basis for a report written by Potter and Vuth on the outcomes from the funding for HIVOS's Arts Collaboratory.
11. Humans of Phnom Penh can be viewed at: https://www.facebook.com/HoPPCambodia

References

Agnew, J. A. (2011). Space and place. In J. A. Agnew and D. N. Livingstone (Eds.), *The SAGE handbook of geographical knowledge* (pp. 316–330). London, United Kingdom: SAGE.

Barton, C. & Cheang, S. (2006, 16 June). More Bassac squatters face eviction. *Phnom Penh Post*, Retrieved from http://www.phnompenhpost.com/national/more-bassac-squatters-face-eviction

Bates, T. R. (1975). Gramsci and the theory of hegemony. *Journal of the History of Ideas*, 36(2), 351–366.

Brenner, N. (2001). State theory in the political conjuncture: Henri Lefebvre's 'Comments on a New State Form'. *Antipode*, 33, 349–379.

Business and Human Rights Resource Centre (2009). Evictions at Dey Krahorm in Phnom Penh, Cambodia. Retrieved from http://business-humanrights.org/en/evictions-at-dey-krahorm-in-phnom-penh-cambodia-0

Cambodia Living Arts (2013). Website history page. Retrieved from http://www.cambodianlivingarts.org/about-us/history/

Cambodian League for the Promotion and Defense of Human Rights (LICADHO) (2006, 14 June). Frenzied development in Cambodia pushes its people out of the capital to squalid conditions. Report. Retrieved from http://www.licadho-cambodia.org/articles/20060614/39/index.html

Cambodian League for the Promotion and Defense of Human Rights (LICADHO) (2008, 23 January). Dey Krahorm: Mass eviction feared. Statement. Retrieved from http://www.licadho-cambodia.org/press release.php?perm=172

Cambodian League for the Promotion and Defense of Human Rights (LICADHO) (2009a, 24 January). Razing Dey Krahorm: The death of a village. Photo essay. Retrieved from http://www.licadho-cambodia.org/ album/view_photo.php?cat=43

Cambodian League for the Promotion and Defense of Human Rights (LICADHO) (2009b, 8 February). Nightmare at Dey Krahorm: Forced eviction in the heart of Phnom Penh. Report. Retrieved from http://www.licadho-cambodia.org/articles/20090208/85/index.html

Cambodian League for the Promotion and Defense of Human Rights (LICADHO)/LICADHO Canada (2008). Dey Krahorm land case explained, Briefing Paper. Retrieved from http://www.licadho-cambodia.org/reports.php?perm=118

Castells, M. (1977). *The urban question: A Marxist approach*. Cambridge, MA: MIT Press.

Castree, N. (2009). The spatio-temporality of capitalism. *Time and Society*, 18(1), 26–61.

Certeau, M. (1984). *The practice of everyday life*. Berkeley, CA: University of California Press.

Chandler, D. (1992). *Brother number one: A political biography of Pol Pot*. Boulder, CO: Westview Press.

Chandler, D. P. (1984). Normative poems (Chbap) and pre-colonial Cambodian Society. *Journal of Southeast Asian Studies*, 15(2), 271–279.

Charnock, G. (2010). Challenging new state spatialities: The open Marxism of Henri Lefebvre. *Antipode*, 42(5), 1279–1303.

Community Legal Education Centre (2006). Another Bassac eviction scheduled for Friday, 21 July. Retrieved from http://www.clec.org.kh/clecnews.php?cnsID=39

Davies, M. (2016). Everyday life as critique: Revisiting the everyday in IPE with Henri Lefebvre and postcolonialism. *International Political Sociology*, 10, 22–38.

Dick, H. W. & Rimmer, P. J. (1998). Beyond the Third World city: The new urban geography of South-east Asia. *Urban Studies*, 35(12), 2303–2321.

Douglass, M. & Huang, L. (2007). Globalizing the city in Southeast Asia – the case of Phu My Hung, Saigon. *International Journal of Asia Pacific Studies*, 3(2), 1–42.

Edmonds, D. & Warburton, N. (2014, 9 January). Roberto Mangabeira Unger on what is wrong with the social sciences today. *Social Science Space*. Retrieved from http://www.socialsciencespace.com/2014/01/roberto-mangabeira-unger-what-is-wrong-with-the-social-sciences-today/

Eimer, D. (2014, 9 February). Vann Molyvann: The unsung hero of Phnom Penh architecture, *Phnom Penh Post Magazine*. Retrieved from [full URL overleaf] http://www.scmp.com/magazines/post-magazine/article/1421349/vann-molyvann-unsung-hero-phnom-penh-architecture

Ekers, M. & Loftus, A. (2013). Revitalizing the production of nature thesis: A Gramscian turn? *Progress in Human Geography, 37*(2), 324–252.

Elias, J. & Louth, J. L. (2016). Regional disputes over the transnationalisation of domestic labour: Malaysia's 'maid shortage' and foreign relations with Indonesia and Cambodia. In J. Elias & L. Rethal (Eds.), *The everyday political economy of Southeast Asia* (pp. 196–217). Cambridge, United Kingdom: Cambridge University Press.

Falser, M. (2015). Cultural heritage as performance: Re-enacting Angkorian grandeur in postcolonial Cambodia (1953–70). In R. Craggs & C. Wintle, (Eds.), *Cultures of decolonization, transnational productions and practices, 1945–70* (pp. 142–152). Manchester, United Kingdom: Manchester University Press.

Foley, D. L. (1960). British town planning: One ideology or three? *The British Journal of Sociology, 11*(3), 211–231.

Gill, S. R. & Law, D. (1989). Global hegemony and the structural power of capital. *International Studies Quarterly, 33*(4), 475–499.

Grant Ross, H. (2015). The civilising vision of an enlightened dictator: Norodom Sihanouk and the Cambodian post-independence experiment (1953–1970). In M. Falser (Ed.), *Cultural heritage as civilising mission* (pp. 149–180). Cham, Switzerland: Springer International Publishing.

Grant Ross, H. & Collins, D. (2006). *Building Cambodia: 'New Khmer Architecture' 1953–1970*. Bangkok, Thailand: The Key Publisher Company.

Grovogui, S. N. & Leonard, L. (2008). Uncivil society: Interrogations at the margins of neo-Gramscian theory. In A. J. Ayers (Ed.), *Gramsci, political economy, and international relations theory: Modern princes and naked emperors* (pp. 169–188). Basingstoke, United Kingdom: Palgrave Macmillan.

Harvey, D. (1990). *The condition of postmodernity*. Oxford, United Kingdom: Blackwell.

Harvey, D. (2001). *Spaces of capital: Towards a critical geography*. New York, NY: Routledge.

Hobson, J. M. & Seabrooke, L. (2006). The case for an everyday international political economy. Working Paper no. 26. International Center for Business and Politics, Copenhagen Business School, Copenhagen, Denmark.

Hul, R. & Yin, C. C. (2014a, 4 September). Tenants of White Building in dark on demolition. *Cambodia Daily*. Retrieved from http://www.cambodiadaily.com/news/tenants-of-white-building-in-dark-on-demolition-67516/

Hul, R. & Yin, C. C. (2014b, 5 September). City Hall backtracks amid White Building outcry. *Cambodia Daily*. Retrieved from https://www.cambodia daily.com/news/city-hall-backtracks-amid-white-building-outcry-67556/

Keyes, C. (1995). *The golden peninsula: Culture and adaptation in mainland Southeast Asia*. Honolulu, HI: University of Hawai'i Press.

Kiernan, B. (1996). *The Pol Pot regime: Race, power and genocide in Cambodia under the Khmer Rouge, 1975-79*. New Haven, CT: Yale University Press.

Lefebvre, H. (1976). Reflections on the politics of space. *Antipode, 8*(2), 30-37.

Lefebvre, H. (1984). *Everyday life in the modern world* (Trans. S. Rabinovitch). (2nd ed.). New Brunswick, NJ: Transaction Publishers.

Lefebvre, H. (1991). *The production of space*. Oxford, United Kingdom: Blackwell.

Louth, J. (2011). From Newton to Newtonianism: Reductionism and the development of the social sciences. *Emergence: Complexity and organization, 13*(4), 63-83.

Louth J. (2012). Complexity, capacity and Cambodia: The neoliberalisation of space and scale. In P. Taylor & P. Wagg (Eds.), *Work and Society: Places, Spaces and Identities* (pp. 196-218). Chester, United Kingdom: University of Chester Press.

Louth, J. (2015). Neoliberalising Cambodia: The production of capacity in Southeast Asia. *Globalizations, 12*(3), 400-419.

Ly, D. & Muan, I. (2001). *Cultures of independence: An introduction to Cambodian arts and culture in the 1950's and 1960's*. Phnom Penh, Cambodia: Reyum Institute of Arts and Culture.

Merrifield, A. (1993). Place and space: A Lefebvrian reconciliation. *Transactions of the Institute of British Geographers, 18*(4), 516-531.
Muong, V. (2015, 28 March). At home in the White Building. *Phnom Penh Post*. Retrieved from http://www.phnompenhpost.com/post-weekend/home-white-building
Nelson, R. (2012, 25 September). The White Building. *Art Monthly Australia*.
Osborne, T. & Rose, N. (1999). Governing cities: Notes on the spatialisation of virtue. *Environment and Planning D: Society and Space, 17*, 737-760.
Pack, S. (1989, 30 April). Cambodian odyssey. *Press-Telegram*, 1-5.
Panh, R. (Director), Panh, R., & Sénémaud, A. (Writers). (2005). *The Burnt Theatre* [Motion Picture]. Cambodia/France.
Phnom Penh reports membership of new KNUFNS Central Committee (1979, 30 October). *Kampuchea Review, 4*, H1.
Potter, M. & Koam, C. (2012). *Songs From The Building – trailer*. Retrieved from https://vimeo.com/68345891
Potter, M. & Vuth, L. (2014). *Snit Snaal*. The White Building Archive website. http://whitebuilding.org/en/collections/snit_snaal
Sa Sa Art Projects (2010-2016). Project descriptions on Sa Sa Art Projects website. http://www.sasaart.info/projects.htm
Sam-Ang, S. (1990a). Preserving a cultural tradition: Ten years after the Khmer Rouge. *Cultural Survival Quarterly, 14*(3). Retrieved from https:// www.culturalsurvival.org/publications/cultural-survival-quarterly/cambodia/preserving-cultural-tradition-ten-years-after-khmer-rouge
Sam-Ang, S. (1990b). A talk with Chheng Phon, Minister of Information and Culture. *Cultural Survival Quarterly, 14*(3). Retrieved fromhttps://www.culturalsurvival.org/publications/cultural-survival-quarterly/cambodia/flowers-forest-talk-chheng-phon-minister-information-and
Saphan, L. (2013). Prince Norodom Sihanouk and the political agenda of Cambodian music, 1955-1970. *International Institute for Asian Studies Newsletter*. Retrieved from http://iias.asia/the-newsletter/article/norodom-sihanouk-and-political-agenda-cambodian-music-1955-1970

Sen, D. & Cuddy, A. (2015, 3 February). Cracks leave tenants in fear. *Phnom Penh Post*. Retrieved from http://www.phnompenh post.com/cracks-leave-tenants-fear

Shozi, K. (2014, 5 March). When development hurts the poor – the struggle for land rights in Cambodia, Engineers Without Borders website. Retrieved from http://www.ewb.org.au/announcements/2/11348

Simone, A. (2008). The politics of the possible: Making urban life in Phnom Penh. *Singapore Journal of Tropical Geography, 29*(2), 186–204.

Sisovann, P. & Quinn, F. (2007, 19 December). Resistance continues in two Tonle Bassac evictions. *Cambodia Daily*. Retrieved from https://www.cambodiadaily.com/archives/resistance-continues-in-two-tonle-bassac-evictions-2-79717/

Sochivy, P. (2009). The 'Nid d'abeille' in Casablanca, built in 1952 by ATBAT (Atelier des Bâtisseurs) in Centre De Formation Régionalaux Métier Du Patrominie, Unpublished Powerpoint presentation.

Springer, S. (2011). Articulated neoliberalism: The specificity of patronage, kleptocracy, and violence in Cambodia's neoliberalization. *Environment and Planning A, 43*: 2554–2570.

Stott, M. (2009). An urban story through the Building in Cambodia, unpublished document.

Turnbull, R. (1999, 25 July). Dance: Reconstructing Khmer classics from zero. *New York Times*. Retrieved from http://www.nytimes.com/1999/07/25/arts/dance-reconstructing-khmer-classics-from-zero

Un, K. & Hughes, C. (2011). The political economy of good governance. In C. Hughes and K. Un (Eds.), *Cambodia's economic transformation* (pp. 199–218). Copenhagen, Denmark: NiAS Press.

Unger, R. (2014). *False necessity: Anti-necessitarian social theory in the service of radical democracy: from Politics, a work in constructive social theory*. London: Verso.

Van den Bosch, A. (2012, 24–25 October). Asian artists: Speaking for the voiceless. *Asian Currents*.

Vickery, M. (1999). *Cambodia 1975–1982*. Chiang Mai, Thailand: Silkworm Books.

Vuth, L. (2014, 2 March). A presentation by Vuth Lyno: Sa Sa Art Projects, *Asia Art Archive in America* (Transcribed by Hilary Chassé, edited by Jane DeBevoise). Retrieved from http://www.aaa-a.org/programs/a-presentation-by-lyno-vuth-sa-sa-art-projects/

Ward, C. & Hall, P. (1998). *Sociable cities: The legacy of Ebenezer Howard.* New York, NY: John Wiley & Sons.

Wilson, J. (2011). Colonising space: The new economic geography in theory and practice. *New Political Economy, 16*(1), 373–397.

Yin, C. C., Heng, S., & Blomberg, M. (2014, 26 August). Residents say 7NG is buying up White Building. *Cambodia Daily*, Retrieved from https://www.cambodiadaily.com/news/residents-say-7ng-is-buying-up-white-building-67136/

CHAPTER ELEVEN

EXPLORING THE FORMATION AND REPRODUCTION
OF NEOLIBERAL SUBJECTIVITIES:
A SOCIO-COGNITIVE APPROACH

Rodolfo Leyva

Introduction
Following the 2007-2008 global financial crisis a number of prominent academics, journalists and activists were quick to predict the demise of neoliberalism (Grantham & Miller, 2010; Stiglitz, 2008). This prediction, however, was rather optimistic, and underestimated the significant degree to which neoliberal ideology has entrenched itself into our socio-political fabric. Indeed, while governments across the globe responded differently to the crisis, seven years later the majority of them, at least at the policy level, are unwavering in their belief that neoliberal-derived pro-market strategies will solve the looming and increasing problems of unemployment, social inequality, and climate change to list a few (Braedley & Luxton, 2010). This staying the course approach would be understandable to an extent if the events of 2007-2008 were outliers or relatively anomalous incidents in an otherwise prosperous and harmonious three decades of neoliberal globalisation. However, although several elites and multinational corporations have certainly benefited during it, the neoliberal era has been marked by frequently recurring global financial crises, deep recessions, and skyrocketing levels of socio-economic inequality and wealth concentration (Albo, Gindin, & Panitch, 2010; Chang, 2010; Chomsky, 2011).
    Neoliberal globalisation has also generated the rise of an ever expanding and unsustainable global consumer culture that is both undermining psychological well-being (Kasser, Cohn,

Kanner, & Ryan, 2007) and depleting and devastating the natural environment (Ellwood, 2002). Yet despite these consistent and detrimental outcomes, in much of the northern hemisphere neoliberal ideological hegemony has not been supplanted (Hall & Rustin, 2015). This seems to be particularly the case for the US and the UK where neoliberal hegemony has arguably not even faced serious unsettling as, to all extents and purposes, outbursts of public unrest and popular social movements have been relatively short-lived, subdued or co-opted to Reed's (2014) argument that:

> Today [in the US], the labor movement has been largely subdued, and social activists have made their peace with neoliberalism and adjusted their horizons accordingly. Within the women's movement, goals have shifted from practical objectives such as comparable worth and universal childcare in the 1980s to celebrating appointments of individual women to public office and challenging the corporate glass ceiling. [...] The movement for racial justice has shifted its focus from inequality to "disparity," while neatly evading any critique of the structures that produce inequality. (p. 1)

But how exactly has or can neoliberalism inflect and shape our 'common-sense' understandings of what is politically, economically and culturally viable? The scholarly literature seeking to explain the hegemony of neoliberalism offers a number of valuable explanatory accounts that describe various interlocked systemic imperatives and structural, discursive and civil society components that enable neoliberalism to endure (Albo et al., 2010; Braedley & Luxton, 2010; Gill, 2003; Hall, 2011; Mirowski & Plehwe, 2009). However, largely missing from this literature are in-depth understandings of the role that micro-level cognitive mechanisms play in the processes of neoliberal hegemony. In the few works where cognitive explanations are evoked, they are often broadly framed in terms that, irrespective of intent, are mired in or very much reflect the Marxist conception of

Formation and Reproduction of Neoliberal Subjectivities

'false consciousness' (e.g. Harvey, 2005; Gill, 2003). This theoretical *deus ex machina*, no matter how sensitively it is applied even in more sophisticated Gramscian works,[1] effectively suggests that the majority of the 99%[2] consciously, albeit misguidedly and/or at times begrudgingly, adapt and consent to varying neoliberal ideas, norms and values. In doing so, they thus consciously submit and contribute to the everyday reproduction of the neoliberal social order even though they are to, varying degrees, subordinated, marginalised and generally negatively affected by it (Braedley & Luxton, 2010; Davies & Niemann, 2002; Hall & Rustin, 2015). These works however, do not provide an account of the specific mental frameworks that constitute a neoliberal false consciousness or of the cognitive mechanisms and processes through which one is developed. Moreover, while power and ideological mystification are important contributing factors, as Bourdieu (2000) argues, these do not, at least in the first instance, sufficiently account for how these systems are able to evolve and adapt to changing times; particularly given that they tend to engender demonstrably unequal, unjust, and exploitative societies.

Therefore, this chapter argues that in order to better understand how individuals hold and reproduce societal discursive practices that run counter to their interests and that contribute to their and their group's disadvantaged social position, contemporary sociological accounts require a more comprehensive and empirically testable conceptualisation of the dynamics between social structures and mental structures. This, in turn, can benefit from a deeper engagement with recent advancements in the cognitive sciences. As Ridgeway (2006) argues, it is in the coupling of cognitive theories with sociological theories that we can begin to better understand, explain, and explore how individuals internalise, reproduce, modify, and alter macro-level social patterns, such as dimensions of stratification, social institutions or widely shared sociocultural norms and values. Therefore, this chapter continues with a review of leading theoretical tenets from the respective literatures on socio-neurocognitive development, social cognition, and neoliberal hegemony. This is followed by a section that lays out a working but testable cognitive-sociological model for explaining and exploring how institutionally and culturally prevalent neoliberal discourses can potentially shape people's socio-cognitive frameworks and corresponding dispositional attitudes, values and practices.

Mental architectures and processes: the computational paradigm

The mainstay of cognitive science posits that the mind is a computational information-processing centre largely consisting of evolutionarily endowed, hierarchically organised and interconnected neural mechanisms known as modules (Barrett & Kurzban, 2006; Sperber & Hirschfeld, 2004). Modules are associated with and anchored across particular regions of the brain and are hypothesised to be informationally encapsulated structures with domain-specific functions (Bussey & Saksida, 2007). That is, each module is believed to be autonomous, and to possess a genetically determined syntactic algorithm with fixed parameters that are designed to only, and mandatorily, process certain sensory inputs to perform distinct cognitive tasks, e.g. visual pattern recognition (Fodor, 2001). Because of their computational property, modules enable us to rapidly process, parse, remember and react to the constant stream of sensory information that we encounter every day (Sperber & Hirschfeld, 2004). However, although there seems to be a general consensus that modules perform low-level cognitive functions, there is an ongoing debate as to whether high-level functions (e.g. reasoning) are performed strictly by modules or domain-general neural networks, or from an interaction between domain specific and domain general mechanisms (see Barrett & Kurzban, 2006).

Formation and Reproduction of Neoliberal Subjectivities

I will sidestep this debate as it does not undermine or relate to the central arguments of this chapter.

A particularly important module for the purposes of this chapter is referred to as the 'medial temporal lobe memory system', which is located along the parahippocampal cortex, hippocampus and entorhinal cortex (Bussey & Saksida, 2007). As such, this module houses multiple memory systems e.g., working, episodic, semantic (Bussey & Saksida, 2007), and stores, generates and interconnects smaller cognitive mechanisms known as schemas (Ghosh, Moscovitch, Colella, & Gilboa, 2014; van Kesteren, Ruiter, Fernandez, & Henson, 2012. A schema (aka a script or mental representation) is a partially informationally encapsulated, generative and subjective knowledge structure that can contain information about either; the self, culture, abstract concepts, institutional norms, or an imaginary or real material aspect of the external world (Brod, Lindenberger, Werkle-Bergner, & Shing, 2015; Chiao et al., 2010). Moreover, schemas are acquired throughout life via exposure to and interaction with external environments. However, a schema's content, or data as it were, is thought to be fragmented and generally granulated. Hence, singular units have to link directly to associative and distributive networks of interrelated schemas in order to form more complex and cohesive representations (Ghosh & Gilboa, 2014). Correspondingly, recent evidence indicates that schemas are encoded and subsequently developed in neural networks via anchoring and reconstructive processes (van Kesteren et al., 2013; Chiao et al., 2010) enabled and reinforced by neuronal dopaminergic substrates and reactions (see, e.g. Tse et al., 2011). Additionally, findings from several neuroimaging and other types of experimental studies show that initial schema encoding or subsequent augmentation often occurs when incoming information is contextually, semantically, and/or conceptually congruent or otherwise associated with pre-existing schema networks (Tse et al., 2011;

van Kesteren et al., 2013). So for example, one's schema for, say, dogs will likely be formed and syntactically defined upon first encountering or learning about dogs. This schema's base syntax can over time modify and expand itself in accordance with new information that corresponds to one's continued learning about and exposure to dogs or dog-related stimuli. These semi-informationally encapsulated and generative properties also allow a schema to connect to related schemas, which, following the previous example, could include a cat schema.

Schema instantiation, reification and modification are also essentially the processes that enable attitudinal development. According to Bohner and Dickel (2011) an attitude is an "evaluation of an object of thought [and attitude objects range] from the mundane to the abstract, including things, people, groups, and ideas" (p. 382). While there is disagreement in this literature on the more intricate nature of attitudes and how they are organised in memory, a middle ground suggests that attitudes are effectively affect-type schemas that are tightly connected to and/or subsumed within information-type schemas (see Bohner & Dickel, 2011). For example, one's attitudes on political parties will be necessarily tied to one's knowledge on politics and politicians. Also, depending on the context of their formation, valence strength,[3] and frequency of activation, affect-type schemas can be durable and potentially lifelong, as is often the case with political attitudes (Lieberman, Schreiber, & Ochsner, 2003), or ad hoc and relatively disposable. Overall, however, affect-type schemas and affective states in general, can have a powerful subliminal effect on motivation, judgement, behaviour and the development of information-type schemas (Pinheiro et al., 2013). As Forgas (2013) notes: "Affect is integrally linked to an associative network of memory representations, and affective states can selectively prime associated constructs that are more likely to be used in subsequent constructive cognitive tasks" (p. 226).

Formation and Reproduction of Neoliberal Subjectivities

Furthermore, schemas are believed to lie dormant in long-term memory waiting to be activated and retrieved in working memory, where they can then be consciously deliberated or acted upon. According to Evans's (2008) more unified version of the dual-processing system paradigm, this occurs through the activation of system 1 – associated with implicit/tacit (i.e., reflexive, automatic, nonconscious, offline) processes – which then delivers cued schematic information to system 2 – associated with explicit/agentic (i.e. reflective, controlled, conscious, online) processes. Correspondingly, situational frequency and contiguity can cause individuals to develop anticipatory, or what can be described as dispositional-behavioural schemas. These can take the form of implicit attitudes, ideas, preferences, expectations, attentional biases or bodily reactions, which when activated, can manifest automatically beyond conscious control or awareness. Yet despite their power to propel people to nonconscious cognitive, affective and/or behavioural reactions, in certain situations and to varying extents, a schema's automatic function can be superseded through concerted conscious effort (Lieberman et al., 2003). This is especially the case when individuals experience situations that run counter to their expectations, as this can induce an aversive arousal state (i.e. cognitive dissonance). Given that people have a strong inclination to maintain cognitive consonance (Randles, Inzlicht, Proulx, Tullett, & Heine, 2015); instances that activate internal inconsistency can to varying degrees, force individuals to consciously engage with and then potentially alter their corresponding dispositional-behavioural schemas (Lieberman et al., 2003). However, this same inclination can also orient people to reify their existing schemas, as well as unconsciously avoid information that may induce cognitive dissonance (e.g. alternative political facts, news and ideologies).

To summarise, a schema's content, complexity, consolidation, weight, saliency, and connection to and co-activation with other schemas are largely determined by the frequency and socio-environmental and affective context in which it is activated and accessed (Ghosh & Gilboa, 2014; Robin & Moscovitch, 2014). However, once instantiated, schemas can:

- Store and organise memories, affects, knowledge and ideas; including their respective attributes and relationships to other related schemas (Robin & Moscovitch, 2014). This includes information such as, motives, intentions, situations, and goals that "enable or inhibit certain behaviours, and causal sequence of events, as well as the specific behaviours themselves" (Baumeister & Bushman, 2011 p. 152).
- Enable the processing of affective, contextual, semantic and discursive meanings and associations (Schröder & Thagard, 2013).
- Facilitate learning by enabling the rapid integration of new associations linked to incoming information (Tse et al., 2011).
- Embody an individual's mental representations of their self, as well as the shared cultural beliefs, norms and values of their respective social group (Chiao et al., 2010).

Social cognition, subjectivity formation, and social reproduction

Having outlined above some of the major neurophysiological properties and socio-cognitive functions of schemas, this section provides an overview of their key role in the interrelated processes of subjectivity formation and social reproduction. To start with, social cognition theory suggests that individual human agents begin to develop their unique cognitive and affective architectures at least as early as infancy via their exposure to and interaction with people and social institutions (Bandura, 2001). Social institutions can be understood as patterned distributions of behaviours and material resources, which explicitly and implicitly impose upon agents specific and organised forms of social information and order, e.g. shared cultural histories, values, norms, relationships between different social institutions and situational expectations (Ridgeway, 2006). These relatively stable sources of information, as noted by Hewer and Roberts (2012) work: "alongside more dynamic sources of knowledge such as the internet and multi-media broadcasting. [...] The result is a continuous and overwhelming flow of information, which either endorses or challenges the status quo" (p. 175).

Over time, agents generate and form their unique subjectivities from engagement with the discursive data and cultural repositories available to them, and through social experiences, rewards and sanctions. Agents are, to a meaningful extent, able to develop their subjectivities consciously, as their cognitive faculties enable them to deliberatively take in, modify and even dismiss the social information that they are exposed to (Bandura, 2001). However, social information that is most institutionally salient, socially valued, sanctioned, and repeatedly experienced, for example during the formative years in a family, is more likely to become encoded in an agent's schematic architecture, and thus concurrently enacted in mostly dispositional forms (Schröder & Thagard, 2013; Chiao et al., 2010). One leading explanation for this is that as Ridgeway (2006) puts it, social institutions effectively function as external modular organising schemas, which can "become the basis for actors' initial expectations for one another's behaviour" (p. 9). Moreover, these also organise and constrain "a broad range of behaviour in a manner consistent with the structural conditions framing the situation, even when that behaviour is not directly and materially constrained by those conditions" (Ridgeway, 2006, p. 9). It therefore follows that the more cultural and political-ideological, discursive, affective and material convergence and integration there is between the major institutions of any given society, the more likely it is that their respective ideas, values, norms and discursive practices will anchor themselves in an agent's schema networks (Schröder & Thagard, 2013). The more these become embodied and reinforced, the more they can place durable neurocognitive parameters that can significantly shape an agent's sociocultural and political-economic knowledge and dispositions (Lieberman et al., 2003; Chiao et al., 2010). These can also block, hinder and/or distort an agent's development of schemas for, and/or intake of information corresponding to, opposing political ideas (Amodio, Jost, Master, & Yee, 2007). In aggregate, these micro-level conditions can lead to macro-level sociocultural inertia (Henrich & Boyd, 2002; Schröder & Thagard, 2013).

However, the generative and ultimately physically, biologically and socially constrained nature of human cognition means that an agent's encoding of even the most institutionally and ideologically salient and widely disseminated forms of social information is likely never an exact mental replication of the source data (Henrich & Boyd, 2002). Our unique cognitive faculties, social experiences, cultural-geo-historic specificities, social positioning and agency lead us to process, recombine, and reproduce even dominant social information in fuzzy, incomplete, novel and/or permutated ways that can mildly to significantly differ from individual to individual and from generation to generation. This inherent and non-linear sociocognitive dynamic can go towards explaining why we, for instance, are not institutional drones or carbon copies of our parents, and why societies are to varying degrees, divergent and always changing (Hewer & Roberts, 2012). In other words, society does not permanently stamp us, it instead provides us with foundational socio-institutional algorithms that we are to some meaningful extent free to consciously modify and act upon. Therefore, while relatively homeostatic, any given set of hegemonic ideological and socio-institutional arrangement is never permanently fixed as societies are inherently chaotic systems that are sensitive and continuously subject to spontaneous micro- and mezzo-level agent-based modifications.

Although the social-cognition model (SCM) of subjectivity development and social reproduction is in many ways similar to Talcott Parson's structural functionalism and Pierre Bourdieu's field theory, it differs from these classic sociological theories in the following ways. First, unlike Parson's 'oversocialised man' or Bourdieu's 'habitus', the SCM is based on empirically tested accounts of how people's socio-neurocognitive architectures are developed and augmented through social interactions. Second, the SCM posits that said architecture is composed of schemas that contain modifiable but specific content. This very much differs from Bourdieu's (2000) unfalsifiable habitus construct, which is effectively a content-free and all-purpose general learning, relatively fixed, and reactive mechanism (Burawoy, 2012; Lizardo, 2004). Third, the SCM offers comprehensive understandings of both automatic and deliberative cognition and agency. Fourth, the SCM emphasises the important role of context, prior knowledge and affect in modulating socio-neurocognitive development and processing. Fifth, the SCM does not reduce subjectivity formation or social reproduction to either socio-structural or cognitive-structural determinants, nor to conscious or nonconscious agency. Rather, the SCM explains subject formation and social reproduction as the products of dynamic and mutually reinforcing biological-genetic, cognitive-affective and institutional-discursive mechanisms and processes, which in turn enable and are enabled by volitional, dispositional, habituated and spontaneous human practices. Lastly, as I will demonstrate in the penultimate sections of this chapter, the SCM provides an explanatory framework that can be used to modify the habitus formulation, and hypothesise about what the content of a neoliberal habitus might entail.

Neoliberalism: a first approximation

Before elaborating on the discussion above, it is first necessary to define neoliberalism briefly. Neoliberalism refers to a political-economic paradigm based on an ideology that calls for the state implementation, facilitation and enforcement of free-market economic systems and logic across national and global settings, and effectively across all forms of human organisation and decision-making (Braedley & Luxton, 2010; Hall & Rustin, 2015). Initially rising to prominence in the 1980s in the United Kingdom and the United States following the elections of Margaret Thatcher and Ronald Reagan respectively, neoliberal discourses and policies have significantly shaped the twenty-first century world order (Albo et al., 2010; Gill, 2003; Harvey, 2005). Moreover, neoliberalism has been influenced by several Western epistemic communities (e.g. Austrian and Freiburg Schools of Economics, the Mont Pelerin Society), and taken on a number of provincial characteristics thereby morphing into several strands (Plehwe, Walpen, & Neunhöffer, 2007; Steger & Roy, 2010).[4] However, this section will focus on outlining the key premises and policy prescriptions associated with the dominant US and UK strands of neoliberalism.

As can be interpreted from the works of leading and self-described neoliberal scholars, the core of neoliberal theory and ideology is premised on an essentialist conception of human nature. This conception paints human beings as predominantly possessive and instrumentally rational individuals that, while capable of altruism, will primarily behave in ways that are in accordance with their perceived self-interests (Friedman, 2002). From this ontology follows the key normative position that despite their self-interested predispositions, people's motivations and actions can and should be channelled for progressive socio-economic development, but only via political-economic systems that engender relatively unfettered market forces, negative forms of freedom, and the legal protection and appropriation of private capital (Hayek, [1960] 1994). Conversely, any attempts to harness the powers of the state to redistribute wealth and regulate markets for the public good, however benevolent and well intentioned, will have disastrous socio-economic outcomes. This is primarily because these objectives as traditionally advanced by state socialism and to a lesser extent by Keynesian forms of capitalism, require excessive government economic intervention that distorts the natural pricing equilibrium mechanisms of supply and demand. Invariably, this results in the inefficient and wasteful allocation of finite resources and services (Friedman, 2002). Additionally, these political-economic systems necessarily infringe on individuals' freedom to utilise their capital as they choose, which has the consequent effect of stifling the psychological incentives necessary for entrepreneurial innovation and economic growth. Coupled, these cumulative macro and micro effects inevitably generate high inflation, stagnant economies and unproductive state dependent citizenries, which can in extreme cases lead to despotism (Hayek, [1960] 1994).

However, far from a hands off approach, neoliberals argue that a sound and prosperous economy and free society necessitates state intervention to enforce contracts and protect property rights (Hayek, [1960] 1994) and shore up markets in times of economic crisis (Friedman, 1948). Furthermore, a minimal degree of funding for public services and private enterprises through fiscal revenues is consistent with neoliberal theory (e.g. negative income tax), provided that these are not "inimical to the initiative and functioning of the market" (Hartwell, 1995, p. 42). Nonetheless, neoliberals emphatically propose that the scope of the welfare state should be massively reduced. They further propose that welfare and all public institutions such as those that provide health and education should be fully or partially privatised, and have to compete for public funds by operating as market apparatuses. This entails the implementation of neo-managerial policies and corporate style accountability metrics and targets to eliminate wastefulness, incentivise positive performances and measure outcomes and customer satisfaction. They also propose that the primary function of welfare and education institutions should be to socialise and train individuals to be self-reliant, entrepreneurial and responsible (Chubb & Moe, 1990; Friedman, 2002).

At the macroeconomic level, neoliberals advocate for monetary policies aimed at controlling inflation (Friedman, 1948). It is postulated that in favouring monetary over fiscal policies, governments and central banks can help to increase and stabilise the real value (as opposed to nominal value) of financial assets. Doing so puts more money into the hands of individual investors and entrepreneurs, and incentivises them to make investments. This will in turn lead to the creation of jobs and more efficient economic growth than can be achieved by means of government fiscal stimulus policies. Additionally, to maintain international competitiveness and induce and accelerate economic growth, neoliberals further posit that countries should:

1) Dismantle trade barriers,
2) Cut corporate and income taxes, as well as government public expenditures,
3) Eliminate or significantly reduce financial, labour and environmental regulations,
4) Privatise their natural resources,
5) Partially or fully privatise state enterprises and services, and
6) Focus on producing exports.

In so doing, countries can gain from their comparative advantages in factor endowments, maintain market credibility, achieve fiscal solvency, and attract foreign direct investment. Although these policy prescriptions may not equate to an ideal free-market system, neoliberals more or less agree that they can best preserve individual political and economic freedom whilst simultaneously generating efficient national and international markets in addition to the skilled and flexible workers needed to maintain and compete in them. It is thus hypothesised that if all the policy prescriptions described above are sufficiently enacted, this will over time usher a prosperous and dynamic, but stable global economy that benefits everyone (Friedman, 2002; Hartwell, 1995).

Neoliberal hegemony in the UK and US
It cannot be stressed enough that neoliberalism has been a consciously articulated political project enacted by interlocking groups of elite intellectuals, politicians and businesspeople who continue to utilise their power to enact their ideal and normative conceptualisation of how each major institution of contemporary society as well as individual agents, should ideally function (Hall, 2011; Plehwe et al., 2007). This ideal conceptualisation can be construed as a sort of neoliberal societal algorithm designed for "competitive globalisation, inspiring and imposing far-reaching programmes of state-restructuring and rescaling across a wide range of national and local contexts" (Peck & Tickell, 2002, p. 381). However, at this juncture it is important to note that US and UK societies are like all others, marked by ideological breaks, ruptures and points of contestation that are generated by the constant dynamism of competing forces. Indeed, the neoliberal era has seen multitudes of resistance from the anti-globalisation movements of the 90s, to the Occupy encampments of the 2010s, to the recent rise of far-right nativist groups. Moreover, many factions and individuals operating within the major social institutions of the UK and US disagree with the neoliberal paradigm, and actively work against it. Examples of this include nationalist elites who push forward protectionist economic policies, and conservative educationalists who believe education should emphasise the classic humanities instead of a narrow economistic pedagogy.

That said, the fact remains that several major US and UK institutions have, to a varying but considerable extent, been restructured and thus behave according the neoliberal paradigm. As Peck and Tickell (2002) argue, from the 1980s–1990s neoliberal policies in the UK and the US underwent two major transitions. In the first stage, during the Reagan and Thatcher eras, the state 'rolled-back' (i.e. lifted economic regulations and reduced the size and funding for social-welfare programmes), while in the second stage, during the Clinton and Blair eras, the state 'rolled-out' (i.e. implemented neo-managerial social policies and workfare programmes designed to regulate or discipline public service workers and government aid recipients via strict yet arbitrarily generated metrics and performance outcomes). Contemporary UK and US neoliberal policies, while varying, are arguably a mix of these two forms of governance. Education policies over the past 30 years for example, have instituted the implementation of market-inspired accountability metrics to measure schools' competence and rank, which in some cases determines their funding (Slater, 2015). Although other factors are considered, these metrics are primarily based on how well students perform on high-stakes standardised tests. It is also worth noting that as a result of these policies, teachers have been increasingly trained in, and pressured to focus on, 'teaching to the test' classroom practices (Brown, 2010; Sloan, 2008). While these pedagogic practices vary at national and local levels, they are generally modelled on rote learning and behaviourist approaches to education, as they are specifically designed to train students to attain an automated and uncritical acceptance of predetermined answers (Boyles, 2004). Moreover, students are usually told that their test scores will largely determine whether and which university they can attend, which will in turn determine what types of jobs they can expect to attain. As such, current public education by and large functions as yet another institutional environment where individuals are further

Formation and Reproduction of Neoliberal Subjectivities

socialised to place a higher value on competition and individualism, than on co-operation and communality.

The influence of neoliberal ideology can also be observed in the mass media's carefully spun and widely circulated sound-bites and opinion pieces that call for the reduction or elimination of welfare services and taxes, the privatisation of public institutions, and the removal of financial, labour and environmental regulations. Incidentally, these messages are very often developed by neoliberal think-tanks like the Adam Smith Institute, Heritage Foundation, Centre for Policy Studies and Institute of Economic Affairs.[5] This ideological saturation is also often coupled with an erosion of criticisms of corporate practices and neoliberal policies, along with a near constant demonisation and misrepresentation of egalitarian ideals, welfare recipients, and redistributive policies (Chomsky, 2011). The few independent non-corporate press organisations that report non-elite interests, critical voices and substantive policy debates are marginalised, constantly under-funded and have very limited communicative reach. Meanwhile, rather than helping to inform democratic deliberation, public broadcasts continue to be co-opted, cheapened, stripped of substance by media conglomerates, or worse still, turned into manufacturers of ridiculous infotainment that celebrates the opulence of the rich and famous (Coleman, 2013; McChesney & Nichols, 2009).

Correspondingly, popular culture now disseminates discourses of competition, individualism and self-interestedness that are markedly more emphatic and exaggerated than those of pre-neoliberal era popular cultures (Kasser et al., 2007). For example, a study by DeWall, Pond, Campbell and Twenge (2011), conducted a psycholinguistic and statistical analysis of the lyrics from the US's Hot 100 Billboard songs from the years 1980–2007. Notably, the findings show that since 1980, the words 'I' and 'Me' have appeared more frequently in popular music lyrics, while more pro-social words like 'We' and 'Us' have significantly dwindled. The researchers argue that the rise in the self-centered and antisocial lyrics found in popular music correlates with several large-scale psychometric survey results that suggest that the Millennial generation (which was born during the neoliberal epoch), is more narcissistic and self-interested than previous generations. Indeed, it is somewhat of an understatement to state that despite the advent of the internet, the range of cultural and political ideological messages that US and UK residents are directly or indirectly exposed to via mass media-culture has been rather narrow (McGuigan, 2010), and is becoming narrower and narrower.

All these institutional and discursive changes have also coincided with a significant weakening of labour unions and increase in the commodification of public spaces and leisure (Coakley, 2011; Davies & Niemann, 2002; Peck & Tickell, 2002), This further limits the range of counter-hegemonic discourses that contemporary Britons and Americans can be exposed to, as well as diminish their probability of encountering counter-hegemonic discourses. In tandem, this discursive and institutional convergence results in a conjuncture where most US and UK residents currently have no choice but to be repeatedly exposed to and interact with institutionally and culturally omnipresent neoliberal discursive formations. Repeated exposure to these formations may thus lead a sufficient number of Britons and Americans, or a critical mass of them, to develop socio-cognitive frameworks, or habituses that broadly and to varying degrees reflect a neoliberal syntax. This syntax can in turn orient them to mostly dispositional social practices, which contribute to the wider processes of neoliberal hegemony and reproduction.

A working model of neoliberal habitus and subjectivity formation

But what exactly might a neoliberal habitus consist of? The conceptual limitations and vagueness of the habitus construct

Formation and Reproduction of Neoliberal Subjectivities

have been well-documented (Burawoy, 2012; Lizardo, 2004), and have been briefly discussed in this chapter so I will not go over them in any more depth. Nonetheless, the habitus concept offers a useful and pliant conceptual device that can be modified and retrofitted with the empirically substantiated theoretical insights from the literatures discussed throughout this chapter to create a provisional and ideal-type characterisation of a neoliberal habitus and concomitant subjectivity. Thus, the conceptualisation of habitus offered here is defined as an individual's consciously and non-consciously acquired and contextually activated collection of related content specific schema networks, which in aggregate form a particular major component of the self, such as a role, identity, or sociocultural and/or political-economic framework. Additionally, these schema networks operate at the dispositional level, but fuel and can be modified and acted on via agential deliberation. Lastly, this conception of habitus indicates that an agent can develop multiple habituses, which can theoretically vary in size or weight and consolidation, as well as converge, overlap, be totally separate from, or conflict with one another. In this regard, said conceptualisation accounts for the capacity of individuals to develop multiple roles, identities and cultural and political scripts, and to hold and act on these even when they contain inconsistent elements.

Furthermore, the following proposed neoliberal habitus model is like most initial theoretical abstractions, a messy first approximation in need of further conceptual refinement and supplementation, as well as empirical verification. Additionally, this model is meant to be understood as a collection of salient cognitions, high-valence attitudes and corresponding social practices that reflect neoliberal norms and values, and which follow a hypothetical sliding continuum that goes from low to high variants. Hence, for instance, holding a strong acceptance of capitalism is not by itself sufficient to reflect a neoliberal habitus. This attitudinal disposition would need to be present along with most or all of the other relevant characteristics described in the model overleaf in order to gauge an individual's level of neoliberal subjectification. However, the associated weighting of these characteristics and the contexts in which they may develop and are consciously or unconsciously internalised, articulated, reified or contested, still need to be fleshed out. Moreover, the model only lists a few key and hypothetical schemas and practices, and should by no means be interpreted as a robust list or diagnostic. *A la* Weberian tradition, this model sacrifices the subtleties and complexities of social reality, but can nonetheless be used to explore and compare how, why and the extent to, and context in which, real cases diverge from or converge with it.

Furthermore, testing this model necessitates the exploration of dispositional schemas. Therefore, the experimental methods used by cognitive psychologists should be considered, as these can to some meaningful extent capture people's nonconscious attitudes and behaviours. For example, priming methods such as lexical-decision tasks or the implicit associate test are reliable instruments for capturing people's implicit racial attitudes (Bohner & Dickel, 2011). These can be tweaked to explore if and the degree to which people's implicit attitudes on, for example, welfare programmes and recipients, poverty, human nature, etc. converge with, or diverge from, what is outlined in the neoliberal habitus model. Otherwise, I propose that the model can be used to develop psychometric instruments (e.g. attitudinal Likert scales), but additional instruments would also be needed to measure the extent to which:

a) Major social institutors act in accordance with neoliberal ideology and disseminate neoliberal cultural and political discursive practices;

b) UK and/or US participants interact and are exposed to these institutions and discourses;

Neoliberal habitus

(Note: The following schemas are hypothesised to be highly salient and distributed along associated networks such that activation of one should in many instances theoretically prime the activation of others)

Dispositional and/or conscious attitudes and conceptual schemas	Corresponding dispositional and/or conscious social practices
<ul><li>An acceptance of capitalism as the only viable economic system.</li><li>A view that connects happiness and/or success in life with financial and material success.</li><li>A high-valence negative attitude towards unions and economic regulations.</li><li>A belief that market solutions are more effective than government intervention in solving social problems.</li><li>An underdeveloped understanding and/or high-valence negative attitude towards more egalitarian political-economic systems.</li></ul>	<ul><li>Consumption of media that valorise and promote conspicuous consumption, wealth attainment, free-market systems, and personal responsibility narratives.</li><li>Continuous acquisition of economic and human capital, or attempts to do so.</li><li>Supporting either through financial means or via the electoral process liberal-democratic and/or more authoritarian forms of government that prioritise order, stability and the enforcement of property rights over human rights.</li><li>Consumption of goods and services in instances when it is known that they stem from exploitative conditions and/or have negative environmental impacts.</li><li>Supporting financially, and/or through the electoral process, de-regulation and anti-union policies and politicians.</li></ul>
<ul><li>A pre-occupation with satisfying self-concerns, coupled with a general disregard for the concerns of others.</li><li>A belief that people are inherently selfish and greedy.</li><li>A belief that schools should be primarily focussed on jobs training.</li><li>A belief that good careers are solely or mostly those that pay the highest salaries.</li></ul>	<ul><li>Consumption of, and/or investing in, companies that produce goods and services in instances where it is known that they stem from exploitative conditions and/or have negative environmental impacts.</li><li>Overtly and ruthlessly competitive, particularly in the workplace.</li><li>Instrumentalist selection of schools, friends, careers and politicians.</li><li>Instrumentalist treatment of co-workers, friends and other relationships.</li></ul>
<ul><li>A belief that one's socioeconomic status is principally determined by personal effort and choices.</li><li>High-valence negative and judgemental attitudes towards welfare recipients and impoverished peoples.</li><li>A belief that people are paid fairly according to their effort.</li><li>A belief that welfare programs are overly generous and should be reduced and means tested.</li></ul>	<ul><li>Callous actions towards the homeless and/or other individuals suffering from poverty.<ul><li>e.g. supporting welfare reform policies that place more stringent conditions on the amount of benefits that can be claimed.</li><li>e.g. opposing the development of homeless shelters and group homes near one's residency.</li></ul></li><li>Minimal contributions to charities.</li></ul>

c) UK and/or US participants are implicitly or explicitly rewarded and/or sanctioned respectively for abiding by or failing to conform to the norms and values of the respective institutions they inhabit. The reason for these added measures is that this model predicts that if the extents for a), b) and c) are high or large, then so will a participant's level of neoliberal subjectification. This, however, will likely vary by age, class, gender, religion, corporate media exposure, regional upbringing and level of education amongst other demographic and psychographic factors. How these factors mediate or moderate the internalisation of neoliberal norms and values must thus also be examined, as this can also provide insights on the variables and conditions that enable people to resist and reject neoliberal ideology. Overall, this is admittedly a very simple and still provisional model. Nonetheless, it is to the author's knowledge, the first to lay out clear and testable sociological propositions about 1) the actual sociocultural dispositions and behaviours that typify a neoliberal subject, and 2) the cognitive-affective mechanisms that explain how individuals acquire and reproduce neoliberal ideology.

Conclusion
In closing, neoliberalism may not mark the end of history, but it is still the 'common sense' of our time. Current sociological explanations for neoliberal hegemony require a more in-depth conceptualisation and formalisation of the specific habitus and concomitant subjectivity that can result from the extended interaction with institutionally and culturally prevalent neoliberal discursive formations. Although this social phenomenon is incredibly complex, the onus of sociology is to attempt to make sense of this complexity without succumbing to structural reductionism or post-structuralist relativism. This chapter thus outlined and argued for a cognitive-sociological model to

Formation and Reproduction of Neoliberal Subjectivities

explore cognitive, affective and social processes and structures, the ways in which they enable, constrain and mediate individual thought and action, and the ways that this in turn helps to sustain or challenge the current neoliberal conjuncture. While this model in no way captures the complexity of these dynamic mechanisms and processes, it incorporates rich theoretical insights from the cognitive sciences, and offers an initial, modifiable and falsifiable framework for how to more robustly conceptualise and empirically explore them.

Notes
1. There is an increasing attention by Gramscian theorists and others to the ways that people's everyday practices become inflected through neoliberal structural and discursive mechanisms in ways that help to contribute to neoliberal hegemony (e.g. Davies & Niemann, 2002). While highly insightful, these theorists still tend to take for granted or overlook an analysis of the super-ordinal cognitive structures and processes that engender said everyday practices.
2. The 99% is a term that moved into popular usage following the Occupy movement's use of the slogan 'We are the 99%'.
3. In psychology the term valence generally refers to the negative or positive orientation and strength of an emotion that is tied to a specific object, idea, person or event. For example, arachnophobics have a very strong fear of spiders, which can be construed as a high-valenced negative emotion.
4. Following the 1991 fall of the Soviet Union, there has been a concerted effort (broadly referred to as the 'Washington Consensus') by elite Western policy-makers and supra-national institutions such as the IMF, World Bank and WTO to impose neoliberal policies on developing and semi-developed countries via, for example, structural adjustment programmes and multilateral free-trade agreements (e.g. 1994 NAFTA). Despite this, countries have not totally abided by the 'Washington Consensus'. As such, neoliberalism has taken on a number of provincial characteristics and morphed into several strands (e.g. German ordoliberalism, Chinese state capitalism, Brazilian new

capitalism). While these strands largely differ in the extent to which the state should intervene to curb social inequalities, they nonetheless all champion free markets, trade liberalisation, financialisation and supply-side economics, and are thus arguably part of a family of neoliberal models (Mirowski & Plehwe, 2009).
5. There are some important differences between these Mont Pelerin Society aligned think tanks (Mirowski & Plehwe, 2009), and other similar ones such as the Cato Institute, which adopts a more right-wing libertarian position. However, they all generally promote neoliberal policy prescriptions as detailed above.

References

Albo, G., Gindin, S., & Panitch, L. (2010). *In and out of crisis. The global financial meltdown and left alternatives.* Oakland, CA: PM Press.

Amodio, D. M., Jost, J. T., Master, S. L., & Yee, C. M. (2007). Neurocognitive correlates of liberalism and conservatism. *Nature Neuroscience, 10*(10), 1246–1247.

Bandura, A. (2001). Social cognitive theory: An agentic perspective. *Annual Review of Psychology, 52*(1), 1–26.

Barrett, H. C. & Kurzban, R. (2006). Modularity in cognition: Framing the debate. *Psychological Review, 113*(3), 628–647.

Baumeister, R. F. & Bushman, B. J. (2011). *Social Psychology & Human Nature.* Belmont, CA: Wadsworth, Cengage Learning.

Bohner, G. & Dickel, N. (2011). Attitudes and attitude change, *Annual Review of Psychology, 62*, 391–417.

Bourdieu, P. (2000). *Pascalian mediations.* Palo Alto, CA: Stanford University Press.

Boyles, D. R. (Ed.). (2004). *Schools or markets?: Commercialism, privatization, and school-business partnerships.* New York, NY; Abingdon, United Kingdom: Routledge.

Braedley, S. & Luxton, M. (Eds.). (2010). *Neoliberalism and everyday life.* Montreal, Canada: McGill-Queen's University Press.

Brod, G., Lindenberger, U., Werkle-Bergner, M., & Shing, Y. L. (2015). Differences in the neural signature of remembering schema-congruent and schema incongruent events. *Neuroimage, 117*, 358–366.

Brown, C. P. (2010). Children of reform: The impact of high-stakes education reform on preservice teachers. *Journal of Teacher Education, 61*(5), 477–491.
Burawoy, M. (2012). The roots of domination: Beyond Bourdieu and Gramsci. *Sociology, 46*(2), 187–206.
Bussey, T. J. & Saksida, L. M. (2007). Memory, perception, and the ventral visual-perirhinal-hippocampal stream: Thinking outside of the boxes. *Hippocampus, 17*(9), 898–908.
Chang, H. J. (2010). *23 things they don't tell you about capitalism*. London, United Kingdom: Bloomsbury Publishing.
Chiao, J. Y., Harada, T., Komeda, H., Li, Z., Mano, Y., Saito, D., Parrish, T. B., Sadato, N., & Iidaka, T. (2010). Dynamic cultural influences on neural representations of the self. *Journal of Cognitive Neuroscience, 22*(1), 1–11.
Chomsky, N. (2011). *Profit over people: Neoliberalism and global order*. New York, NY: Seven Stories Press.
Chubb, J. E. & Moe, T. M. (1990). *Politics, markets, and America's schools*. Washington, DC: The Brookings Institution.
Coakley, J. (2011). Ideology doesn't just happen: Sports and neoliberalism. *Journal of ALESDE, 1*(1), 67–84.
Coleman, S. (2013). Debate on television: The spectacle of deliberation. *Television & New Media, 14*(1), 20–30.
Davies, M. & Niemann, M. (2002). The everyday spaces of global politics: Work, leisure, family. *New Political Science, 24*(4), 557–577.
DeWall, C. N., Pond Jr., R. S., Campbell, W. K., & Twenge, J. M. (2011). Tuning in to psychological change: Linguistic markers of psychological traits and emotions over time in popular US song lyrics. *Psychology of Aesthetics, Creativity, and the Arts, 5*(3), 200–207.
Ellwood, W. (2002). *No-nonsense guide to globalization*. New York, NY: New Internationalist/Verso.
Evans, J. S. B. (2008). Dual-processing accounts of reasoning, judgment, and social cognition. *Annual Review of Psychology, 59*, 255–278.
Fodor, J. A. (2001). *The mind doesn't work that way: The scope and limits of computational psychology*. Cambridge, MA: MIT Press.

Forgas, J. P. (2013). Don't worry, be sad! On the cognitive, motivational, and interpersonal benefits of negative mood. *Current Directions in Psychological Science, 22*(3), 225–232.

Friedman, M. (1948). A monetary and fiscal framework for economic stability. *The American Economic Review*, 245–264.

Friedman, M. (2002). *Capitalism and freedom.* Chicago, IL: University of Chicago Press.

Ghosh, V. E. & Gilboa, A. (2014). What is a memory schema? A historical perspective on current neuroscience literature. *Neuropsychologia, 53*, 104–114.

Ghosh, V. E., Moscovitch, M., Colella, B. M., & Gilboa, A. (2014). Schema representation in patients with ventromedial PFC lesions. *The Journal of Neuroscience, 34*(36), 12057–12070.

Gill, S. (2003). *Power and resistance in the new world order.* New York, NY: Palgrave Macmillan.

Grantham, B. & Miller, T. (2010). The end of neoliberalism, *Popular Communication, 8*(3), 174–177.

Hall, S. (2011). The neo-liberal revolution. *Cultural Studies, 25*(6), 705–728.

Hall, S. & Rustin, M. (Eds.). (2015). *After Neoliberalism?: The Kilburn Manifesto.* Chadwell Heath, United Kingdom: Lawrence & Wishart Limited.

Hartwell, M. (1995). *A history of the Mont Pelerin Society.* Indianapolis, IN: Liberty Fund Inc.

Harvey, D. (2005). *A brief history of neoliberalism.* Oxford, United Kingdom: Oxford University Press.

Hayek, F. ([1960] 1994). *The road to serfdom.* Chicago, IL: University of Chicago Press.

Henrich, J. & Boyd, R. (2002). On modeling cognition and culture. *Journal of Cognition and Culture, 2*(2), 87–112.

Hewer, C. J. & Roberts, R. (2012). History, culture and cognition: Towards a dynamic model of social memory. *Culture & Psychology, 18*(2), 167–183.

Kasser, T., Cohn, S., Kanner, A. D., & Ryan, R. M. (2007). Some costs of American corporate capitalism: A psychological exploration of value and goal conflicts. *Psychological Inquiry, 18*(1), 1–22.

Lieberman, D. M., Schreiber, D., & Ochsner, N. K. (2003). Is political cognition like riding a bicycle? How cognitive neuroscience can inform research on political thinking, *Political Psychology*, 24(4), 681–704.
Lizardo, O. (2004). The cognitive origins of Bourdieu's habitus. *Journal for the Theory of Social Behavior*, 34(4), 375–401.
McChesney, M. R. & Nichols, J. (2009). *The death and life of American journalism: The media revolution that will begin the world again.* New York: Nation Books.
McGuigan, J. (2010). *Cool capitalism.* London, United Kingdom: Pluto Press.
Mirowski, P. & Plehwe, D. (Eds.). (2009). *The road from Mont Pelerin: The making of the neoliberal thought collective.* Cambridge, MA: Harvard University Press.
Peck, J. & Tickell, A. (2002). Neoliberalizing space. *Antipode*, 34(3), 380–404.
Pinheiro, A. P., del Re, E., Nestor, P. G., McCarley, R. W., Gonçalves, Ó. F., & Niznikiewicz, M. (2013). Interactions between mood and the structure of semantic memory: Event-related potentials evidence. *Social Cognitive and Affective Neuroscience*, 8(5), 579–594.
Plehwe, D., Walpen, B. J., & Neunhöffer, G. (Eds.). (2007). *Neoliberal hegemony: A global critique.* New York, NY: Routledge.
Randles, D., Inzlicht, M., Proulx, T., Tullett, A. M., & Heine, S. J. (2015). Is dissonance reduction a special case of fluid compensation? Evidence that dissonant cognitions cause compensatory affirmation and abstraction. *Journal of Personality and Social Psychology*, 108(5), 697–710.
Reed, A. (2014). Nothing left: The long slow surrender of American liberals. *Harpers.* Retrieved from http://harpers.org/archive/2014/03/nothing-left-2/
Ridgeway, L. C. (2006). Linking social structure and interpersonal behavior: A theoretical perspective on cultural schemas and social relations. *Social Psychology Quarterly,* 69(5), 5–16.
Robin, J. & Moscovitch, M. (2014). The effects of spatial contextual familiarity on remembered scenes, episodic memories, and imagined future events. *Journal of Experimental Psychology: Learning, Memory, and Cognition*, 40(2), 459–475.

Schröder, T. & Thagard, P. (2013). The affective meanings of automatic social behaviors: Three mechanisms that explain priming. *Psychological Review, 120*(1), 255–280.

Slater, G. B. (2015). Education as recovery: Neoliberalism, school reform, and the politics of crisis. *Journal of Education Policy, 30*(1), 1–20.

Sloan, K. (2008). The expanding educational services sector: Neoliberalism and the corporatization of curriculum at the local level in the US. *Journal of Curriculum Studies, 40*(5), 555–578.

Sperber, D. & Hirschfeld, A. L. (2004). The cognitive foundations of cultural stability and diversity. *Cognitive Sciences. 9*(1), 40–47.

Steger, B. M. & Roy, K. R. (2010). *Neoliberalism: A very short introduction*. New York, NY: Oxford University Press.

Stiglitz, J. (2008). The end of neoliberalism. *Project Syndicate*. Retrieved from https://www.project-syndicate.org/commentary/the-end-of-neo-liberalism

Tse, D., Takeuchi, T., Kakeyama, M., Kajii, Y., Okuno, H., Tohyama, C., Bito, H., & Morris, R. G. (2011). Schema-dependent gene activation and memory encoding in neocortex. *Science, 333*(6044), 891–895.

van Kesteren, M. T. R., Beul, S. F., Takashima, A., Henson, R. N., Ruiter, D. J., & Fernández, G. (2013). Differential roles for medial prefrontal and medial temporal cortices in schema-dependent encoding: From congruent to incongruent. *Neuropsychologia, 51*(12), 2352–2359.

van Kesteren, M. T. R., Ruiter, J. D., Fernández, G., & Henson, N. R. (2012). How schema and novelty augment memory formation. *Trends in Neurosciences, 35*(4), 211–210.

Index

A

Abe, Shinzō
Abenomics, 14, 20
abjection, 132, 135, 160
Aboriginal and Torres Strait Islander, 92
accumulation, 163, 182, 231, 254, 259, 266
Afghanistan, 58, 64, 98
Africa, 63, 231
agency, 8, 19, 33, 70, 124, 134, 141–142, 147, 157–158, 234–235, 239, 294, 295
allosexual, 150
allosexuality, 148
anarchism, 261
Archer, Margaret, 134, 142, 145, 148, 155–158
asexual, 12–13, 134–135, 148, 150–153, 155–157, 159
asexual community, 134–135, 149, 151, 153, 157
asexuality, 146, 148, 150–153, 157, 159
non-asexual, 150
asylum seekers, 10–11, 84–85, 88, 90–95, 97–100, 103–104
Australia, 10–11, 45, 84–85, 87–88, 92, 94–104, 106, 108–109, 115–118, 122, 124, 125–126, 129–130, 132–133, 172, 177, 206, 282
High Court, 98
White Australia Policy, 93
Australian Labor Party, 10, 84–85, 87–88, 97–99
autogestion, 245–246, 248, 252

B

Balkans, 16, 230–231, 252–253
Blair, Tony, 3, 107, 115, 300
New Labour, 3, 107
Bosnia Herzegovina, 16, 230, 231–232, 236, 246, 249
Bosnian, 16, 237, 240, 248
Mostar, 16, 232, 236, 238, 240–241, 242–244, 246–247, 250
Bourdieu, Pierre, 125, 129, 158, 287, 295, 308–309, 311
habitus, 295, 302–304, 306, 311
Brazil, 308
Brown, Gordon, 52, 77, 79
Brown, Wendy, 32, 48, 55, 63, 79
Butler, Judith, 72, 75, 82

C

Cambodia, 16, 22, 93, 254, 259–264, 267, 274, 278–284

313

Khmer Rouge, 16, 260, 263–265, 277, 281–282
Phnom Penh, 16, 254, 259, 260, 263–267, 270, 272–274, 277–279, 281–283
the White Building, 16–17, 254–255, 258, 260–261, 267, 272–277, 281–282, 284
Cameron, David, 107
Canada, 21, 49, 63, 104, 108, 129, 266, 279
capitalism, 2–5, 15, 19, 20–22, 39, 61, 110, 130, 176, 182–184, 186, 201, 206, 233, 245, 247, 255, 258–263, 267, 279, 297, 303, 308, 310
Centrelink, 124
Chile, 4
China, 308
Christianity, 78, 235
cis-gender, 151
citizenship, 8–9, 11, 25–35, 38, 43–47, 50, 86, 92, 96, 100, 107, 110, 112, 115, 125, 127, 248
civil society, 6, 16, 90, 240, 244, 248, 286
class, 5–6, 54, 65, 68, 70, 74, 114, 129, 132, 147, 185, 189, 206, 231, 245, 247, 261, 263, 270, 306
climate change, 36–37, 285
Clinton, Bill, 72, 79, 107, 300

Clinton, Hillary, 79
Cold War, 230–232, 248
collectives, 276
Colombia, 210
counter-conduct, 232, 235, 246, 250
critical realism, 143, 157
Croatia, 230

D

Dayton Peace Agreements, 230
Department of Work and Pensions, 121
depoliticisation, 10, 63
determinism, 11, 134, 155, 255
disability, 11, 68, 106–112, 115–116, 119–125, 127–132
disablism, 128, 131
division of labour, 76, 256

E

ejaculation, 13, 161–162, 164–176, 178–180
emancipation, 76
emancipatory, 17, 55, 58–59, 234, 258–259, 267, 276
emotions, 11, 110–111, 127–128, 132, 309
entrepreneurial, 86, 91–92, 135, 154, 163, 182–183, 198, 201, 213, 240, 297–298
entrepreneurial self, 135, 154
entrepreneurial subject, 91

Index

intimate entrepreneurship, 163, 175
environment, 2, 9, 25-26, 31, 34-36, 40, 43, 46-47, 56, 286, 298
environmental activists, 25
environmental citizenship, 9, 25, 30-31, 34-35, 44, 46-47
environmental issues, 25, 34, 43
environmental problems, 38, 41, 47
environmental rights, 31
environmental sustainability, 36
environmentalism, 41
environmentality, 9, 26, 35, 39
United Nations Environment Programme, 35, 38, 50
ethnography, 76, 184, 207, 227, 249
European Union, 16, 20, 35-36, 50, 232, 236-237, 239-240, 248, 250
everyday life, 15, 17, 45, 64, 113-114, 117, 121, 147, 154, 180, 208, 212, 223, 241, 244, 247-249, 254, 258, 267, 279
exploitation, 16-17, 43, 100, 235, 259

F

feminism, 54, 65-66, 68, 70, 81-82, 170
Fetter, Frank, 34
financial crisis, 213
floating signifier, 9, 12, 52
Foucault, Michel, 6-8, 10, 12, 16, 21, 23, 29, 49-50, 53, 60, 79-82, 88-89, 101-104, 134-142, 154-159, 206, 232-235, 237, 245, 250-253
biopower, 103-104, 234-235, 251
Foucauldian, 20, 89-90, 134, 144, 235, 237
France, 48, 63, 81-82, 87, 138, 158, 233, 251, 261-262, 282
Friedman, Milton, 1, 5, 86, 101, 296-299, 310
Chicago School, 5, 24

G

Geertz, Hildred, 217, 228
gender, xii, 54, 57, 65, 82-83, 129, 146, 159, 164, 170, 177, 190, 201, 205, 306
Germany, 44, 48, 63, 130, 231, 250
Gillard, Julia, 97-98, 101-103
globalisation, 23, 31, 50, 73, 92, 185, 231, 285, 299, 309

315

governmentality, 9, 21, 25,
29–30, 35, 42, 48–49, 53,
59–63, 77, 81, 87–90, 97–98,
101–104, 135, 191, 232–234,
247, 250, 261
Governmentality, 21, 29, 49,
60, 101–104, 230, 232
Gramsci, Antonio, 21, 102,
257, 278, 309
   Gramscian, 6, 49, 86–87, 90,
280, 287, 307
Greece, 5
Guatemala, 210

H

Hall, Stuart, 17, 21, 96, 102,
286–287, 296, 299, 310
Harvey, David, 2, 6, 14, 19–20,
22, 31, 49, 86–87, 102, 181,
200, 204, 209, 224, 232, 235,
244, 251, 255–256, 258, 276,
280, 287, 296, 310
Hashimoto, Ryutaro, 182
hate crime, 112–113, 131
Hawke, Bob, 93
Hayek, Friedrich von, 1, 3, 85,
102, 297, 310
   Mont Pelerin Society, 3, 24,
296, 308, 310–311
hegemony, 6, 11, 34, 46, 85, 87,
90, 97, 107, 117, 250, 259,
278, 280, 286, 288, 302,
306–307
   hegemonic, 1, 13–14, 85–86,
90, 99, 163–164, 173–175,
178, 181, 184, 201, 246,
257–259, 294, 302
heterogeneity, 54, 60, 144
heteronormative, 164–165, 176
heterosexuality, 71, 140, 147,
152, 159, 162, 165, 170–171,
175, 177, 179
heterotopia, 232, 235, 244–245,
248
Howard, John, 85, 95–96, 102
   Howard Government,
95–96, 100

I

identity, xii, 2, 9–10, 12, 14, 16,
26, 66, 74, 84–85, 92, 95–96,
99–100, 102, 113, 120, 127,
134–136, 138, 142, 148,
150–152, 154–155, 158–160,
184, 191, 200–202, 219, 222,
226–227, 232, 236, 240, 254,
270, 271, 303
ideology, 2–6, 18–19, 53, 55,
87, 90, 128, 156, 164, 176,
185, 188, 190–191, 200–201,
230, 236, 239, 255–257, 259,
261–262, 280, 285–287,
293–294, 296, 299, 301–302,
304, 306
Indonesia, 94, 104, 207–210,
213, 215, 219, 226, 228–229
   Surabaya, vi, 207–211,
213–214, 217, 219, 225,
227–229

Index

inequality, 2, 5–6, 17, 61, 63, 114, 231, 285, 286
institutions, 1, 4, 8, 10, 17–18, 26, 29, 52, 58–59, 86–87, 89, 106, 124, 126, 146, 181, 185, 186, 200, 202, 240, 257, 263, 277–288, 292–293, 297, 299, 300–301, 304, 306–307
International Monetary Fund, 3–5, 20, 23, 31, 106–107, 307
Bretton Woods, 4, 31
international political economy, 257
international relations, 8, 19
Islam, 20, 57, 73, 78

J

Japan, 14, 20, 22, 63, 181–190, 192–193, 198, 200–206
Liberal Democratic Party, 182

K

Kaplan, Robert, 230
Keating, Paul, 93
Keynes, John Maynard
Keynesian, 19, 86, 89, 181, 297
Koizumi, Junichiro, 186–187

L

leaky body, 171, 173
Lebanon, 92
Lefebvre, Henri, 8, 16, 22, 232, 235–236, 242, 244–246, 248–249, 252, 255–260, 266–268, 273, 276, 279, 281
Lefebvrian, 17, 254
representational spaces, 258
representations of space, 257
spatial practice, 256
liberalism, 79, 82, 85–87, 102, 135, 154, 205, 233, 308

M

Malaysia, 98
masculine identities, 161
memory, 17–18, 264, 275, 289–291, 310–312
methodological individualism, 2
Middle East, 58, 79, 231
Mill, John Stuart, 85, 103
Millennium Development Goals, 56
Mitterrand, François, 87, 100
modernity, 54, 144, 161, 178, 245, 261

N

NAFTA, 307
Nakasone, Yasuhiro, 182
Nauru, 96–98
neoclassical economics, 4, 20
neoliberal subjectivity, 1, 232, 234, 236
masculine subject, 13, 162
neoliberal subject, 6–7, 14

neoliberal subjectivities, 1, 135, 159
neoliberalism, 1–4, 6–14, 16, 18–19, 21, 23–26, 29–35, 39, 42, 43–45, 47–48, 53–55, 59–63, 65–67, 77, 82, 84–94, 96–110, 112–124, 126–128, 130, 132, 134–135, 150, 154–155, 158–159, 162–165, 168, 170, 173–176, 181–186, 188–192, 194–196, 199–202, 206, 215, 219, 225, 227, 231, 232–236, 239–240, 246–247, 254–255, 257, 259, 266, 268, 275, 285, 286–288, 295–297, 299–304, 306–308
marketisation, 14, 181–182, 203
neoliberal cosmopolitanism, 233, 236
neoliberal geopolitics, 231, 233, 240
neoliberal governance, 11–12
neoliberal governmentality, 8–10, 50, 61, 91
neoliberal hegemony, 8, 19, 250, 299, 311
neoliberalisation, 8, 25, 31, 236, 252, 281, 283
neoliberalisms, 18
privatisation, 3–5, 31, 86, 182, 186, 238, 242, 247, 301, 308
roll-back, 1, 181
roll-out, 181, 300
sexual subjects, 163
Neoliberalism, 130, 132
New Right, 31, 108, 115, 119
New Zealand, 96, 101
Newtonian, 255–256, 258, 281
non-linear, 7, 22, 294
norm circles, 143–148
normativity, 136, 138, 143–146, 155–156
Norway, 95
Nussbaum, Martha, 113–114, 131

O

OECD, 11, 106–108, 131
ontology, 6, 18, 96, 156–157, 257, 296
orgasm, 161, 164–165, 168–169, 170, 172, 174–175, 177–179
orientalist, 57

P

Pakistan, 52, 54, 58–59, 63–64, 66–68, 75, 80
Papua New Guinea, 96–99
patriarchy, 57, 67, 70, 74, 176
pedagogy, 9, 25–29, 35, 39–40, 45–46, 53, 74, 177, 299, 300
Pinochet, Augusto, 1, 4, 20
political economy, 21–22, 102, 251–252, 257, 281, 283
pornography, 173

Index

postcolonial, 262, 280
postcolonialism, 279
post-structuralism, 13, 155
problematization, 12, 139-142, 154-157

Q

queer theory, 147

R

Reagan, Ronald, 1-2, 31, 89, 107, 114, 296, 300
refugees, 11, 84, 88, 92-94, 96, 99-100, 103-104
religion, 20, 73, 78, 306
Rudd, Kevin, 97, 102, 104, 132
Russia, 63

S

Sartre, Jean-Paul, 7
scientific, 4, 137, 139, 166, 169, 172, 255-257
self-determination, 56, 65, 68
Sen, Hun, 266
sexual assumption, 150, 152-153, 155
sexual attraction, 148-149, 151, 153
sexuality, 10, 12-13, 53, 59, 68-70, 77, 139-140, 146, 148-149, 162-166, 168, 170, 177-178, 180
shame, 7, 11-12, 106, 111, 113-117, 122-123, 126-127, 130-132, 173-174
shame-rage spiral, 125

Sihanouk, Norodom, 260, 262-263, 280, 282
social institutions, 217, 226, 293
social movements, 97, 132, 235, 259, 286
social relations, 152, 189, 225, 227, 242, 266, 274-276
social reproduction, 292
socialism, 3, 85, 200, 261, 297
socio-cognitive, 285
Southeast Asia, 22, 262, 276, 279, 281
Soviet Union, 233, 307
space, 10, 15-17, 19, 22, 27, 38, 40, 43, 54, 70, 91, 94, 97, 99, 123, 125, 150, 152, 207, 209, 215-216, 224-226, 230, 233, 242-244, 246-247, 249, 254-261, 263, 266-270, 273, 275-276, 281-282, 284, 311
public space, 242, 268
Spain, 192-193
spatio-temporality, 224, 279
structural violence, 122
subjection, 74, 135, 138, 156
subjectivation, 136, 138
subjectivity, 1, 6-8, 12-13, 16, 21, 23, 25, 28, 30, 48, 54, 60-63, 65, 67, 72, 76, 117, 134-137, 140, 145, 154-155, 158-159, 162, 189, 191-192, 195, 201-202, 206-207, 232, 239, 253, 274, 292, 295, 302, 303, 306

subjectivities, 6, 8, 12, 14, 18-19, 53, 70-71, 73, 106, 109, 123, 134-135, 154-155, 175, 177, 183-184, 190, 192, 227, 236, 247, 293

T

Thatcher, Margaret, 1, 3-4, 21, 31, 89, 296, 300
Thatcherism, 6, 23
Thatcherites, 3
third world, 55, 57-58, 74, 82

U

Unger, Roberto, 8, 23, 254, 267, 279, 283
United Kingdom, 3, 6, 11, 31, 35, 44, 62-63, 69, 78, 82, 92, 106-107, 109, 115-118, 120-124, 126, 129, 148, 157, 173, 186, 269, 281, 286, 296, 299-300, 302, 304, 306
United Nations, 35, 52, 56, 59, 64, 69, 77, 83, 93
United States, 31, 33, 43, 45-46, 55-56, 63-64, 67, 70, 72, 107-109, 115, 129, 131, 186, 210, 233, 236-237, 248, 250, 252-253, 260, 286, 296, 299-302, 304, 306, 309, 312
utopia, 8, 224, 237, 248, 258, 261, 262
utopianism, 237, 262, 267

V

Vietnam, 92-93, 264
voluntarism, 134, 155

W

Washington consensus, 4, 203, 307
welfare, 11, 31, 50, 74, 84, 88- 89, 91, 100, 106-109, 112-113, 115-119, 120, 123, 125-126, 128, 130, 181-182, 185, 201, 214, 297, 300-301, 304
   disability welfare, 106, 109, 112, 120
   welfare queens, 115
   welfare scrounger, 115
   welfare state, 89
Workfare, 107, 108, 131
World Bank, 4, 31, 106, 204, 307
World Health Organization, 161, 165-166, 169, 174, 180
World Trade Organization, 31, 307

Y

Yousafzai, Malala, 9, 52, 66-67, 77-80, 82-83
Yugoslavia, 230-231, 243, 250, 251-253